JOHN PEARSON is the bestselling author of several novels and biographies including *The Profession of Violence* (Edgar Allan Poe Special Award from the Mystery Writers of America, and released as the major motion picture *Legend*) and the only authorised biography of Ian Fleming, as well as *Gone to Timbuctoo* (Author's Club Award for best first novel of the year), *The Life of James Bond*, *The Kindness of Dr Avicenna*, *Stags and Serpents: The History of the Dukes of Devonshire* and *The Selling of the Royal Family* (a collective biography of the British royal family). He lives in Sussex.

Also by John Pearson

ALL THE
MONEY
IN THE
WORLD

The Outrageous Fortune and Misfortunes
of the Heirs of J. Paul Getty

John Pearson

**WILLIAM
COLLINS**

William Collins
An imprint of HarperCollins*Publishers*
1 London Bridge Street
London SE1 9GF

WilliamCollinsBooks.com

First published in Great Britain as *Painfully Rich* by Macmillan in 1995
This new edition published by William Collins in 2017

1

A catalogue record for this book is available from the British Library

ISBN 978-0-00-828153-3 (UK edition)
ISBN 978-0-00-828152-6 (US edition)
ISBN 978-0-00-828454-1 (AUS/NZ edition)

Set in BemboStd
Printed and bound in the United States of America.

For my wife Lynette, whose love is worth more than all the money in the world

Money is the last thing that shall never be subdued. While there is flesh there is money – or the want of money; but money is always on the brain, so long as there is a brain in reasonable order.

Samuel Butler – the Notebooks

ACKNOWLEDGEMENTS

To write a book as complex as the story of the Gettys is to incur countless debts of gratitude to those whose generosity with time and memory helped to make it possible; so as well as thanking Gordon Getty for permission to quote from his poem, 'My Uncle's House' on page 263 and E.L. Doctorow for permission to quote from 'Ragtime' on page 86 I would like to thank the following for talking to me: Aaron Asher, Adam Alvarez, Brinsley Black, Michael Brown, Lady Jean Campbell, Josephine Champsoeur, Craig Copetas, Penelope de Laszlo, Douglas and Martha Duncan, Harry Evans, Malcolm Forbes, Adam Frankland, Lady Freyberg, Stephen Garrett, Gail Getty, Gordon Getty, Mark Getty, Ronald Getty, Christopher Gibbs, Judith Goodman, Lord Gowrie, Dan Green, Priscilla Higham, James Halligan, Dr Timothy Leary, Robert Lenzner, Donna Long, Duff Hart Davis, John Mallen, Russell Miller, Jonathan Meades, David Mlinaric, Judge William Newsom, Juliet Nicolson, Geraldine Norman, Edmund Purdom, John Richardson, John Semepolis, June Sherman, Mark Steinbrink, Claire Sterling, Alexis Teissier, Lord Christopher Thynne, Briget O'Brien Twohig, Vivienne Ventura, and Jacqueline Williams.

Paul Shrimpton, kindliest of bankers, managed my overdraft with rare compassion; Julie Powell, my local computer genius, saved me when Word Perfect failed me; Oscar Turnhill checked my facts and punctuation; and Edda Tasiemka of the miraculous Hans Tasiemka Archive found me press reports which no one else so much as knew existed. Ted Green was, as ever, always there when needed, whilst my perfect wife, Lynette, has been my inspiration and consolation and coped so well with being painfully poor as I wrote about the painfully rich.

J.P. 1995

CONTENTS

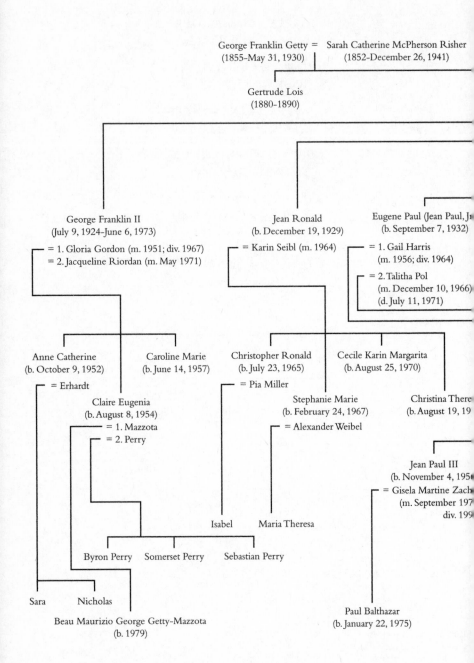

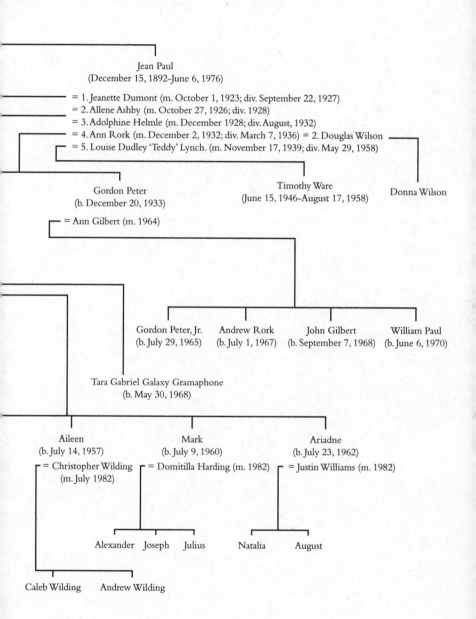

Jean Paul
(December 15, 1892-June 6, 1976)

= 1. Jeanette Dumont (m. October 1, 1923; div. September 22, 1927)
= 2. Allene Ashby (m. October 27, 1926; div. 1928)
= 3. Adolphine Helmle (m. December 1928; div. August, 1932)
= 4. Ann Rork (m. December 2, 1932; div. March 7, 1936) = 2. Douglas Wilson
= 5. Louise Dudley 'Teddy' Lynch. (m. November 17, 1939; div. May 29, 1958)

Gordon Peter
(b. December 20, 1933)

Timothy Ware
(June 15, 1946-August 17, 1958)

Donna Wilson

= Ann Gilbert (m. 1964)

Gordon Peter, Jr.
(b. July 29, 1965)

Andrew Rork
(b. July 1, 1967)

John Gilbert
(b. September 7, 1968)

William Paul
(b. June 6, 1970)

Tara Gabriel Galaxy Gramaphone
(b. May 30, 1968)

Aileen
(b. July 14, 1957)
= Christopher Wilding
(m. July 1982)

Mark
(b. July 9, 1960)
= Domitilla Harding (m. 1982)

Ariadne
(b. July 23, 1962)
= Justin Williams (m. 1982)

Alexander   Joseph   Julius

Natalia   August

Caleb Wilding   Andrew Wilding

INTRODUCTION

JEAN PAUL GETTY was eighty-three, and had had three face-lifts, the first at sixty, but the last had failed, making him look inordinately old. He was reputedly the richest American alive, but recently all he had wanted was to hear Penelope read him G. A. Henty's Victorian boys' adventure stories.

Penelope Kitson – he called her Pen – was a tall, good-looking woman, who had been his closest friend and mistress for more than twenty years and she read well in the no-nonsense voice of the upper-class Englishwoman she was. He had a large collection of the works of G. A. Henty. Possibly they made him think of a daring boyhood he had never had – and a life of physical adventure he wished that he had led.

Getty believed in reincarnation but dreaded dying. Convinced that he had been the Roman Emperor Hadrian in an earlier life, and having been so fortunate in this, his present one, he feared that third time round he might not be so lucky.

Getty reincarnated as a coolie, as the child of a Calcutta slum? Could God have such a twisted sense of humour? All too possible, and the prospect daunted him.

His youngest surviving son, accompanied by his wife, had flown to London from California and had been with him at the house for several days trying to persuade him to 'go home' with them by chartered Boeing. 'Home' was Getty's ranch-house overlooking the Pacific Ocean at Malibu – but the old man was terrified of flying and had not seen Malibu – nor his native USA – for over twenty years. What sort of home was that?

'You know what, Pen? They want to take me back because they think I'm dying.'

He stated the fact in the flat midwestern voice which seemed to count the cost of every syllable – then closed the subject as a book-keeper closes an account. J. Paul Getty, billionaire, was staying put.

He was also refusing now to go to bed.

'People die in bed,' he said – making it clear that he had no intention of doing so if he could help it. Recently he had taken to living in his armchair with a shawl around his shoulders.

Death is harder for the rich to face than it is for humbler mortals, the rich having so much more to lose and leave behind them – this great draughty house for instance. Built between 1521 and 1530 by Sir Richard Weston, a courtier of Henry VIII, Sutton Place had been one of Jean Paul Getty's many bargains when he had prised it from a hard-pressed Scottish duke (Sutherland) in 1959. It was the nearest to a real home that he had ever had, and for all its discomfort and inconvenience he truly loved this red-brick Tudor pile with its twenty-seven bedrooms, its timbered hall complete with minstrels' gallery, its home farm, and its resident ghost (of Anne Boleyn, who else?), all set in bijou Surrey countryside twenty miles by motorway from London.

Then there was Getty's male lion, Nero, growling in his cage outside the house. The old man loved Nero as much as he permitted himself to love almost anyone, and since he fed him personally, Nero would miss him.

After Nero came his women.

'Jean Paul Getty is priapic,' Lord Beaverbrook once warned his granddaughter, Lady Jean Campbell.

'What does that mean, Grandpapa?' she asked him.

'Ever-ready,' he replied.

He always had been. Ever since adolescence in Los Angeles, women had been the one luxury the old miser had never denied himself. How he had enjoyed them in his time! Young and old, fat and fashionably thin, drum-majorettes and duchesses, street-walkers, stars and socialites. Until quite recently he had been taking vitamins in massive doses, together with the so-called sex drug, H3, to maintain his potency. But now all that was over, and it was no longer sex but the rumour of his imminent departure which brought his mistresses to Sutton Place.

He would not be lavish with them – any more than he was lavish with himself. He was courteous with women, but rarely became emotionally involved for long.

Had all his money brought him happiness? There is a certain consolation in the thought of the very rich deriving little pleasure from their wealth, and much of Getty's undoubted popularity originated in that look of crucified affliction with which he had schooled himself to face the world.

As Getty's one-time chief executive, the celebrated Claus von Bülow, put it, he always looked as if he were attending his own funeral. But clever Claus was swift to add that behind that rainy countenance his boss was secretly enjoying life, and that this contrast formed what he saw as the essential comedy of Getty's whole existence. Von Bülow may have had a somewhat special sense of humour, but according to him, Getty always saw the funny side of things.

Perhaps he did, and we will never know what risible delights the old nocturnal joker found in the stillness of the Surrey night with a balance sheet.

For his fortune had achieved surreal proportions, and since most of it was carefully invested and busily creating yet more money, not even Jean Paul Getty ever knew precisely how rich he was. Suffice it to say that his fortune was almost as great as the annual budget at that time of Northern Ireland, where his forebears originated, more than any human being could exhaust in a lifetime of the most extravagant desires. He could have given every man, woman and child in the United States a ten-dollar bill and still been rich.

Few things, of course, would have been less likely, for in contrast with John D. Rockefeller, who habitually dispensed a

freshly minted dime to any child he met, Jean Paul was disinclined to acts of random generosity. Indeed he was disinclined
to generosity, full stop, but his celebrated stinginess was not
exactly what it seemed.

'That's why he's rich,' people used to say. But they were
wrong. Avarice alone could never have accounted for a fraction
of a fortune such as his, and Getty's meanness was less the cause
of his exaggerated wealth than a symptom of something more
intriguing.

The truth was that Jean Paul Getty was a man of passion,
which he had channelled single-mindedly into the creation of
his massive fortune much as a great composer pours his soul
into a symphony. His real love was not for women, who were
incidental, but for money, which was not, and he had proved
himself a faithful and romantic partner during his lifelong love
affair with wealth, jealously acquiring it, and making it increase,
in massive quantities, across a period of more than sixty years.

His avarice was an incidental aspect of this love. How can
one bear to waste the object of one's adoration? How could he
squander that delightful substance which, with death approaching, offered him his greatest hope of immortality?

Vast wealth surrounded Jean Paul Getty like a nimbus, dispensing godlike qualities not vouchsafed to poorer mortals.
Through money he was able to create continual movement
across the world, from the security guards with their fierce
Alsatians padding in the darkness near the house, to his oil refineries working round the clock, his tankers ploughing distant
oceans, his oil wells pumping wealth up from the depths of the
sea and the furthest reaches of the desert.

But there are limits to the god-like powers that wealth
bestows on mortal billionaires, and nothing could relieve him of
the final act required of him. He had always been a quiet, lonely
man, and during the night of 6 June 1976, still sitting in his
favourite armchair, silently and quite alone, he died.

★

Death is a great diminisher, and it was strange how insignificant America's richest man appeared once he was dead. In accordance with his wishes his body was laid out in state in the great hall of Sutton Place like a tudor nobleman. 'He always liked to think he was Duke John of Sutton Place,' one of his mistresses remarked. But a dukedom was one thing even his enormous fortune could not buy, and the only mourners watching by the bier were security men making sure that, even now, the body wasn't kidnapped.

Later, and again in accordance with his wishes, a memorial service was held at the smart Anglican church of St Mark's, North Audley Street, in Mayfair. As an event it was curiously in character. Another duke (Bedford this time) delivered the address to a dry-eyed, fashionable congregation; just one of Getty's surviving sons, though suffering the severe effects of heroin and alcohol addiction, managed to attend; and the vicar never got his service fee.

Not that one could blame Jean Paul for that, for by then he had made the journey he had always dreaded – by air-freight in his coffin in a Boeing's cargo hold to California – and he was currently residing in a funeral parlour at Hollywood's Forest Lawn cemetery while the family and the Los Angeles authorities argued over where to bury him.

But there still remained one area where the vital force of this inscrutable old man was very much alive – in his last will and testament, which had been duly published by his London lawyers. It was a fascinating document – as much for what it left out as for what it stated – and it served to emphasize the mystery of the whole baroque relationship between the dead man, his enormous fortune and the members of his very scattered family.

A will is an opportunity to deliver those one loves a final judgement before going off to meet one's own. It was an opportunity Jean Paul appreciated, having lived his life in the shadow of the will made by his father half a century before. And like Papa, he made the most of it.

For the past ten years, whenever his lawyer, energetic, white-haired Lansing Hays, had flown in to see him from Los Angeles, there would always be some change which Getty wanted made to the fearsome document, always somebody to add to – or angrily subtract from – the list of legatees. Getty was a man of some precision, and his will became a finely tuned expression of his wishes.

He had never bothered overmuch with humble people, and the humble people in his life received scant crumbs from America's richest table. Léon Turrou, his trusted security adviser, and Tom Smith, the half-Indian masseur Getty relied on to relieve his pains in his last years, both said he promised to remember them and both were bitter to discover they had been forgotten. The gardeners at Sutton Place got three months' wages; the butler, the po-faced Bullimore, six; and even his faithful secretary, Barbara Wallace, who had mother-henned him for some twenty years, was lucky to receive $5,000.

Remembering him, she is more generous than he was with her. 'That's how he was,' she says. 'I loved him and what counted was not the money but the memory of working with the most extraordinary character I've ever known.'

Others were less charitable, for he also used his will to make clear what he thought about the women in his life. His legal adviser, chaste Miss Lund, received $200 a month – possibly to put on record what he thought of chastity. But then, the unchaste Nicaraguan Mrs Rosabella Burch fared little better, so he may have had some other reason.

The only female friend who did do well was Mrs Kitson, who received some $850,000 worth of Getty Oil stock. When the value of shares in Getty Oil doubled in the early eighties, she would finally be the only person to become a dollar millionaire from reading G. A. Henty.

Again, the frugality of these personal bequests was totally in character and was probably intended to emphasize the big surprise within this deeply pondered document. For in one untypically grand gesture, Jean Paul Getty had decided to

dispose of the mass of his personal fortune in its entirety, uncon-
ditionally and without the faintest reservations.

He'd always been a man for sly surprises, and, apart from
Lansing Hays, had given nobody the slightest hint of how he
would be opening the sluice-gates on this vast amount of money
to benefit one unsuspecting legatee – the modest J. Paul Getty
Museum at Malibu, which he had been quietly creating in the
grounds of his ranch-house but had never dared to visit.

In museum terms the Getty legacy was vast. At his death his
personal assets were computed at nearly a billion dollars (around
2 billion today allowing for subsequent inflation). With this
money, the strange museum he had had meticulously created in
the form of an ancient Roman villa on the shores of the Pacific
Ocean became overnight the most richly endowed institution
of its kind in modern history.

According to the old man's personal assistant, Norris Bramlett, 'This was his hope of immortality. He wanted the Getty
name to be remembered as long as civilization lasted.'

It was also, as he knew quite well, a highly tax-efficient way
of disposing of a large amount of capital. In California, the
museum counted as a charity, and provided its directors spent 4
per cent of the value of the capital on acquisitions every year,
the US Internal Revenue Service would not assess taxes on it.
Getty had always been viscerally opposed to paying taxes – and
unlike simpler citizens who feel the same, he rarely had.

Beyond these facts, the will gave not the faintest explanation
as to why his money had been left like this, and why no
conditions were imposed upon the way the museum trustees
spent it. When Getty's rival oilman, Armand Hammer, created
his own much smaller museum in Los Angeles, he tied up everything in minutest detail. The steel baron Henry Clay Frick had
almost made it legally impossible to change an aspidistra in the
atrium of the Frick Collection in New York – let alone a picture. But should the trustees of the J. Paul Getty Museum in
their wisdom suddenly decide to sell the whole collection, using

the assets to create a bicycle museum, a bicycle museum is what the J. Paul Getty Museum will irrevocably become.

But just as the will shed little light upon the old man's reasons for bequeathing everything in this way, so it also left obscure a more intriguing mystery: the financial fate of the members of his family, or, as he liked to call them, the 'Getty dynasty' – the children and the grandchildren of three of his five failed marriages. Since the will made so little mention of them, what of their future? Had he simply forgotten them, or had they been collectively disinherited?

When archaeologists unearthed the tombs of some of the richest pharaohs, they sometimes found, concealed behind the burial chamber, a further chamber crammed with still more splendid objects where the spirit of the dead resided. Something similar had happened with the money left by Jean Paul Getty, for it was typical of the old man's covert nature that behind his personal fortune, which he bequeathed to his museum, he had been slowly building up a second, even greater, fortune which resided in a trust not covered by his will.

This massive trust had always been completely separate from Getty's personal fortune, and had grown with a lifetime's winnings from the secret game he had been playing with the world for over forty years. This was where he stacked away the vast amounts of money which, according to the complex rules by which this game was played, some of his descendants would inherit – and some, emphatically, would not.

Although this trust had suited Jean Paul Getty's purposes as a sort of monster tax-proof money-box, it was originally created as a so-called 'spendthrift trust' to placate his formidable mother, Sarah, who had known him well enough to distrust his motives. It was through her insistence that the trust was established in the mid 1930s to protect the financial interests of her grandchildren from what she saw as Getty's 'spendthrift' tendencies, and appropriately it bore her name – the Sarah C. Getty Trust.

It was strange to have the century's richest miser publicly proclaimed a 'spendthrift'. What was stranger still was the way he seemed obsessively compelled to go on adding to the trust, creating this prodigious pile of untaxed capital. When finally split between its beneficiaries in 1986, the trust was valued in excess of 4 billion dollars – since when the resultant capital has more than doubled in value yet again.

One might have thought, as Sarah presumably did, that this spendthrift trust would guarantee to her descendants all the benefits and pleasures wealth can bring to those who journey down the rocky road of life: freedom from anxiety and care, the best of everything, faithful friends, and – dare one whisper it? – happiness.

Reader, think again!

The great unanswered mystery of the Getty fortune is why it has apparently devoured so many of its beneficiaries.

Why should this massive reservoir of wealth have proved to be not just the largest, but probably the most destructive major fortune of our time? And why, when millions die for want of money, and countless millions slave, scheme, murder, labour, subjugate themselves for such pathetic glimpses of the stuff, should something as pleasurable as money bring such misery and havoc as it has to Getty's heirs?

The human wreckage started piling up within the old man's lifetime. One son had killed himself three years before he died. By then another son appeared intent on doing much the same through alcohol and heroin addiction. A third son, disinherited in child-hood, had grown increasingly embittered at the way he had been treated by his father. Only the fourth and youngest son was cur-rently enjoying what by normal standards one might term a rea-sonably fulfilling life – but at the cost of cutting himself off from anything to do with Getty Oil or his father's other businesses.

By the time the old man died, the blight was starting to afflict the next generation too. Getty's eldest grandson had been kidnapped by the Italian mafia, losing his right ear in the pro-cess, and then embarking on a life of drug addiction, drink, and dissipation which would end by almost totally destroying him. Later his sister would end up suffering from Aids.

Indeed, in the years following on Jean Paul Getty's death, there were times when the family itself appeared intent on self-destruction, as brother battled through the courts with brother over this vast and poisoned legacy. As one journalist put it, by the 1980s the name of Getty had become 'a synonym for family dysfunction'.

Great fortunes can clearly have disastrous effects upon the heirs – generally by swamping them with too much money at an early age. But with the Getty family, undiluted lucre was never at the root of all their misery. None of J. Paul Getty's sons was raised in pampered luxury – nor even in the expectation of inheriting enormous wealth. Nor were the grandchildren. Rather the contrary.

Balzac, who was fascinated by great fortunes, and by the havoc that he saw them bring to the *nouveaux riches* families of France's Second Empire, believed that, as he wrote, 'behind every great fortune lies a great crime'.

But even here the Gettys would have baffled him. For although there may have been a modicum of dirty-work and double-dealing in the creation of the Getty fortune, there was no actual crime to put one's finger on – and certainly no 'great' one.

There was, however, something more intriguing, which Balzac would have loved – the infinitely complex character of Getty himself. The story of his fortune is essentially the story of his life, and the contradictions and obsessions of this most eccentric Californian always played a crucial role in his achievement. They played an even greater part in the troubled heritage he left behind him, so much so that what happened to his children and his children's children also forms a part of Jean Paul Getty's legacy. Some were destroyed by it; some, though badly scarred, have come to terms with it; and some of the younger generation, all too well aware of what has occurred, are seeking to offset the dangers for the future.

How all this happened forms an extraordinary chronicle of the effect of vast amounts of money on a group of very vulnerable human beings. To understand it, one must begin with the strange creation of the fortune, and the character of the solitary, frightened, womanizing puritan who made himself the richest human being in America.

PART ONE

CHAPTER ONE

FATHER AND SON

J EAN PAUL GETTY was no novice to great wealth and the problems it could bring to its possessors. He was in fact a second generation millionaire himself – his father, George Franklin Getty, had started the family fortune with the profits from the Oklahoma oil boom of 1903. But just as with a great tree it is hard to picture the sapling out of which it grew, so the vastness of Jean Paul Getty's fortune almost totally obscures the lesser fortune which preceded it. It also obscures the fact that without his father and *his* fortune, the Getty billions could never have existed.

When Jean Paul was already in his sixties, as rich as Croesus, and immensely proud to be sleeping with a duchess, with the sister of a duke, and with a distant cousin of the Tsar of Russia, one of his odder habits was to recite part of Lincoln's Gettysburg Address, which he knew by heart, to those he particularly wanted to impress. On concluding, he would casually mention that Gettysburg happened to derive its name from an ancestor of his, one James Getty, who bought the site of the historic town from William Penn in person, and endowed it with his name.

It might seem odd that the richest American felt obliged to produce this sort of ancestral credit rating. What is odder still is that the story was totally untrue. Gettysburg got its name from a family called Gettys, and Jean Paul's ancestors had no connection with the place at all.

More to the point, his father's history, far from requiring

enhancement with the sort of phony origins sometimes indulged in by the English aristocracy, was one of those tales of achievement of which any son, particularly an American, might well have been extremely proud. But then, Jean Paul had reasons of his own to feel ambivalent about his father – and the part their curious relationship had played in the whole bizarre creation of his fortune.

Jean Paul himself was born in Minneapolis in 1892. His father, George, a powerful, godly man, was thirty-seven at the time. His mother, Sarah, *née* Risher – dark eyes, tightly piled-up hair, and the down-turned mouth of the dissatisfied character she was – was three years older, of distant Dutch and Scottish origins.

The Gettys themselves originated from Northern Ireland, arriving in America at the end of the eighteenth century and going through the melting pot of the American immigrant experience. As a result, George began life as the offspring of poor farming folk in Maryland. His father died when he was six, leaving the boy to labour with his mother in the fields until his uncle, Joseph Getty, famous as a local hell-fire temperance preacher, sent him to school in Ohio.

George was a strong, hard-working boy and the adversity following his father's death left him with an iron resolution to raise himself from poverty. Meanwhile from Uncle Joe he learned the rigid precepts of fundamentalist Christianity, together with a lifelong hatred of the demon drink, and a steadfast faith in the saving grace of God to lift humanity from poverty and sin.

It was while at Ohio University, and studying to become a teacher, that George first caught the eye of Sarah Risher. She had no intention of spending her life married to a schoolmaster, so she made George promise to become a lawyer – offering the money from her dowry to pay his fees through law school.

It is appropriate that Sarah Getty's name is still enshrined within the massive trust which came to dominate the fortunes of her family, for throughout the marriage sharp-eyed Sarah was the mover, egging on her dutiful, hard-working, younger partner to make money and succeed.

Within a year of their marriage in 1879 George had already taken his law degree at the University of Michigan, and Sarah was urging their move to thriving Minneapolis – where her husband turned his legal talents to the insurance business and began to prosper. By their early thirties George and Sarah owned their own house in the most fashionable part of Minneapolis, drove a coach and pair, and were people of substance and promise in the booming capital of the North Star State of Minnesota.

Far from weakening their puritan ideals, success made both Gettys stronger in the faith. From puritan Uncle Joe, George had imbibed a Calvinistic sense of good and evil, and worldly wealth was seen as evidence of heavenly favour. According to this practical belief, God rewarded those who hearkened to his word – and smiled on those whose way of life forswore the devil and his works.

As zealous methodists, George and Sarah were serious and self-denying. Having signed the pledge in his early twenties, George remained a lifelong and dedicated teetotaller. And until the age of thirty-five, his life had seemed a story-book example of the benefits which flow from Christian conduct. He had responded to the word of God. He had laboured in the vineyard. Now the time had come for George, like Job, to face his period of tribulation.

When he was being hailed as his country's richest human being, one of the few possessions Jean Paul Getty genuinely treasured was a sepia photograph of a small girl he had never seen. She had ringlets, a large bow in her hair, and soulful eyes.

This was his sister, Gertrude Lois Getty, who was born in

1880, soon after George and Sarah's marriage, and died in the typhoid epidemic which swept Minnesota in the winter of 1890. Sarah also caught this fearsome illness and, although she recovered, it gave her a tendency to deafness which steadily grew worse, making her virtually stone deaf at fifty.

For George and Sarah the taking of their only child, 'the sunbeam of the family', was a loss which tried their faith as Christians. Of the two, George appeared the more affected, and for a period he turned to spiritualism in an attempt to find his daughter, and underwent a deep religious crisis.

When he finally emerged from it, he was more steadfast in the faith than ever, and actually abandoned Methodism for the stricter creed of Christian Science, whose principles he adhered to firmly for the remainder of his life.

As if to show that God approved this change of creed, it was shortly afterwards that George received a sign. In her fortieth year Sarah, who had conceived but once before, discovered she was pregnant. And on 15 December 1892, the arrival of a son was like an early Christmas present to replace their daughter.

In their gratitude to God, how could the Gettys fail to treasure such a child? And George had further reasons for rejoicing in the newborn Jean Paul Getty. Here was an heir at last to carry on the name, and inherit what was steadily accruing from the lucrative insurance business in the thriving cities of the Midwest USA.

Sarah named the child after her husband's Getty cousin, John, but it was very much in character that she also had to give the child a touch of European sophistication by making the name not 'John' but 'Jean'. With time the name would be compressed to the bare initial, J. in J. Paul Getty, and within their family its owner would be generally referred to by the name of Paul. But there was something more prophetic than Sarah can have realized when she gave her child this personal connection with

Europe. Europe and its culture were to act as magnets to her son and many of the members of his family in the years ahead.

Despite the Gettys' middle-class prosperity, life with two strait-laced, ageing parents, haunted by a vanished daughter, offered little in the way of sociability or mirth, and Paul, though cosseted and protected, had a lonely and loveless childhood. His mother actively discouraged contact with other children from fear of fresh contagion. And while over-protective with her son, she was careful not to show him too much love in case she lost him as she lost his sister.

Years later Paul told his wife that as a child he was never cuddled – nor did he have a birthday party or a Christmas tree. His one great interest was his postage stamp collection, his closest friend a mongrel dog called Jip.

Undoubtedly this claustrophobic childhood put its mark on him, and he would always be a loner, wary of his fellows, and keeping his thoughts and feelings to himself.

'I have long been able to exercise a considerable degree of control over my display of emotions,' he proudly wrote when he was over eighty.

But in childhood, the tedium of life in this rigid little family clearly affected him in other ways as well. Instead of passively accepting the grey horizons of nineteenth-century puritan America, he secretly rebelled, and throughout his life, part of him would always struggle to escape the boredom and restriction of humdrum domesticity. He would never be entirely at ease within a family. Instead he would be always on the move, and until the onset of old age would never settle anywhere for long. Left to his own devices, Paul Getty would have been a wanderer.

With business booming, God appeased, and his home in Minneapolis in order, George Franklin Getty had every reason to be happy – particularly when he suddenly received a further sign of heavenly approval.

In 1903, when Paul was ten, the Lord directed George to Bartlesville, a one-horse town in what was legally still Indian Territory in Oklahoma, to settle an insurance claim. At the time he had no way of knowing the stupendous outcome of this unexciting journey. Bartlesville was buzzing with the beginnings of the Oklahoma oil bonanza. Under this barren landscape lay some of the largest oil reserves within the USA. And George had arrived just in time to benefit from them.

'There are men,' wrote his son, 'who seem to have an uncanny affinity with oil in its natural state. I am inclined to think that my father had a touch of this himself.'

Perhaps he had, but, to start with, it was little more than passing speculation that led George to invest 500 dollars in 'Lot 50' – a lease to the oil rights on 1,100 acres of virgin prairie outside Bartlesville.

But the Lord had directed George aright. When drilling started on Lot 50 that October, it almost instantly struck oil, and one year later, George had six oil wells in production. The price of crude was 52 cents a barrel at the time and Lot 50 was averaging 100,000 barrels every month.

Apart from heavenly guidance, there were more prosaic factors to George's rapid creation of a fortune. He had already saved considerable reserves of capital from the insurance business; he knew the law; and he conducted his affairs the honest and self-denying way.

Within the next three busy years, George propelled his company, which he called Minnehoma Oil (a name concocted, not from some romantic redskin maiden, but from the business-like elision of the two words Minnesota and Oklahoma), into a thriving company. By 1906, George Getty was a millionaire.

CHAPTER TWO

A SOLITARY CHILDHOOD

PAUL WAS TEN when he arrived in Bartlesville and got his earliest glimpse of George's famous 'Lot 50' oil well. He was deeply disappointed. Knowing that Bartlesville was in Indian territory, he had gone there expecting redskins, squaws and wigwams. Instead he saw a makeshift boom-town, reeking of oil, and peopled with men in grimy overalls.

But it was a formative experience for any boy to watch his father suddenly grow rich so very easily and something he would not forget. Having this intimate *entrée* to the oil business, it would not be difficult for him to do the same – should he ever need to. And from the start of Minnehoma, George took it for granted that his son would naturally join him in the company and ultimately succeed him at its head. He even encouraged his infant son to use his pocket money to buy two Minnehoma shares.

'Now I have to work for you,' he told him, handing him the share certificates. George had a habit of dispensing nuggets of his homespun wisdom. 'A businessman is only as good as his sources of information,' was one of them. 'Let your deeds speak louder than your words,' another.

But throughout childhood and adolescence, Paul stayed obtusely uninspired by his father's words – and by the oil business, having interests of his own to occupy his time.

Later in life, he would always speak of George with considerable piety and reverence. 'He was a great man, and a genuine philosopher,' he solemnly intoned. 'He taught me everything I know.'

In fact Paul taught himself everything he needed, and father and son would often clash with one another. According to his cousin, Hal Seymour, 'Paul and his father just seemed to get in one another's way when they were together in the house.'

In character Paul was closer to his mother than to solid George. He had inherited her down-turned mouth, her restlessness, her locked-in nature; then, as he grew, a further similarity revealed itself between them. Sarah's deafness made her particularly isolated, and Paul began to emulate her solitariness. Even his voice would bear the traces of their close relationship. The measured diction that became a sort of Getty trademark was something that he learned from talking with a mother who was hard of hearing. And like his mother, he increasingly relied upon his own company. It was now that Cousin Hal remembered him as being 'exceptionally solitary, even for an only child'.

Unlike his parents, he found little pleasure in the joys of Christianity; his one true passion was for reading. By the age of ten he had discovered those works of G. A. Henty which he would be enjoying in his eighties.

As a boys' adventure writer Henty had inspired a generation of Victorian schoolboys, transporting them from the boredom of the dusty schoolroom to the most colourful periods of history, peopled with its most exciting characters. *Under Drake's Flag, With Clive in India, With Moore at Corunna*: even the titles were an invitation to a solitary only child to escape from a closed-in Christian home in Minnesota to the richer, more exciting world outside.

Now that George was rapidly becoming rich, and was frequently away in Oklahoma, Sarah decided it was time for one more move – from the flat farmlands and freezing winters of Minnesota to sunny California. She claimed her health was delicate, and that she needed warmth and a change of scenery. As usual, George agreed with her.

After visiting San Diego, which they thought provincial, the Gettys decided on a plot of land on newly laid-out South Kingsley Drive, on a corner with the still unsurfaced stretch of Wilshire Boulevard lying beyond the Los Angeles city limits. There they built themselves a house.

As a family the Gettys had few close friends and the move had cut them off from those they had. They drank not, neither did they sin – and Sarah's growing deafness heightened the sense of isolation of the family. In the days before efficient hearing-aids, it was hard for any family with a mother suffering this most antisocial of afflictions to be open and at ease with those around them. So more than ever now the Gettys were thrown back upon their own resources. They were self-sufficient and reclusive people. These were habits Paul learned early, practised all his life and passed on to his children.

George tried to be as strict with his son as with himself, but the more exacting George became, the more sullen was his son's reaction. He was wilful, as solitary children often are; and George, as parents often do, imagined that the cure was discipline. So, shortly after moving to Los Angeles, Paul was sent as a day boy to the local military school – which inevitably he hated. Drill, marching, uniforms and discipline were not for him. He stayed for nearly four years, acquired few friends, showed zero aptitude for soldiering, and when he finally escaped was grateful for the peace and privacy of his own room in the house at South Kingsley Drive.

It used to be a commonplace of educational theory that teenage boys who read too much and were left to their own devices were particularly at risk to sexual temptation. This certainly applied to Paul, and the hearty discipline of the military school had failed to cure him. As something of a bookworm – he was known to his classmates as 'Dictionary Getty' – he had remained stolidly resistant to healthy group activities such as marching, field-days and team games of all types. The result was predictable. Together with his-love of reading went an obsession with the opposite sex which stayed with him for life. In matters sexual he had finally discovered something he was good at.

Perhaps it was his manner, which was always courteous and charming with the other sex. ('Paul never said "no" to a woman – or "yes" to a man,' as somebody remarked.)

Or possibly it was simply knowing what he wanted, which in matters sexual, as in those of business, tends to bring results. At all events, by his fourteenth birthday Paul was apparently boasting of losing his virginity.

If true, this was more of an achievement for a boy from a rich Christian family in California than it would be today. By Getty standards, it was also seriously sinful, placing him on collision course with all those strictly held and practised puritan beliefs solemnly maintained by George and Sarah.

Paul was increasingly getting on his father's nerves – and vice versa. A period supposedly studying economics at the University of Southern California at Los Angeles was followed by a further period supposedly reading law at Berkeley. But universities, it seemed, were not for him and as a thoroughly discontented seventeen-year-old, he soon returned to South Kingsley Drive.

By now Paul was very much his mother's precious only child, the gift of God and a consolation for her deafness and advancing years. So rather than lose him totally, she schooled herself to overlook his faults, and tended to support him in his battles with his father.

As something of a bait – and a way of keeping him at home – Sarah arranged that he should have a private entrance for his room, with his own latch-key. It was typical of Sarah that, having done this, she was soon objecting to the friends he started bringing home, but there was little she could do about them –

any more than she and George could really interfere with their son's developing interest in the night life of Los Angeles.

Without telling them, Paul began borrowing his father's car, an impressive four-door Chadwick tourer, which he would silently roll out of the garage when his parents were asleep and use to tour the local nightspots with his friends to pick up girls.

One night, after Paul had visited a roadhouse with companions Sarah would have disapproved of – and met some girls she would have disapproved of even more – disaster struck. One of the girls spilled red wine on the car's upholstery, and although they did their best to mop it up, nothing could remove the stains.

When George saw what had happened, he must have realized the truth – that Paul was not just borrowing the family barouche for reasons of nocturnal pleasure, but indulging in his particular *bête noire*, the demon drink itself. But George's reaction set an important precedent for future relations in the Getty family. No bellow of paternal rage disturbed the peace at South Kingsley Drive. As usual when it came to Paul, Sarah almost certainly restrained him, and not a word was said about the incident.

However, George had ways of registering paternal disapproval. The next time Paul tried borrowing the car when his parents were in bed, he found the back wheel firmly padlocked to a ring cemented to the garage floor.

When Sarah made the family migrate 2,000 miles south-west from frozen Minneapolis to radiant Los Angeles, this stretch of Southern California had yet to become the overpopulated paradise at the far end of the great American rainbow it is today. Its golden landscape was unsullied, its ocean unpolluted, and its perfect year-round climate was still unaffected by the products of the oil industry that was making George's fortune.

The Gettys were early *émigrés* from the East in search of happiness – but even here happiness eluded them. The outdoor pleasures of the golden state were not for George and Sarah. As

far as George the dedicated oilman was concerned, life still centred on the Oklahoma oilfields over 1,000 miles by railroad to
the east. And Sarah found Los Angeles sadly deficient in culture
and amenities. Thus it was very much in character that the house
the couple built was more of a harking back to old world memories than a celebration of the new.

In his mid sixties Paul would finally succumb to buying
himself a permanent home – the stately Tudor pile of Sutton
Place. And here, among the orange groves off rural Wilshire
Boulevard, was surely its precursor – the Tudor-style mansion
with its mullioned windows, gimcrack gables, and freshly stained
Elizabethan beams. As a house it presumably belonged to the
distant world of another imagined Getty ancestor. Nostalgia was
its keynote, and a few years later, when George felt rich enough
to take Paul and Sarah off on their first extended holiday
together, they travelled to Europe.

This was still the period when the heroes and heroines of
novelists like Henry James and Edith Wharton were taking it for
granted that only in Europe could they discover truly civilized
existence. Europe, in those far-off days, was still the fountain-
head of history, art, and serious sophistication for the American
élite.

But this obsession with Europe was far more typical of East
Coast millionaires than Californian *nouveaux riches* like George
and Sarah. And it is interesting that at the very moment when
expatriate New York movie-makers just up the road in the
Hollywood hills were beginning a counterculture which would
conquer Europe with a home-grown vision of America, the
Gettys should have undertaken this laborious journey to New
York, then on to Europe for a carefully planned, three-month
tour by road of all the major capitals. From this moment it was
the old world, rather than the new, that captured the imagination of Paul Getty.

As so often in the family, the incentive for this journey came
from Sarah. Left to his own devices, George would have been
content to mind the store in Oklahoma. But Sarah was insistent

and so off they went – shipping the famous Chadwick tourer with them, collecting a chauffeur in Liverpool whose accent they could barely comprehend, then driving on rapidly to France, determined to experience and see as much as possible.

The Gettys were energetic rather than indulgent travellers – something else that set a pattern which their son would copy. In Paris they enjoyed a fortnight at the Hôtel Continentale – haunt of bourgeois businessmen and commercial travellers – rather than the Ritz, which George could have easily afforded. Then it was off along the dusty roads to Monte Carlo, Rome, Geneva, Amsterdam, before heading back across the Channel, seeing London, and returning on the liner *Aquitania* to New York.

For the young man with the wavy hair and the practised pale blue eye for any girl he saw, this bumpy journey was a formative experience. He loved travel, and he positively enjoyed hotels, excited by the richness and the possibilities of adventure in these European cities. But he must have felt inhibited by the presence of two aged parents, one a strict Methodist with hearing problems, and the other a teetotal, moralistic, born-again Christian Scientist. Eighteen-year-old Paul Getty couldn't wait to return and start enjoying all these fascinating places on his own.

Once back on South Kingsley Drive, Sarah was happy that her restless son evinced such interest in European culture, and, despite her fears of losing him, seems to have supported his ambition to return to Europe once he told her that he wished to study at Oxford University.

George was less enthusiastic. Oxford's dreaming spires were not for him, but Sarah talked him into granting Paul an adequate allowance – in the form of a banker's draft for 200 dollars a month – and in August 1912, after a brief trip to Japan, the twenty-year-old son and heir was once more crossing the Atlantic – on his own.

He travelled in considerable style, for this was very much the journey of the indulged scion of an American millionaire, with echoes, however faint, of those European grand tours on which English aristocrats once dispatched their offspring to obtain some culture and knowledge of the world before returning home to their inheritance. This European trip would have its own profound effect on Paul – but not exactly in the way his parents were expecting.

From the start it was a considerable undertaking for a solitary, more or less philistine young American to make such a journey on his own. But just as with his women, Paul was distinctly knowledgeable and self-assured when it came to getting what he wanted. He had already hustled George into obtaining him a letter of introduction from one of his former legal cronies, the lawyer William Howard Taft, who now happened to be Republican President of the USA. And once in Europe he grandly purchased a second-hand Mercedes tourer, ordered several suits from Savile Row, and then set out for the unlikely object of his journey – Oxford University. He arrived there in November, when term had already started.

Oxford before the First World War was very much a closed society, and this unknown, unconnected young American, who had failed to complete a university course at either Los Angeles or Berkeley, had little in the way of learning or formal education to commend him.

Luckily this hardly mattered, as the standard of education among most Oxford undergraduates of the period was lamentably low, and Paul was not in Oxford on a quest for learning. Like Jay Gatsby, what he wanted was quite different – the right to call himself an Oxford man, which, with customary single-mindedness, he more or less obtained.

The letter from the President of the USA provided his introduction to the President of fashionable Magdalen College, the comfortable classicist Dr Herbert Warren, who spent some time with this self-possessed young Californian and ended by recommending someone in his college to 'tutor' him in economics. Paul also became a non-collegiate member of St Catherine's Society, which was not yet a fully accredited Oxford college, but which permitted him to attend lectures if he wished – something rarely practised by the majority of undergraduates at the time. And he had little difficulty finding lodgings in the centre of the city.

But although he later claimed that while at Oxford he had 'more or less lived at Magdalen', and insisted that 'the men at Magdalen accepted me as one of their number', he was not a member of Magdalen College or at Oxford University. Not that this ever stopped him tacitly implying that he was – and in later years he always made great play of how his time at fashionable Magdalen had subtly infiltrated him into the bosom of the British upper classes.

'The first close friend I made at Magdalen,' he would fondly reminisce, 'was the brother of the present Earl of Portarlington, George Dawson-Damer.' Running George a gilded second was 'His Royal Highness, the Prince of Wales', who also chanced to be at Magdalen. 'We,' said Getty casually, always 'called each other "David" and "Paul" and formed a close, warm friendship that was to endure for almost half a century.'

It was never very clear how long Paul actually spent at Oxford or whether he did obtain the 'diploma' that he claimed – nor how really 'close and warm' was that lifelong friendship with the future King of England – but little of this really mattered. What was important was that here at Oxford, Paul had seen at last a world he thoroughly admired and envied. Some of his Magdalen friends invited this rich young Californian home to enjoy that fashionable institution of the period, the Edwardian weekend, and later he would write nostalgically of how the houses he had visited were 'frequently stately country manors which, in that last blaze of the Edwardian era, were still at the height of their splendour'.

Here, in vivid contrast with simple sunny California, and the grimy oil wells of Oklahoma, was a world of titled aristocrats, stately homes, grandiose art – and wonderfully sophisticated women. Here was a world that would haunt him for the remainder of his life.

There are essentially two sorts of snob – insiders attempting to keep the vulgar 'out', and spellbound outsiders trying to convince themselves that they are 'in'. Paul was emphatically in the second category – and henceforth one important part of his ambition would be to stake his claim within that illusory yet sacred zone of titles, deference, ancient wealth and European royalty which he had glimpsed at Magdalen during that golden time before the lamps went out all over Europe.

After Oxford, Paul was in no hurry to return to California. He was becoming a compulsive traveller, seriously intent upon escape, and rather than become immersed in the tedium of South Kingsley Drive, he was soon at the wheel of the Mercedes *en route* to what he had decided was to be his favourite city, Paris. Summer was spent in Russia, autumn in Berlin, and just before Christmas he was in Vienna, planning to spend the beginning of 1914 on the sights of Egypt.

But money had become a problem – which inevitably brought him into conflict with his father. Two hundred dollars a month meant fairly basic travel, and requests for more produced a sour response from George, who was becoming increasingly exasperated by this European 'gallivanting' of his wayward son.

By now Paul had been in flight for more than a year, and it was on the eve of his twenty-first birthday – which was spent aboard a rusty coaster, sailing to Alexandria – that his requests for money finally exploded into bitter conflict with his father.

Thoroughly aggravated by what he saw as his son's 'continuing extravagance and self-indulgence', George informed him that he was taking back 15,000 shares which he had placed in Paul's name in Minnehoma Oil. This produced a venomous riposte from Paul, showing something of the anger and resentment which, when thwarted, he could summon up against his father.

After a sharp demand to be permitted to retain the shares, Paul attacked him for his meanness to his only son – reminding him that when William Randolph Hearst reached twenty-one, *his* father had actually presented him with the *San Francisco Examiner* together with the newspaper building, which was worth at least 3 million dollars.

He bitterly continued that he had no intention of being 'cheated out of my birthright', and ended by saying that his father's attitude left him no alternative 'but to deal with the matter as I would with an opponent'.

Once more it seems that Sarah smoothed things over. Soon she was writing affectionately to Paul, saying how much she wished that she could 'fly to see him', and by early summer she had even persuaded George to make another transatlantic crossing so that they could meet their wayward son in Paris, relish the reunion, and travel home together.

June 1914 saw the Gettys reconciled and staying once again at the Hôtel Continentale; and it was there that Paul disclosed his real ambition for the future. Since he had every intention of continuing to travel and indulge in cosmopolitan society, he was going to become a diplomat – or, failing that, a writer.

Sarah appears to have supported him. George said nothing.

Despite his limitations, George Getty was not stupid, and in some ways he understood his son far better than Paul understood himself.

Instead of squandering precious time and money touring Europe, Paul should be safely settled in the one place where a son of his should obviously be – in the family business, learning the ropes, taking decisions, and being groomed as his successor.

Great events were now on George's side. With France and Germany on the brink of war, Paul could not return to Europe as he hoped in the autumn of 1914 to start learning diplomatic French and German. This gave George his chance to offer him a deal, which he knew that Paul would not refuse.

This was a straightforward business proposition, a stake of $10,000 for Paul to seek his fortune in the Oklahoma oilfields as he had done himself eleven years before. George emphasized that this was not a gift, but an investment by Minnehoma Oil. Any profit would accrue to the company, and Paul would be entitled to 30 per cent commission. Paul agreed.

Conditions had grown tougher than when George had arrived at Bartlesville and stumbled into the Oklahoma oil bonanza. Competition had increased, large companies like Standard Oil were moving in, and it was that much harder for the individual wild-catter to find his plot of oil-rich land, purchase his lease on the mineral rights, and make his fortune. But since Oklahoma was a massive area, containing one of the largest natural oilfields in the USA, there were still discoveries – and fortunes – to be made by anyone sufficiently determined. George was sure that once Paul had his first real taste of money and success, he would have him hooked.

CHAPTER THREE

THE FIRST MILLION DOLLARS

FOR A YOUNG man with a ruthless disposition, a little capital, and a resilient physique, the oil industry was the bargain basement of the twentieth century. Ford would produce their millionth motor car by the end of 1914, and war in Europe made the demand for oil increase dramatically. Then, as the century progressed, America's thirst for oil would go on growing – and the oil industry would inevitably grow with it.

It was at Tulsa, in the heart of Oklahoma's oil-rich territory, that Paul arrived to try his luck in the late autumn of 1914. In his pale grey suit, starched collar and fedora hat, the quietly spoken Oxford man from California must have been an unlikely figure among the speculators, drillers, engineers and drifters who thronged the lobby of the newly built Tulsa hotel.

But despite his manner and appearance, Paul was not as soft and overcivilized as he seemed. At twenty-two he measured five feet ten inches and was physically extremely strong and very conscious of his body. As a loner he had continued his hatred of team sports, but he was obsessive over strengthening his physique. He swam a lot, used weights and dumb-bells to improve his muscles, practised judo, and around this time was confident enough as a boxer to go several rounds with his friend, the future world heavyweight champion, Jack Dempsey.

Heavyweights in training often like to take on lighter fighters to improve their speed, and Dempsey's verdict was that Paul was 'well built, pugnacious by nature, and quick. I've never met anyone with such intense concentration and willpower – perhaps more than is good for him,' he said.

During that winter and the spring of 1915, Paul needed all these qualities as he drove the length of Oklahoma in his battered Ford, searching for that plot of oil-rich land to make his fortune. He had great determination, spurred on by his desire to match his father's original achievement.

It took practically a year before he succeeded. In August 1915, after bluffing several other would-be purchasers, he secured his first oil lease for a rock-bottom $500. His luck held. His well on the so-called 'Nancy Taylor Lease' was soon producing over 1,000 barrels daily, and with crude oil prices reaching $3 a barrel late that autumn, his capital began accruing. Encouraged by success, he started buying further leases which proved even more productive, and by the summer of 1916, his percentage on the profit he had made for Minnehoma Oil passed the magic figure of a million dollars.

He was all of twenty-three – and a millionaire. Convinced that there were more important things to life than oil, he decided to retire.

This should have been the moment he was waiting for – the precious time to realize his true ambitions. And but for the war he might have done so, sailed for Europe, and the Getty story would have had a different ending.

But war was making Europe inaccessible. Paul always claimed that around this time he volunteered to be a flier, and while he waited for his papers to arrive (they never did) he had no alternative but to return to South Kingsley Drive. His old room with its private entrance was awaiting him, crammed with his personal possessions lovingly tended by his mother. Rather to his surprise, he found himself enjoying being home.

As he later wrote, 'Southern California was an ideal place for anyone seeking to enjoy himself. It had a wonderful climate, spectacular scenery, and then as later, it abounded with exceedingly attractive, largely unattached young women.'

It was those 'largely unattached young women' who particularly appealed to him, and during the summertime of 1916, with a million dollars in the bank, he made the most of them.

'In my experience,' he used to say, 'money is the only absolutely certain aphrodisiac' – but a smart car also helped, and he bought several in succession – a Cadillac convertible, an early Chrysler, a bright red Duesenberg.

At South Kingsley Drive, with his private key, he came and went exactly as he pleased, and sometimes even brought his women home there for the night.

'Rather the "deep deep bliss" of the double bed at South Kingsley Drive, than the "hurly-burly" of the back seat of a Duesenberg,' as Mrs Patrick Campbell might have said.

George and Sarah must have known what was going on, and according to their own strict Christian principles, their son had now become a hopeless sinner. But had they told him so, they would have run the risk of losing him – and that was something Sarah wouldn't contemplate. So George and Sarah kept their feelings to themselves, Paul continued down the primrose path – and peace and harmony obtained in South Kingsley Drive.

But for Paul there was now one all-important factor in this pleasant situation – the fact that he had made himself a millionaire. Thanks to his money he had also made himself completely independent, and George was effectively deprived of any power to tell him what to do. This meant that Paul was able to enjoy his early twenties in a sort of endlessly extended spoiled childhood, indulged by his mother, tolerated by his father, and enjoying all the pleasures of a rich and thoroughly emancipated modern adolescent.

It was a lesson in the moral power of money, which would have a significant effect on Paul and his parents for the future.

Money effectively removed the moral imperative from everyday existence, and, thanks to his money, Paul could live a virtual double life – which clearly suited him.

He no longer needed to assert himself against his puritanical Papa, nor would he ever cease to be, at least in theory, the devoted only child of 'beloved Mama' either. Never needing to grow up, he would protest his love for them both most touchingly until they died. But at the same time he could also be a sort of licensed puritan, and make the most of many things his parents disapproved of – fast cars and faster women, night clubs and bootlegged gin, high life, and lower company.

As a result, the moral sense of Paul Getty seemed strangely contradictory, as he followed several lines of least resistance – eager for freedom, yet anxious for his parents' love, essaying all manner of escapes, yet always returning like a wayward child to the house on South Kingsley Drive.

As a Christian, George was presumably counting on the fact that his son's unedifying life of sin could not go on for ever. This was the time for Christian patience. God in His wisdom would surely make His presence felt, just as He did to the apostle Paul on the Damascus road. Once this happened, his benighted son would see the error of his ways, become reborn in Christ, and George and Sarah could finally rejoice in one more sinner saved.

It was an optimistic theory, and to a point it worked. Paul's idle, hedonistic life could not continue. Something had to bring it to a close. But when it did, it was certainly not what George had bargained for – and Paul failed to react as his parents prayed he would.

The girl's name was Elsie Eckstrom, and she claimed in court that she had been a virgin before Paul plied her with alcohol, drove her home, and forcibly deflowered her at South Kingsley Drive.

Paul's lawyer counterclaimed that Elsie was no virgin but an *habituée* of roadhouses and nightclubs, who drank and danced and slept around and got no more than she deserved.

The truth about Elsie is no longer particularly important – but what nobody denied in court was that sexual intercourse took place beneath the parental rafters of the Getty residence and that a baby daughter, born in 1917, was christened Paula.

After much unwelcome publicity with banner headlines in the *Los Angeles Times* during September 1917, Paul reluctantly produced $10,000 for Miss Eckstrom and the baby, and what was presumably the first offspring of the man destined to become his country's richest citizen vanished from the scene, along with any further scandal. To this day the Getty family has heard no more of her.

But what was intriguing was that, as in the Sherlock Holmes story of the dog that didn't bark in the night, there was still no outburst, no disclaimer, no evident reaction from the Getty family. Shortly afterwards, however, Paul left his life of idleness in California and returned to work for Minnehoma in the oil-fields of Oklahoma.

George Getty could console himself with the thought that his son, although a sinner, was clearly dedicated to the family business and showing extraordinary flair in the oil industry. He had energy and drive and vision, was a tougher businessman than George had ever been, and would make an admirable successor at the head of Minnehoma when George decided to retire.

In fact Paul was already showing signs of taking over as the driving force in Minnehoma. During 1919, it was his idea to extend the company's operations from Oklahoma to the freshly discovered coastal oilfields of California. Initially George was not enthusiastic, but Paul insisted, and Minnehoma's Californian operation proved highly profitable, more than doubling the capital value of the company (which led to the restructuring of Minnehoma under the new name of George Getty Inc.).

Now, too, Paul showed signs of actively enjoying life on the oilfields – learning the skills of the oil engineer, proving himself against the toughest workers on the rigs, boozing and whoring with them in the evenings, and fighting with his fists when necessary. It was a man's life, and this one-time, would-be intellectual found himself thoroughly enjoying it. No more was heard of literature or diplomacy. 'Nothing,' Paul would write, 'can adequately describe the emotion and triumph one experiences when he [*sic*] brings in his first producing well.'

Despite this, George was far from happy with his son. Paul had not repented of his trespasses – nor did he show the slightest sign of doing so. George also had his doubts about his probity, as he watched him taking risks, and underwriting deals he personally would not have sanctioned. There may have been an element of jealousy as well, the professional jealousy of the older man who fears his son displacing him, and the sexual jealousy of the ageing puritan who glimpses, in his son's behaviour, something of the fun he might have had himself.

For with the end of war in Europe, Paul was growing restless and had started taking longer holidays and travelling abroad – first to Mexico and then to his beloved Europe. It was not hard to imagine what Paul was doing on his travels, and George and Sarah must have felt that their son's last chance of salvation lay in finding a good wife, settling down in California, and raising a family.

CHAPTER FOUR

MARITAL FEVER

O N EMERGING FROM adolescence, young girls possess a special kind of beauty and, though no longer children, are briefly free from the demands which come so swiftly with maturity. It was this fragile, transitory stage of femininity which seems to have excited Paul Getty in his thirties.

Not only did he like young virgins, but, being very rich, he could afford them. They flattered his ego, kept him young, and had few of the more exacting expectations of older women. Living life exactly as he wanted, he was never very sympathetic to the emotional demands of others.

Although an important factor in his sexuality, this taste for Lolita-style nymphets was also a cause of many subsequent dramas and disasters in the family. It led him into five failed marriages, all with women almost young enough to have been his daughters.

The first began in 1923, when at thirty he suddenly proposed to seventeen-year-old Jeanette Dumont, a dark-eyed, half-Polish high-school beauty. Acting not unlike an anxious adolescent himself, he kept the romance secret from his parents, and it was not until he and his child-bride returned to Los Angeles from a secret wedding at Aventura, Mexico, in October that he broke the news to them that he was married.

In fact they were delighted, and rapidly became extremely fond of their schoolgirl daughter-in-law. They helped to find the newly-weds an apartment close to South Kingsley Drive, and, when Jeanette discovered she was pregnant, did all they could to make their son feel happy at the prospect of a family.

But a family was the last thing Paul desired. Nor did he desire Jeanette once the virgin bride turned into a pregnant and dependent wife. Far from approaching parenthood with joy, he bucked away and, like the spoiled only child he was, made angry efforts to escape.

With his precious freedom under threat, it was now that the aggressive side of Getty's nature soon became apparent. Gravid Jeanette was cruelly neglected as he returned to the night-life of Los Angeles with more responsive partners. When she complained, bitter rows ensued.

According to subsequent divorce-court testimony it was now that he yelled at her – 'I'm sick and tired of you, sick and tired of being married.'

According to the same source, he later 'beat and bruised her', even threatening to kill her. Then he left her.

But despite these ructions, it was somehow typical Paul that when the son he didn't want was born, on 9 July 1924, he proudly named him 'George Franklin Getty II' – in honour of his father.

George, meanwhile, was far from well. Early in 1923, at the age of sixty-eight, he suffered a major stroke on the Brentwood golf course in Los Angeles, which affected his speech and the right-hand portion of his body.

With his father out of action, Paul took charge of the company. Later he would always claim that, due to bad management and the squandering of capital on unprofitable oil leases, George Getty Inc. was actually running at a loss. But by saying so, and trying to increase efficiency, he made few friends among the old guard in the company. When his father gamely struggled back to work some six weeks later, he was greeted by numerous complaints about 'the boy' from old employees, angry at the way they had been treated in his absence.

But during his period in charge of the family company, Paul had also been pondering the future – and envisaging George Getty Inc. growing from the relatively simple oil-producing operation that it was into an oil conglomerate, capable of refining and marketing a range of petroleum products for the rapidly expanding US market. This was clearly where the future lay – but it was not what his father or his senior directors wished to hear.

Finally, George's gathering resentment turned to anger when, on top of everything, people told him how Paul had been behaving to Jeanette.

'That boy deserves a spanking,' was his astonishing reaction. For George could barely shuffle round the office with a stick, let alone administer his burly son a 'spanking'. Which did not stop his rage increasing even further when he heard that Paul, having summarily walked out on wife and baby, was about to be involved in a scandalous divorce.

Even Sarah turned against him now, confiding to a friend that she seriously believed that Paul had been 'taken over by the Devil'.

Far from being cured of marriage by Jeanette and all the trouble that had followed, Paul remained firmly in the throes of what he later called 'matrimonial fever'. Like an alcoholic on a bender, he was more enthusiastic for the married state than ever.

The truth was that he loved marrying but hated marriage. Marrying was exciting and romantic, but marriage brought the obligations and restrictions of a family, and he had been escaping from obligations and restrictions almost all his life. But none of this prevented him from getting firmly entangled once again – before he was even legally disentangled from Jeanette.

The beginning of 1926 found him back in Mexico in the bright red Duesenberg, hot on the trail of oil concessions in the

Gulf of Mexico, at intervals between studying Spanish at the university in Mexico City.

At the university he became involved with two pretty students, Belene and Allene Ashby, daughters of a Texas rancher, and, amative as ever, he conducted love affairs with both at once. Belene was the prettier, but Allene was just seventeen, and the chance of marrying another nymphet proved too much for the nympholeptic Paul Getty.

So, that October, he and Allene Ashby drove to Cuernavaca in the Duesenberg and married. In his enthusiasm he seems to have overlooked the fact that, since his divorce from Jeanette was still not finalized, he had not only landed in a second marriage, but had also committed bigamy.

Mexico being Mexico, no one mentioned this or seemed to notice. And unlike her predecessor, Allene not only avoided pregnancy, but quickly changed her mind about being Mrs J. Paul Getty. Paul was developing cold feet too, and they parted swiftly, painlessly and fairly amicably.

But Paul was too well known by now to marry incognito – even in Cuernavaca, Mexico. Somehow the news seeped back to South Kingsley Drive, and early that December George Franklin Getty called his lawyer.

One of the qualities George Getty shared with Paul was a marked ability to hide his feelings. During this period, and despite his weakened state of health, he had managed to disguise his anger at his son's behaviour, and amity was apparently restored within the Getty family – so much so that after the dramas when he left Jeanette, Paul must have felt that he had been forgiven.

But with illness, George's religious views were manifestly hardening. In 1913 he had already advanced from membership of the Third Church of Christ Scientist in Los Angeles, and joined the worldwide organization of the First Church in Boston, Massachusetts. Now illness had evidently made him take his church's teachings more seriously than ever, for that autumn he had become 'a class-taught student of Christian Science', attending a concentrated two-week instruction course on the message of the founder of Christian Science, Mrs Mary Baker Eddy. Within the teachings of that formidable lady, George would have discovered the most damning condemnation of his son's behaviour.

'Infidelity to the marriage convenant is the social scourge of all races,' wrote Mrs Baker Eddy.'It is "the pestilence that walketh in darkness, the destruction that wasteth at noonday".'

'The commandment, "Thou shalt not commit adultery," ' she added, 'is no less imperative than the one, "Thou shalt not kill." '

Strong words. But for the dedicated Christian Scientist there was no evading them. And George had recently become an even more devout believer.

He must, however, have confined these feelings to his lawyer and himself. Certainly he didn't criticize Paul openly, and 1927 started with a seemingly united Getty family, as Paul and parents happily embarked on a joint holiday to the continent of Europe.

Even in 1927 it was unusual for a twice-married man of rising thirty-five to take a lengthy European holiday with two aged parents, but despite his philandering, Paul remained as deeply involved with them as ever. He was still the same dutiful, attentive son who had gone on holiday with them before the war, and the unlikely trio seem to have enjoyed themselves.

They went to Rome, then travelled on to Switzerland and Paris – even staying at the faithful Hôtel Continentale. As usual, Sarah was happy to be back in Europe, but George's fragile health seems to have forced them into an earlier-than-planned return by transatlantic liner.

Being in no hurry to return himself, Paul saw them off, then rented an apartment by the Eiffel Tower and remained in Paris. The loving son had done his bit. The sophisticated man of pleasure could take over.

★

One can imagine the relief with which he set about enjoying Europe once he was free to travel, please himself, and follow any passing love affair that caught his fancy. This had become his favourite means of exercise and relaxation, and from Paris he proceeded to Berlin, where the night-life particularly appealed to him. He had started learning German, and there was no shortage of pretty women willing to help this rich foreigner learn their language.

But business called him back to California. His father was clearly losing his grip on the company, and Paul was needed as a trouble-shooter, boosting production from various Getty properties in California. It was demanding work, and George effectively acknowledged this by offering him a third of the capital of George Getty Inc. for $1 million. It may have seemed odd for a father to be offering to sell his son part of a company he would presumably inherit, but there were doubtless tax advantages to the sale. Certainly Paul did not seem at all concerned over the arrangement, particularly as George permitted him to pay a quarter of the price in cash and the rest in notes of promise.

With much to do, it was not until early summer that Paul escaped again to Europe. His first stop was Amsterdam for the 1928 Olympics, where he saw the Finnish runner Nurmi set a new Olympic record in the 10,000 metres. Then it was time for rather different games.

Paul had always loved Vienna, but at first he barely recognized it as the city he remembered from before the war. Yet although the old prosperity had gone, he was reassured to find that at the Grand Hotel at least 'the service, food, wines and furnishings were as superior [sic] as they had been before the war.' He was just starting to enjoy them when a fresh attack of matrimonial fever hit him rather badly.

It was another seventeen-year-old – a striking blue-eyed blonde this time – and he saw her dining with an older couple in the hotel restaurant. Afterwards he tried his luck and sent a note inviting her to dinner two nights later. Since she was young and foolish, she accepted.

He soon discovered she was not the fast young woman he had expected, but a schoolgirl barely out of a North German convent, who was holidaying with her parents and a girl friend in Vienna. Her father, the Herr Doktor Otto Helmle, was the rich and powerful head of the Badenwerk industrial complex in Karlsruhe. Her name was Adolphine – but everybody called her Fini.

Paul was now thirty-six, and after many years perfecting courtship patterns with young girls he found they worked as well as ever. Instead of attempting to disguise his age, he played the sophisticated, sympathetic older man, speaking German with an accent that amused her.

Fini was intrigued. Her admirer was closer to her father's age than hers, but he was so much more polite and cultured than the few boys she had met. Since he was so amusing and attentive she found it hard to refuse him when he suggested that they meet again. He was persistent – and soon there were other things she found it harder to refuse. They became lovers, and when she returned to Karlsruhe he followed. When he spoke of marriage, she insisted he discuss it with her father – and in Fini's father, Paul Getty met serious opposition.

An upright, old-style German Catholic who loved his family, and exemplified the bourgeois virtues, Dr Helmle seems to have instantly taken against Paul – and vice versa. Faced with this divorced American who had clearly bewitched his beloved Fini, the Herr Doktor indignantly refused permission for the match – and from that point on, the romance became less a love affair between Paul and Fini than a battle of wills between Paul and Dr Helmle.

True to his nature, Paul set his heart on winning – and finally did so by persuading the infatuated Fini to ignore her father and elope with him to Cuba. In an attempt to save her daughter's reputation, Frau Helmle travelled with her, and Paul and Fini were duly married in December 1928, a few days after his divorce from Allene Ashby was finalized. From Cuba they went on to Los Angeles, where Paul introduced his latest wife to George and Sarah.

Hoping that Paul was settling down at last, they greeted Fini warmly, and were happy when they moved into a nearby apartment. But just as with Jeanette, the reality of married life started to repel Paul once his wife was pregnant. He was increasingly absent and she was miserable and lonely. Soon she was feeling morning-sick, then home-sick. When her parents wrote suggesting she return to Germany to have the baby, Paul did nothing to prevent her going. But nor would he go with her.

Instead he insisted on going to New York to witness at first hand the Wall Street crash of October 1929. It impressed him deeply as the death knell of a whole financial era. Pondering the future, he left for Germany and reached Berlin in time to be with Fini when she had her baby. At first he was affectionate to her, and it seemed as if the marriage would continue. They called the baby Ronald, and for a few days Paul appeared excited by the prospect of a second son.

But not for long. Fini wished to take the child to see her parents back in Karlsruhe. Paul refused to go with her – and there, effectively, the marriage ended.

For Dr Helmle returned to the attack, insisting that his daughter stay in Karlsruhe and file for divorce. Paul made no objection, having found a pretty girl in a Berlin dance-hall and moved her into his apartment. But Dr Helmle proved as tough as his son-in-law, and, advised by a top divorce lawyer, was soon demanding heavy damages for his daughter.

At this point Paul decided it might be advisable to save the marriage, and had actually begun a fresh reunion with Fini in Montreux when, on 22 April, he received news that sent him rushing back to California. George had had a second stroke and was dying.

★

It took Paul nine days by train and transatlantic liner to return to South Kingsley Drive. He arrived to find his father just alive, but his deaf mother so distraught that she could only communicate in writing. As a dedicated Christian Scientist George was refusing to see a doctor, and the sickbed squalor was considerable. This, at least, was something Paul was able to alleviate. He calmed his mother, insisted on summoning a doctor, and then for thirty days he kept vigil by the sick man's bed.

George died on 31 May 1930, with Paul and Sarah at his bedside. Both were overcome with grief. It was, wrote Paul, 'the heaviest blow, the greatest loss, I had suffered in my life'. But worse was to come. The next day, when the will was read, Paul discovered that his father had bequeathed his fortune not to him, but to his mother, Sarah.

Control of the all-important Getty oil interests passed to the executors. Paul's son, the three-year-old George F. Getty II, received $350,000. And although Paul was 'remembered' with a derisory $250,000, his father had effectively disinherited him.

CHAPTER FIVE

GETTY'S SECRET

As was to be expected from a man who spent a lifetime developing the inscrutable expression of a Chinese poker-player, Paul gave the outside world no sign of the extent of his disaster. Because of this, there has always been a mystery over what he really felt about the way his father treated him.

Outwardly he seemed completely unaffected, behaving almost as if the will had not been written. Since he'd been so close to both his parents, how could anything have altered? Dearest Papa had loved him, and Paul had loved him in return. That was all that mattered and could never change.

Two days after George's death he devotedly inscribed a note for the press praising his father's virtues. 'His loving kindness and great heart, combined with a charming simplicity of manner made George F. Getty the idol of all who knew him. His mental ability was outstanding to the last. I, his son and successor, can only strive to carry on to the best of my ability, the life work of an abler man.'

There is no reason to doubt his sincerity when he wrote this. Forty years later he would still be piously insisting that 'the love, respect, and admiration I had for my father were boundless. His death was a blow that only passing years have numbed.'

But the 'blow' was more serious than simple grief for somebody he loved. For if nothing else, the will had inflicted a serious financial injury on him – and was a grave setback to his personal ambitions.

It also came as a complete surprise. Until that moment when the will was read, Paul had been regarding himself as his father's inevitable successor – and with reason. For years he had been helping to enrich the family company. He had initiated some of its most profitable ventures, and even before he bought his third of its capital for a million dollars, he had been permitting money that was really due to him to be ploughed back into George Getty Inc. He must have counted on the fact that this would all descend to him.

Thus George F. Getty had inflicted a considerable punishment on his son; and however calm he may have seemed in public, it was not in Paul's nature to accept punishment from anyone.

In fact he was deeply angered at the way he had been treated. Many years later, Getty's then accountant, who was on close terms with him at the time, told his biographer, Ralph Hewins, that 'When his father died, Paul was swindled and hurt, and has since built up a protective armour.' Claus von Bülow, who became Getty's 'chief executive', says much the same. He believes that after George's death, Getty spent the rest of his life proving himself against his father's judgement. 'Dad was going to eat his words. And when that is your attitude,' he added, 'it becomes an obsession.'

But why, if Getty had this deep obsession, did he always say how deeply he had loved his father?

During the days following George's death, Paul clearly had to face the fact that he would never publicly admit – that his father had done more than simply disinherit him.

Through all those years of Paul's affairs and broken marriages, father and son had carefully avoided any real confrontation over that most sensitive of subjects – Paul's blatant 'immorality'. But suddenly pretence was over. In his will George had done what he had never dared do face to face – deliver judgement on his son in the strongest terms at his disposal. Mrs

Baker Eddy had declared adultery and the breaking of marriage bonds akin to murder. Now, by disinheriting his only son and heir, George was rejecting him as firmly as he might have done a murderer.

For Paul this rejection went against the very basis of the wonderfully seductive way of life he'd been perfecting since his early twenties. Thanks to his own precocious fortune, Paul had managed to remain like a pampered child, immune to criticism and paternal pressure. In his role of spoiled only son he knew that however he behaved he could always count upon affection and forgiveness from his parents. But no longer. By disinheriting him, George had made it clear that Paul was not forgiven – which left him with a serious dilemma.

His obvious reaction should have been indifference. George was dead, Paul was relatively young and still extremely rich, and he could live his life exactly as he wanted. Why agonize about the judgement of a father now departed?

From someone who appeared so cold and ruthless, this is certainly what one might have expected – but it didn't happen. George would always mean too much to Paul to be forgotten. 'Dearest Papa' would always be the keeper of his conscience.

This left Paul a second possibility: doing what his father had clearly wanted him to do – repent, reform, and settle for a godly, moral life like George and Sarah's. But this was equally impossible. Paul was getting on for forty, which was far too old to give up all those harmless pleasures which for twenty years had made his life worth living.

But there remained a third solution. If he could reverse his father's judgement, and somehow make him posthumously 'eat his words', his problems would be over. He would be freed to live exactly as he wanted, travel as he had before, enjoy his women, treat his wives and children as he pleased, and still refuse to settle down.

The only way to do this was to make a fortune large enough to answer George's evident belief that Paul's immorality disqualified him from managing the affairs of George Getty Inc. For a puritan like George F. Getty, godliness was closely linked to credit-worthiness, just as making money was a sign of virtue. So Paul could still redeem himself by producing a financial triumph – which was the origin of that continuing obsession which von Bulow would notice thirty years later. From now on this obsession was to drive him forward until he ended up creating the largest fortune in America.

It is here that one discerns the uniqueness of Paul Getty both as a businessman and as a human being. By any definition, he was something of a freak, a forbidding combination of relentlessly acquisitive business genius with the emotional development of a sex-starved adolescent.

Henceforth the businessman would operate in overdrive, always attempting to increase that stock of money which would provide the adolescent with his alibi before his parents. As a businessman he possessed formidable resources – originality, strength of will and an obsessive mastery of detail.

Now all these qualities were ruthlessly applied to the task before him – and it was now that he also really started to enforce such strict control over his own expenditure. He had never been lavish with himself – still less with others – but now every petty meanness held a deeper meaning – to add, however insignificantly, to the all-important pile of wealth and quietly inform the ghostly keeper of his conscience that he was not the immoral profligate his father had rejected.

Similarly, any personal acquisition was decided henceforth strictly on a profit basis. As a good puritan, George F. Getty was a dedicated self-denier; so Paul set out to beat him here as well. He would permit himself no self-indulgence in the purchase of a place to live, a work of art, even a piece of furniture, unless he could convince himself that it would appreciate in value.

The result was a strangely dedicated life, with everything within it geared to one overriding purpose – the accumulation of ever larger quantities of capital. For then and only then could the adolescent in him be permitted to continue as he had before Papa's demise – pursuing his teenage girls, refusing to shoulder any real responsibility as husband or as father, always on the move, and always able to believe that he could count on his parents' love behind him.

As a recipe for happy living, Paul Getty's system left a lot to be desired, but as far as business was concerned, his quaint psychology became a real source of strength, soon setting him apart from the happy ranks of other massively successful multi-millionaires. For past a certain point, the makers of all large fortunes face the problem of maintaining motivation. Why continue? Why bother with acquiring yet more money when one has all the Impressionist paintings, private jets, and Park Lane mansions one can live with?

There inevitably comes a point where even the most driven wealth-acquirer needs some external motive to continue – like buying political power, creating an art collection, building a great ancestral home or even, if all else fails, using the money for philanthropy.

That mordant critic of the social scene, the economist Thorstein Veblen, in his classic *Theory of the Leisure Class*, invented a phrase to describe the way the great nineteenth-century American *nouveaux riches* like the Vanderbilts and Rockefellers once employed their surplus wealth in competitive display. He called it 'conspicuous consumption': the building of the great Rhode Island mansions which they barely used, the throwing of the massive parties which none but the hideously rich could equal. Driven by such sumptuary competition, they sometimes reached the point which Veblen identified as 'conspicuous waste' – the spending of very large amounts of money simply to defeat their rivals in a war of pointless ostentation.

Such problems never troubled Paul Getty. Far from requiring any outside interests, he had a perfect built-in system of obsessive motivation. Far from ever getting bored with money, the more of it he had, the more profound would be his sense of satisfaction. He would have regarded the idea of conspicuous consumption as unthinkable, the notion of conspicuous waste a gross obscenity.

He personally required none of the outward trappings of success. On the contrary, he wanted privacy and quiet to enjoy the solitary game that he was playing. Just as he had no need for others to envy or applaud him, so he felt no obligation to share any of his winnings with the multitude. He was completely self-obsessed and self-sustaining. All he required to ensure that his father 'ate his words' was money – and as much of it as possible. As long as he could go on making it, he could live his life exactly as he wanted. As long as he could make Papa stay silent, his money would have served its most important purpose.

CHAPTER SIX

MATERNAL TRUST

WHEN THE DIRECTORS of George Getty Inc. made Paul their president, they did so in the evident belief that as a minority shareholder owning only a third of the capital he would have no power to make serious decisions. Thanks to his father's will the head of the company, with two-thirds of the capital, was eighty years of age, stone deaf, overweight, and lonely – his mother Sarah.

Luckily for Paul she loved him dearly – and he did his best to ensure that her love continued. She still called him 'dearest child', just as he referred to her as 'beloved Mama'. Twice and sometimes thrice a week he used to call at the house on South Kingsley Drive to take her out. By now she could barely walk. A lift had been installed to get her to her bedroom, and she required a servant on each arm to reach his Cadillac. Sometimes he drove her through the foothills of the Santa Monica hills, but what she really liked was to feed the sea-lions that still basked along the beach at Malibu.

It must have been a strange sight – sea-lions barking from the water's edge, overweight widow dressed in black, and neatly suited middle-aged son throwing herrings to the beasts at her direction.

But what must have been still stranger was their conversation. For the sea-lions offered Paul his finest chance to influence his mother and persuade her to transfer her power in the company to him.

There would have been a strong temptation for a tired old lady to agree. She, after all, had had little experience of business. She was very lame and old, and Paul could be remarkably persuasive when it came to getting what he wanted.

But Sarah had always been obstinate, and despite Paul's arguments, something held her back. In the first place she believed that George's wishes ought to be respected. Since he had seen fit to place her in this position of responsibility, she had a duty to accept it. Second, she knew her son. She loved him dearly. He was all she had, but she also knew how rash and harebrained he could be, and during such dangerous economic times as the early thirties, wildness could lead a company like George Getty Inc. to disaster.

Worse still, if she understood him properly, Paul was suggesting the complete reversal of much that dear Papa had stood for. Papa had built the company by discovering oil, buying leases on the land, and then producing it. He was an oil man, not a smart financier, and he believed in sticking to the things the company did best. He had always had an honest Christian dread of debt. She could hear him now. 'The last thing to do is borrow. The first thing to do is always to repay your debts.'

It was over this that her arguments with Paul invariably began. What Paul had set his heart on was expansion, extending the company into every branch of the oil business – refining, marketing, and finally creating a network of gasoline stations selling Getty products nationwide. When she asked him where the money was to come from, he replied that the company had capital in reserve, and he was perfectly prepared to borrow too if necessary. He had even coined a motto of his own, which he repeated when she mentioned his father's fear of debt. 'Buy when everyone else is selling, and hold on until everyone else is buying.'

In fact he was convinced that the Wall Street crash of 1929, far from being a dire warning, was actually offering George Getty Inc. the chance of a lifetime by changing the economic landscape of the oil industry. Since oil shares on the New York stock exchange had plummeted, now was the time to buy, thus picking up oil reserves at bargain prices through their undervalued shares.

For Paul this seemed more sensible than developing fresh oilfields as he himself had been doing in the past. It also offered an unrivalled opportunity to achieve his great ambition. By carefully acquiring shares in publicly quoted oil companies, he could slowly gain control of them. Some were highly vulnerable, and he inevitably had his strategy worked out for the companies he wanted. It was time to act before the bargains vanished.

When he explained this to his mother she sometimes became extremely agitated, but he knew exactly how to calm her down.

'Times change, and this is what dear Papa would do himself if he was here,' he'd tell her.

Sarah would usually end by agreeing – but she was never totally convinced that he was right.

During the next three years, Paul pursued his strategy of acquisition with the energy and skill of a raiding general bent on plunder. Anxious as ever to disprove his father, he became a most adroit financier. He was patient, fearless and extremely sharp, but behind each operation lay the thoroughness with which he made his preparations. Everything was checked and counter-checked. Nothing was left to chance.

Even so, his first big stock deal ended in disaster. In September 1930 he finally persuaded a reluctant Sarah to agree to borrow from the Security-First National Bank for the purchase of 3 million dollars' worth of stock of Mexican Seaboard, a Californian company with leases in the oil-rich Kettleman Hills whose shares he considered undervalued.

After the deal, Paul had to leave on a hurried trip to Europe and so couldn't stop the panic when the shares continued dropping. Had he been present, he would have urged his directors to sit tight – as they should have done – but in his absence the bank insisted on selling the shares to repay the loan before they sank still further – thus losing practically a million dollars.

On his return, Paul found the boardroom atmosphere of George Getty Inc. 'decidedly chilly', as he put it, adding that at least 'Mother was vindicated'.

This was the nearest Paul ever came to real disaster. It was a sobering lesson, reminding him that to fail now would mean losing everything and prove that his father had been right. He had no alternative but to continue, even if this meant risking every penny he possessed and calling on any source of credit he could muster.

Typically, instead of playing safe, this was the moment when he raised the stakes. Using all his energy and everything he owned, he started bidding for Pacific Western, one of California's biggest oil-producers, whose shares had fallen in the last twelve months from $17 to $3.

This time he succeeded. By the end of 1931 he was nearly bankrupt – but he was also firmly in control of Pacific Western. His plans were working, and next on his plan of campaign was America's ninth largest oil company, the $200 million Tide Water Oil company. To take it was a daunting proposition for a small unknown outsider – but he needed something big to justify himself against his father, even if this brought him into conflict with his mother.

To begin with she was acquiescent, and he was able to sell off George Getty Inc.'s San Joaquin Valley oilfield for 4.5 million dollars without excessive opposition. This was to be the war-chest with which he planned to finance his campaign.

By March 1932 Tide Water stock had slumped to a record low of $2.50 a share. But Paul knew that over-hasty buying could raise the share price and alert the Tide Water management to the threat he represented. It was time for wariness and anonymity – qualities he had never lacked. By the end of March Paul had somehow acquired a significant holding in Tide Water without anyone in the company knowing who he was, or being any the wiser.

During this period following his father's death, Paul's financial situation remained closely tied in with his private life. Had he lost his nerve, as well as that million dollars on the Mexican Seaboard deal, he would have been tacitly admitting that his father had been right to disinherit him. But since he had such faith in his own future, and since his plans were steadily maturing, he had no need to worry over any criticism from the grave on the subject of his 'immorality'.

As a result, the period following his father's death saw Paul as sexually adventurous as ever, and finally hit by a fresh attack of his old affliction – marital fever.

This time the cause was slightly older than before. But although Ann Rork was all of twenty-one when Paul became involved with her in the autumn of 1930, she had barely changed from the dimpled nymphet of fourteen he had attempted to seduce some eight years earlier. She must have been a precocious adolescent, for Paul had been taking her to bars and night-clubs even then – until angrily warned off by Sam Rork, Ann's extremely jealous father, who had heard about Paul Getty's reputation.

Rork himself was an old-time Hollywood producer, faintly famous as the discoverer of the star of silent movies, Clara Bow, the original 'vamp'. He adored his quick-tongued daughter and encouraged her ambitions to become a star by giving her the juvenile lead in *A Blonde Saint*, a forgettable romantic drama starring the matinée idol Gilbert Roland. But by 1930, Rork, who was badly hit by the great Depression, was more amenable when his daughter's multi-millionaire admirer started calling her again – even if he was now thirty-seven with three failed marriages behind him.

Paul had to break off the romance in the autumn of 1930 to get to Germany as fast as possible in order to contest the divorce proceedings over Fini. Since her father's lawyers in Berlin were still trying to extract punitive damages, Paul was determined to appear in court in person, but his appearance made little difference. Helmle was as difficult as possible. His detectives produced fresh evidence of yet another woman living with Paul during his period in Berlin, and, unable to get the settlement he wanted, Dr Helmle got the case postponed until Paul agreed. As Paul would not agree, he had no alternative but to return to America still legally encumbered with Fini as his wife.

So marriage had to wait as far as dark-eyed, baby-faced Ann Rork was concerned. Not that it seemed to matter deeply. Ann was grateful to her rich protector, and since he insisted that he loved her, she was perfectly prepared to wait.

In August 1931 Paul moved her into an apartment in the New York Plaza and, telling her that he'd like to marry her, asked her if she felt the same. When she nodded, he said, 'Fine. Then we'll get married here. Since we love each other we don't need anybody else, nor do we need a licence or a ceremony.'

And that, it seems, was that. Many years later Ann told Getty's biographer, Robert Lenzner, 'I really thought that Paul was God. His knowledge was so awesome. He was,' she added, 'my first lover, and a very considerate one at that. I was introduced properly. And I certainly hope I pleased him.'

It seems as if she did, for the next few months saw them very much together, first in Germany, and then early in 1932 in Paris, where they stayed in Paul's old bachelor apartment near the Eiffel Tower. But as soon as Ann discovered she was pregnant, the idyll ended and he behaved as he always did at the prospect of a family.

Four years later, Ann's divorce court testimony would catalogue the same old list of grievances as all his wives had done before – neglect, abuse, and the times he left her to go out with other women. She claimed that sometimes she was so unhappy that she had even tried to kill herself by swallowing iodine – which burned her throat, but otherwise failed to harm her.

As these unhappy lovers still weren't married – except in the eyes of Paul Getty's private deity – the relationship would presumably have ended there and then but for the child she was carrying. For just as with his earlier children, George and Ronald, Paul, who hated families, still had a superstitious sense of the importance of his offspring. Not that this meant that he possessed the faintest glimmerings of parenthood, or a vestigial desire to have his children near him. He emphatically did not.

But on a recent visit to San Simeon, William Randolph Hearst had lectured him on his responsibility to father several heirs to make a dynasty. Paul liked the idea of a dynasty, and Hearst's words appear to have impressed him.

There were problems over Ann, however. An heir needed to be born in wedlock, and although he was perfectly prepared to marry her, he was still legally joined to Fini, and getting old for a second bout of bigamy.

As summer ended Paul and Ann were on holiday in Italy, she heavily pregnant, he compulsively unfaithful. In Rome he was off to night-clubs, and in Naples, he dragged her, puffing and protesting, to the very crater of Vesuvius. Then it was back by ship to Genoa, and the ship was still at sea on 7 September when Ann produced a third son for her lover. The baby was premature, extremely small, and when the ship called at the port of La Spezia, the child was registered Eugene Paul Getty.

Paul and Ann returned to California, taking an apartment in the hills of Santa Monica. At first Paul was wary of introducing Ann to his mother as his wife – partly because she wasn't and partly because Fini had been Sarah's favourite. Paul's divorce from Fini had not been finalized until that August – with heavy damages and Fini having custody of two-year-old Ronald, who would spend the next few years with her in Switzerland. Paul was deeply resentful over what he thought a grave injustice and a dreadful waste of money, and as far as Dr Helmle was concerned he would never forgive him – nor forget what happened.

But at least this meant that he and Ann could now legitimize their child by marrying – which they did in Paul's favourite marital rendezvous of Cuernavaca, in December 1932. This also meant that Ann was finally allowed to meet his mother. Understandably, perhaps, the two women never cared for one another, and in later years Ann blamed Sarah for the break-up of her marriage. But in the meantime, Paul had done what he'd never done before. He had bought himself a beach house facing the sea at Malibu, where he and his young family could all live happily together. Except that they didn't. Paul was as firmly bound as ever to his mother, and still kept clothes and possessions in his room at South Kingsley Drive – as well as a so-called 'love-nest' up in Santa Monica where he took his women. Ann felt lonely and neglected as she watched the ocean.

'Since you're so rich, why do you have to work?' she asked him – a question which he didn't deign to answer. By the time their second son, Gordon, was born in December 1933, they were barely speaking to each other.

Legend has it that Paul arrived at the hospital to see his wife and newborn child, glanced at the baby, muttered, 'Uh-huh, it looks like you' – and rapidly departed.

Paul had more important things to think about than babies, being obsessively involved by now in one thing and one thing only – the battle for Tide Water Oil. This ailing giant was a seemingly impossible prize for an isolated aggressor like Paul to conquer, and as he pursued it he displayed a range of qualities which account for much of his subsequent success – total concentration, mastery of detail in the complicated deals involved, a love of risk, and a cool ability to exploit any opportunity which worked to his advantage. He was still pursuing his strange solitary game, which only someone with an absolute obsession had any hope of winning.

He knew that to win he had to have the one thing his father had purposely denied him – full financial control of George

Getty Inc. Not until he had all Sarah's capital in addition to his own could he borrow on the scale he needed. If this had to lead to further battles with 'dearest Mama', so be it.

Now it took more than visits to the sea-lions to convince her, and she fought a long delaying action. Finally he won by endless argument, and as a Christmas present at the end of 1933 she almost gave him what he wanted. As a negotiator she was quite his equal when it came to it, and in a deal which she spec-ified would terminate 'if not accepted by you in writing on or before noon of 30 December' she offered to sell Paul her two-thirds interest in the family company, in return for promissory notes for the purchase price of $4.6 million, bearing a fixed income of 3.5 per cent a year. Businesslike as ever, she signed her offer 'Yours very sincerely, Sarah C. Getty'.

This income from her son was to be her widow's pension, and as a sweetener she offered Paul a timely Christmas present for himself – an additional gift of $850,000 if he accepted.

He had no alternative, for by now his fight for Tide Water was in the open, and he was up against an equally determined enemy – the massive Standard Oil company of New Jersey which was already the major shareholder in Tide Water. But once again Paul was lucky. Federal anti-trust legislation was making Standard disburse its shares – which it was placing in a brand new company called the Mission Corporation.

In this multi-million dollar game of chess, Paul's next move was obviously to purchase as many Mission shares as possible, thereby boosting his holding in Tide Water. But once again he found himself checkmated by his mother.

He was still unable to convince her of the wisdom of George Getty Inc. buying Tide Water stock, and since she owned prom-issory notes from Paul for $4.5 million, she could effectively prevent this happening. For as Paul rapidly discovered, no bank would lend him on the scale he wanted once they learned that he was four and a half million dollars in the red – even to his mother.

So began the last round in this curious contest between

'beloved Mama' and her 'dearest child'. To continue buying into the Mission Corporation, Paul needed Sarah to liquidate his debt. As he reminded her, she had no need of the $140,000 he was paying her each year in interest, since her annual expenses never topped $30,000.

She seems to have agreed, but then like the smart negotiator she was, she switched the argument. What she was really most concerned about, she said, was not herself but future generations of the Gettys. Paul might be right. Time would tell. But when Papa had left her all his money, he was really leaving it in trust for the grandchildren, and for all the unborn Gettys to come after. She couldn't bear to think that by letting Paul have his way she might be depriving future generations of their patrimony.

She had clearly discussed this with her lawyers, for her solution to the problem was ingenious. She would set up 'an irrevocable spendthrift trust' to protect the interests of his children against the possible results of his business speculation, and contribute an initial $2.5 million to it from her own resources. By placing the family capital in a trust the money would be protected against Paul's supposed 'spendthrift' tendencies, and also against his own possible bankruptcy.

He agreed and contributed some over-valued shares he owned in George Getty Inc. so that the trust could begin at the end of 1934 with a capital of $3.368 million.

This was the start of the famous Sarah C. Getty Trust, which would dominate the family finances for many years to come.

Financially the arrangement suited Paul extremely well, since he was appointed principal trustee with absolute power to use the trust's capital according to his judgement for any transaction which involved the family's oil interests – such as acquiring further shares in the Mission Corporation or Tide Water.

It also suited Sarah, since it satisfied her conscience over her duty to the family fortune and her otherwise unprotected grandchildren.

As far as the beneficiaries of the trust were concerned the terms were simple. To satisfy Sarah's primary concern that her son should meet his duties as a father, it made suitable provision for his wife Ann, and his four children, ten-year-old George II, four-year-old Ronald, two-year-old Paul Jr. and one-year-old Gordon. For as long as she remained legally married to Paul, Ann was to receive an annual ten per cent of the trust's income, but payments to the children were unequal. During 1934, the $21,000 of the trust's income remaining after Ann had been paid was shared out as follows. Paul Jr. and Gordon were each paid $9,000. George II was paid nothing as he had already benefited from the $300,000 legacy from his grandfather, the late George Getty. And Ronald's portion was limited to $3,000.

This disadvantage was placed on Ronald because his father seems to have convinced Sarah that Ronald would be receiving substantial money from the will of his maternal grandfather, Dr Helmle. It was a disadvantage which would weigh heavily on him in the future, once the trust itself increased dramatically in value. For a further condition of the trust was that if it earned more than $21,000 a year George, Paul Jr. and Gordon were to share equally in the excess. Ronald was specifically excluded from any further income from the trust beyond his annual $3,000.

A further important clause which was to cause some trouble in the years ahead laid down that Paul, as principal trustee, was to have effective control of how all future payments should be made – either in the form of cash dividends, or further shares within the trust.

As for the future beneficiaries of the trust, his as yet unborn grandchildren, he and Sarah wanted to ensure that they should earn their own livings before inheriting from the trust. It was stated that not until the last of Paul's four boys was dead were the grandchildren as a group to inherit their share of the capital. Although Ronald's inheritance was so strictly limited, there were no such limitations on his children, who would be treated exactly as their cousins.

As it turned out, the founding of the Sarah Getty Trust was an historic moment for the Gettys. For the trust rapidly became a crucial factor in their whole financial future – by becoming the effective guardian of the family's rapidly expanding fortune. What no one, Paul included, seems to have realized at first was the remorseless way the legendary trust would grow. Not only would it provide its principal trustee with precisely what he needed – a source of capital to use as and when required for his business acquisitions – it was also perfectly adapted to his obsession to amass ever larger sums of money for his family to satisfy his conscience.

A 'spendthrift trust' like this was the ideal way to accumulate the great fortune he had set his heart on. Proof against taxation, bankruptcy and personal extravagance, the trust named after Jean Paul Getty's mother would help create the greatest fortune in America.

CHAPTER SEVEN

BOOM TIME

HOWEVER TOUGH THE thirties were upon America and the world in general, they were unusually kind to Paul Getty. Just as the death of his father in 1930 made him dedicate himself afresh to making money, so the creation of the Sarah C. Getty Trust and his acquisition of full control of the family businesses meant that his campaign to capture Tide Water Oil could start in earnest.

On the face of it his chances of success were slim. In 1935 Tide Water had a turnover approaching $100 million against the $1.5 million of George Getty Inc., and by now Tide Water's management were thoroughly aware of the threat Paul represented, and firmly set to block him.

But Paul had the advantages of the small determined operator – speed, surprise, and the challenge of a personal encounter; and the creation of the Sarah C. Getty Trust had given him the financial weapon he needed. He was banned from using the trust to borrow money, but as its sole trustee was otherwise completely free to use its assets to acquire any oil shares he wanted.

Like some modern takeover tycoon, he wanted Tide Water complete with all its assets – refineries, storage capacity, and the marketing network through which he hoped to sell his own oil products. In taking over Tide Water lay his best hope of acquiring the full-scale oil operation he had set his heart on.

Early in the battle he shrewdly recruited David Hecht, a

smart young corporation lawyer, and with Hecht beside him steadily wheeled and dealt his way towards acquiring the crucial shares he needed. He had his strokes of luck – like the New Year's Eve party with Randolph Hearst in 1935 when he heard that the Rockefellers were disposing of a 20 per cent holding in the Mission Corporation and, with Hecht's help, promptly snapped them up. But for the most part, acquisition was a painstaking, concentrated labour, which only somebody as driven and as dedicated as Paul could have accomplished.

He worked inexorably, and by 1936, when he had built up sufficient equity within the Mission Corporation to give him a 25 per cent holding in Tide Water, the financial equivalent of trench warfare started between him and Tide Water's directors. With his total single-mindedness this was something Paul was good at, and by the outbreak of war in 1939 he had practically succeeded.

For by then the long-awaited upswing in the oil industry had come. US automobile ownership and, with it, gasoline consumption, had in fact begun to rise as early as 1936, despite the great Depression, so that the Tide Water shares he had bought for $2.50 at the bottom of the market in 1930 stood at $17.00 by 1938.

It was a spectacular advance, which meant that as well as bringing him so near to controlling Tide Water, his share-buying operations had also made him very rich. By 1938, as owner of George Getty Inc., his personal fortune stood at $12 million, and true to his promise to his mother, he had made the Sarah C. Getty Trust richer still. The trust, which had begun with $3.5 million in 1934, was now worth $18 million.

The money in the Sarah C. Getty Trust was the core of the massive fortune he still needed to create if he was truly to 'make Daddy eat his words'. An important part of his financial strategy was to plough all the profits back into the trust itself, thus ensuring that its capital steadily increased, untouched by spending or taxation.

This was what Mama had wanted, and since the capital within the trust would benefit his children and his children's children yet unborn, he could argue that the money more than justified him now against any criticism of his way of life.

For the trust itself had become his excuse for living the life he wanted, at a time when he was becoming more opposed than ever to family life, which he saw as a dreadful obstacle to his success. Even in old age he was still insisting that life as an ordinary husband would have held him back and stopped him from succeeding – since a family would have diverted his attention, squandered his precious time, and sapped his concentration. As he put it in a moment of extreme exasperation, 'A lasting relationship with a woman is only possible if you're a business failure.'

But if Paul Getty couldn't offer his wives and children his presence or his love, success in business enabled him to give them something he considered more important – large amounts of money for the future. With so much money safely in the Sarah C. Getty Trust, he was free to turn his full attention to perfecting the extraordinary way of life that he was leading.

He was still driven by two overwhelming urges – for sexual adventures, preferably abroad, and for acquiring very large amounts of money. To combine successfully these two activities, he needed to devise a way of managing his business interests – which included the day-to-day running of George Getty Inc. and the battle for Tide Water – during his lengthy periods in Europe.

Since he loved anonymity, and much of his pleasure in travelling abroad was frankly sexual, the last thing Paul required round him was a staff of executives and aides. These were consigned to the Getty offices in Los Angeles, and he taught himself to operate alone or with a single secretary, storing whatever information he needed in his head. He believed that business wasted too much time on paperwork, committees and discussion anyhow. Forgetting nothing, and delegating what

was inessential, he became a great exponent of the role of capitalist as self-sufficient one-man band, making the most minute
decisions with a minimum of red tape and bureaucracy.

Victor Hugo once called Alfred Nobel, the inventor of
dynamite, who also loved living in hotels and hated families, 'the
vagabond billionaire of Europe'. Paul Getty, who was much the
same, was fast becoming his successor.

His favoured method of replying to a letter was to scribble
a reply in the margin and mail it back himself in the readdressed
envelope it came in. He had an obsession with saving stationery,
particularly expensive manila envelopes, which he always kept
and carefully re-used. Any documents he needed stayed in the
old-fashioned steamer trunk which accompanied him everywhere And a crucial item in his business armoury was the small
black book which never left him, containing the telephone
numbers, not only of his countless girlfriends, but also of key
business contacts round the world through whom he personally
conducted all his business.

For the crucial instrument without which his way of life
could not have functioned was the telephone; and as the transatlantic telephone service steadily improved throughout the
thirties, so did the length of time he spent in Europe. It was the
telephone that would finally enable him to leave America for
ever.

As long as the transatlantic lines from Europe to America
were open, Paul was fully operational – whatever else he happened to be doing at the time. The eight-hour time gap between
Europe and California was in his favour, allowing him to meet
a woman, feed her and enjoy her, and be on the telephone again
before the Los Angeles offices closed for the evening.

By combining this highly programmed life of pleasure with
an otherwise puritanical attitude to his existence, he was not as
hypocritical as he sounded. Promiscuous sex, he would have
argued, was nowhere near as bad for a businessman as the marital variety. It took up far less time, cost less, was infinitely less

demanding, and actually added to one's prowess as a business-man. As he put it once, 'Business success generates a sexual drive, and sexual drive pushes business.'

The point was that for Paul, money and success remained the surest proof of virtue, and true to the very rigid rules by which he led his life, he was never profligate or rash in any of his personal behaviour.

He was compelled to live in good hotels during his periods abroad, but this was principally because only good hotels had reliable telephonic switchboards. And even in his favourite Hôtel Georges V in Paris, he always made a point of bargaining for the cheapest suite on offer. He wasted nothing, ate economically, and recorded every cab-fare in his diary. He could fornicate, but not be profligate.

Sex helped business, which in turn brought yet more conscience-money into the sacred coffers of the Sarah C. Getty Trust.

Unsurprisingly in these circumstances, his fourth marriage now collapsed like all the others, the only difference being that Ann Rork Getty was a tougher proposition than her predecessors. In this garrulous would-be actress, Paul had more than met his equal in the marriage stakes.

She would marry four times herself; and even first time round she made it clear that she had no intention of enduring her husband's philandering and bullying for ever. She was gregarious and popular, and instead of gazing sadly from the beach house at the ocean, was soon inviting friends from Hollywood to come and see her. So when Paul did come home, it was often to face a houseful of his wife's guests who treated him with scant respect. Sometimes he even heard them encouraging Ann behind his back.

'He should give you a Rolls, darling.'

'He should dress you in sables instead of mink.'

Unable to cope with such behaviour, he stayed away more than ever – and after one particularly lengthy absence, one of

Ann's friends from Hollywood introduced her to the toughest lawyer in town, who opened proceedings in what Paul called 'an unusually noisome divorce'. 'Noisome' was his word for being publicly taken to the cleaners.

Whatever her failings as an actress on the screen, Ann Rork Getty was a star in the witness-box and made the most of the horror tale of courtship and marriage with Paul – her suicide attempts, his behaviour on Vesuvius, and his unorthodox notions on the role of a father and a husband.

She began by suing for a portion of his fortune, so he was lucky that the massive divorce settlements of the present day State of California hadn't started. As it was she caused him much worry and annoyance before finally agreeing to what she termed 'a beautiful settlement' of $2,500 a month, and $1,000 a month for each of the two children.

Although he was now the father of four young sons, he showed not the faintest interest in any of them; and with the Los Angeles newspapers feasting on the lurid details of his divorce, he decided to escape to New York before continuing abroad. Thanks to his god, the telephone, his affairs could be conducted just as well from there as from Los Angeles, and with the money he was now amassing, he felt justified in taking one of the smartest addresses in the city.

It would be wrong to think that Paul Getty's freshly acquired wealth would make no difference to his way of life. In fact a number of important changes now occurred in his behaviour. But all of them were governed by two crucial principles – they were not to affect his balance-sheets, and not to deflect him from the great financial game that he was playing. Otherwise he seemed quite anxious to upgrade his life in keeping with his earnings.

In New York he moved to an address which by a strange coincidence was the same as the Tudor mansion where he would end his days, Sutton Place. But instead of purchasing an apartment in this fashionable New York block beside the river, he preferred to rent – which was tax deductible and could not be paid for by the company. Also the apartment appealed to snobbish elements within his nature, being owned by the wife of Winston Churchill's cousin, the former heiress Amy Phipps, by this time Mrs Freddie Guest.

Mrs Guest's eighteenth-century paintings and French furniture also appealed to him, enough to make him think about collecting on his own account – which in fact he did, starting buying with considerable knowledge and success. Businesslike as ever, through reading and by visiting museums, he made himself a considerable expert on French eighteenth-century furniture. As he soon realized, the Depression had forced it down in value and he was able to purchase a number of important pieces at knock-down prices.

This would become the principle behind almost all his subsequent collecting. Whatever else, anything he bought had to be a bargain – for only with a bargain could he convince himself he wasn't wasting money. This applied to almost everything he bought – from his socks, for which he refused to pay more than $1.50 a pair, to perhaps the biggest single bargain of this period: the Pierre Hotel, on the corner of 5th Avenue and 61st Street, facing Central Park. When built in 1930, as New York's most exclusive luxury hotel, it had cost more than $6 million. Paul bought it for $2.35 million, for the simple reason that it was such a bargain that he knew that he could never lose on the deal.

One place where Paul's social aspirations showed around this period was over sex. With matrimonial fever once more in the air, it was quite in character for him to start courting Louise 'Teddy' Lynch – a buxom, twenty-three-year-old night-club singer. But Miss Lynch was no ordinary night-club singer. Another Churchill connection, Bernard Baruch the financier, was her uncle, and Teddy herself had serious ambitions as an opera singer.

For Paul, the prestige of having such a smart fiancée led him to contemplate the horror of matrimony once again, for he took unusual care to court Teddy's mother, who didn't object to having this four times married, forty-four-year-old as a potential son-in-law. But neither he nor Teddy seemed in a hurry to get married after the engagement was announced at the end of 1936.

She was an independent young woman who wanted to perfect her singing, and as long as Paul would pay for her singing lessons, she seemed perfectly content to treat him rather as an oversexed avuncular figure, without making great demands upon his time or his fidelity.

This was exactly what he wanted, and his engagement didn't interfere with his womanizing forays to Europe. While he was pursuing Helga and Trudi and Gretchen in Berlin, Teddy would be taking singing lessons back in London. For despite the trouble over Fini, Paul retained his love of Berlin, which, like many foreigners in this period, he treated as his brothel. Like many foreign businessmen he also had a fairly uncritical attitude towards the Nazis, frankly admiring the efficiency with which they seemed to run the country.

He was not an active Nazi sympathizer, but he might all too easily have become involved with them in ways that could have been uncomfortable for his future, had Teddy not diverted his interest and attention to a slightly safer country. In 1939 she wished to study singing in Italy and, tolerant as ever, Paul accompanied her to Rome. It was a strange episode in both their lives. Intent for once on keeping up appearances, Paul suggested that they stayed in separate hotels; while she was singing, he was conscientiously visiting Rome's ruins and museums.

It was during this period that he first became infatuated both with Rome and with Fascist Italy. One evening he took Teddy to *Rigoletto*, and was excited to see Mussolini in the audience. 'The greatest son of Italy since the Emperor Augustus,' he wrote that evening in his diary.

But however much he admired Mussolini, he was becoming

highly concerned now about the effect of war on his personal safety, and was anxious to return to America. Teddy was equally anxious to continue singing. Neither would budge an inch, and the result was the curious compromise of Paul's fifth and final marriage.

At midday on 17 November 1939, he and Teddy met before the mayor of Rome in the historic Campidoglio, the Roman Capitol, and were made man and wife. Afterwards they lunched quietly at the Ambassador Hotel, then said goodbye. Instead of waiting to consummate the marriage, Paul had to catch the afternoon train to Naples, where he boarded the *Conte di Savoia* for New York. Teddy remained in Rome.

CHAPTER EIGHT

WAR AND THE NEUTRAL ZONE

AMERICA'S ENTRY INTO the war in 1941 had a strange effect on Paul Getty. Although he was rising fifty, he wrote like a schoolboy in his diary about doing his duty so that 'dearest Mama and Papa can be proud of me'. But with age he had been growing increasingly fearful for his safety – and what he had seen in Europe had made him obsessed about the power of Nazi Germany.

He volunteered for active service with the US Navy, but must have known he was too old to be accepted. Once rejected, he then made an extraordinary compromise between doing his bit and staying as far as possible from danger for the war's duration.

One of the incidental assets of the Mission Corporation, which he now controlled, was the small, half moribund Spartan Aircraft Company at Tulsa, Oklahoma. Manufacturing aircraft for the war effort was a patriotic occupation, Tulsa was familiar territory, and if anywhere was safe from the threat of the German Luftwaffe during the Second World War it had to be Oklahoma.

Even so, when Paul took personal command of Spartan Aircraft he treated it like some perilous wartime posting, and built himself a bomb-proof, four-roomed concrete bunker by the factory. It was here that he lived and from here that he personally directed Spartan Aircraft from 1942 until the war was over.

He was in fact a great success. As much the workaholic as

ever, he proved an exceptional factory manager, driving the workforce hard, working late himself on any problem, and getting Spartan to produce an excellent single-engined trainer for the US Army Air Force. So eager was he for what he felt would be his parents' approbation that he spent almost all his time in his factory at Tulsa, and when at the end of 1941 Sarah Getty finally expired, aged eighty-nine, his diary entry might have been a young boy's lamentation for his youthful mother: 'Last night, gently and sweetly, my dearest dearest Mummy passed away.'

Around the same time, as if in compensation for the loss of his mother, his adventurous wife, Teddy, finally returned from Italy, where she had been interned by the Italians near Siena. Neither she nor her husband seems to have pined unduly for the other, but they did achieve their long-postponed bridal night together. Anxious to resume her career as a singer, Teddy was still no clinging vine, although she would have liked a modicum of a married life; but when she presented Paul with his fifth son, christened Timothy, in 1946, her husband still opted for duty back in Tulsa rather than married life with Teddy.

Timmy proved an ailing infant. 'Poor poor Timmy' was how Paul wrote about him at his birth. And throughout his short life, Timmy suffered dreadfully, developing a brain tumour at the age of six, which required protracted surgery. But although he always said how moved he was by 'sad little Timmy', Paul seemed as incapable as ever of coping with personal unhappiness – or married life. Teddy often urged that all three of them should live together as a family, but Paul stayed in Tulsa, relying for relief on waitresses, shop-girls, call-girls – anything to save him from the dreaded tentacles of marriage.

By the time the war had ended, something had clearly happened to him. Perhaps it was the onset of the male menopause, while some believed he'd burned out young. Maybe he no longer felt the urge to make his long dead father 'eat his words' by earning vast amounts of money. Whatever the cause, he remained at Tulsa in his precious bunker and, instead of returning to the oil business, organized the change-over of

Spartan Aircraft from making aircraft to creating homes on trailers.

It was an odd activity for a financial genius like Paul Getty. But the challenge of producing mobile homes seems to have intrigued him; he took endless trouble working out details of design and marketing, and was proud when production topped 2,000.

After four years in his bunker, he clearly needed something more than trailers to excite him. Lacking it, he was soon muttering about giving up everything to become a beachcomber. He even got as far as selling out a tranche of holdings in his prized Western Pacific – the only time he ever did – and his biographer Robert Lenzner is convinced he would have continued selling had he not come up against legal obstacles to offloading further shares in the Sarah C. Getty Trust.

This was fortunate for the Getty family. For it left him no choice but to remain in the oil business; and this in turn meant that in 1948, when he recognized the chance of several million lifetimes, he was poised to seize it.

Like so much in the Middle East, where little is what it seems, the so-called Neutral Zone between Saudi Arabia and Kuwait is anything but Neutral. For centuries the Saudis to the south and the Kuwaitis to the north had argued over the ownership of this apparently useless 2,000-square-mile wedge of desert, lying between its neighbours and the Persian Gulf. The issue was finally settled with a typical Arab compromise.

Ignoring the nomadic Bedouin, who were the only human beings poor enough to go there, the area was defined as a kind of no-man's-land and called the Neutral Zone. Its two neighbours retained dual sovereignty – 'an undivided half interest' – over the one thing that might one day be of value, the mineral rights. But for many years there were no takers.

Even when the world's greatest oilfield, the massive Burghan field in Kuwait, was discovered in the 1930s, just a few miles north of its boundaries, the Zone itself continued to daunt prospective oilmen with its inhospitable terrain, its scorching climate, and the geopolitical quagmire of its mineral rights.

With the ending of war in Europe, it was clear that the US oilfields would soon find it hard to satisfy America's booming car economy, and interest focused once again on the Persian Gulf as the likeliest alternative. Even the Neutral Zone, with all its problems, began to be 'tentatively' discussed among the major oil companies.

Inevitably word of this reached Paul Getty – but unlike most senior executives of major oil companies, he was not a tentative man. He was a realist. 'If one is to be anyone in the world's oil business, one must stake one's claim in the Middle East,' he said. And since he decided that he emphatically did want to be someone in the world oil business, he made one of his inspired decisions.

Without having the region surveyed, or placing a foot in the Middle East himself, he decided that he and he alone would have the Saudi concession to the Neutral Zone.

By now he was more concerned for his personal safety than ever, and had decided he would never risk travelling by air. So he had absolutely no intention of venturing to the Neutral Zone himself. Instead he was fortunate to discover the ideal agent within his own organization – Paul Walton, a young geologist who had worked in Saudi Arabia in the 1930s and was currently head of exploration in the Rocky Mountain division of the Pacific Western oil company. Walton knew the Persian Gulf. He knew its people, and its problems. He was anxious to return. So Getty invited him to Paris, and briefed him on his mission.

He did this with his customary obsession with detail, spending four full days with Walton in the Hôtel Georges V until every eventuality was covered – the exact price at which Walton should start bidding for the oil concession, the speed at which he had to move, and the height to which he was prepared to go.

Having done this to his satisfaction, Getty waited.

He was acting entirely on instinct, for at this stage he had not seen so much as a single survey report on the Neutral Zone. But his instinct was as sound as ever. When Walton made his first aerial reconnaissance of the Zone, it was as Paul had suspected. Spread across the desert were a number of the dome-like mounds identical to similar formations covering Kuwait's Burghan field to the north.

As this made it almost certain that the oil deposits of the field continued through the Neutral Zone, Walton was being ultra-cautious when he reported back that the chances of a major oil-find within the Zone were fifty-fifty. (Later he said he would have given higher odds, but he had seen similar perfect sites in Saudi Arabia come up 'dry as hell' and didn't wish to overpitch the prospects.)

It was typical of Paul that even now he was so suspicious and secretive that he had forbidden Walton to send back his news by telephone, wireless or cablegram – all of which might just be liable to interception. Instead he insisted on an anony-mous-looking airmail letter – which took all of nine days to reach Paris from Jiddah. And throughout this period of waiting, Paul, with his sombre face and poker-player's self-control, con-tinued life entirely as usual, betraying not the faintest sign of what was happening.

But once he had the letter he was jubilant. Odds of fifty-fifty are high for the oil business, and he started bidding for the great potential oil bonanza of the Neutral Zone. He was sud-denly prepared to stake his entire personal fortune, the funds in the Sarah C. Getty Trust, and anything further he could raise upon the greatest gamble of his life.

For such a fearful man to take such a bold decision, and such a miserly one to risk so much, even before solving all the mas-sive problems of transporting, refining and marketing the oil he hoped to find, is a measure of the unpredictability of his com-plex nature. It puzzled and astonished even those who knew him best.

But stranger still was the fact that while all this was going on there was not the faintest change in the anonymous life that he was leading. Now in his late fifties, he continued to direct his multi-million-dollar empire from room 801 of the Hotel Georges V in Paris, where he also slept with his women, washed his socks, played teach-yourself Arabic records like background music, and every evening dutifully entered his day's expenses in his diary – 'taxi 5 francs, bus fare 1 franc, newspaper – 10 centimes'.

Yet this was the man who was negotiating to pay the King of Saudi Arabia and the Sultan of Kuwait, as joint owners of the Neutral Zone, a guaranteed million dollars each a year even if no oil was ever found, an unprecedented royalty of 40 per cent on each barrel of oil produced – plus a $20 million down payment for the privilege of wildcatting in an arid desert 2,000 miles away from where he was sitting.

Success in the Neutral Zone did not come easily. Paul soon discovered that the Aminoil syndicate, which included one of the major American oil companies, Phillips Petroleum, had got there before him, and had also purchased a concession to the Zone from the Kuwaitis. As Paul's concession was granted by the Saudis, this meant he had to work in tandem with Aminoil employees – which inevitably led to friction, feuds and terrible misunderstandings.

Nor was it all that easy to strike oil – however convinced Paul might be that it was simply waiting there to be discovered. Not until early 1953 did his Pacific Western technicians finally locate what they were seeking – an oil strike connecting with a virtual underground sea of oil. It was a discovery which, in oil terms, *Fortune* magazine described as 'somewhere between colossal and history making'. But it was only now that Paul showed the true originality and business flair which would make the Getty fortune stratospheric.

Much of the oil in the Neutral Zone was in the form of cheap so-called 'garbage oil', the low-grade crude coming from shallow wells which cost little to produce, but for which there was little real demand. Paul realized that provided he could get this oil to America in sufficient quantities, up-to-date oil refineries would have no difficulty processing it for the ever-growing American domestic market. The problem was to get it there, build suitably large refineries, and market it. Solving this problem was to prove the most ambitious undertaking of his life, and required coordination and financing on a massive scale.

Unwilling to give tanker owners the power to hold him hostage in the future, he decided to construct his own tanker fleet – spending more than $200 million on the massive super-tankers which would carry his cheap oil from the Neutral Zone, not only to America but also to Europe and Japan. (It was typical of Paul that, with the assistance of his well-connected friend, the French industrialist and former air ace, Commandant Paul Louis Weiller, he was able to get these tankers built in French dockyards with a 35 per cent French government subsidy – and then receive the Légion d'Honneur for services to France.)

A further $200 million went on a new refinery at Wilmington on America's eastern seaboard, and $60 million on upgrading the old Avon refinery in California. These were massive undertakings. The Delaware River had to be deepened and port installations built to bring the Getty supertankers up to Wilmington. The number of Tide Water service stations in America was more than doubled to provide outlets for Getty gasoline.

The outlay was vast, but the profits were vaster. From the shallow wells the oil was costing so little to produce that salaries and overheads were minimal. World demand for gasoline and oil continued to increase, and over the next twelve years Pacific Western would build fifteen separate wells in the Neutral Zone, producing a major part of American oil imports from the Middle East and making Pacific Western the seventh largest gasoline producer in the USA.

Since Paul personally controlled the company and he and the Sarah C. Getty Trust were its major shareholders, the profits immeasurably enriched him and his heirs. And in 1956, to ensure that his contribution to the Getty dynasty would be remembered, he changed the name of his thriving company. In place of Pacific Western, it would henceforth be known as the Getty Oil Company.

What was so strange about this whole elaborate operation was that Paul continued to direct almost every detail of it himself. The creation of a great oilfield, of a major tanker fleet, and of port facilities and massive refineries in America were all master-minded by this one extraordinary individual, sitting quietly in Room 801 in the Hôtel Georges V in Paris. He would often work throughout the night, and not bother overmuch with food. But otherwise this whole amazing enterprise barely changed his private way of life at all.

Provided he was always near a telephone, he could continue his travels, his affairs, his personal interests, while his most ambitious business ventures seemed to remain what they had always been – part of the everlasting game that he was playing with the world for his private satisfaction.

When Paul met Penelope Kitson in 1953, she was just thirty-one, an elegant, very self-possessed upper-class Englishwoman, with three children and an unsatisfactory marriage. They became intimate friends, and she enjoyed his company, finding him charming, extraordinarily knowledgeable, and possessed of 'the sharpest brain of anyone I've ever known'.

He made a fuss of her and said he loved her, but from the start something told her that if she ever fell completely in love with him, she'd be at his mercy – so she never did. As an intelligent woman of the world she could see his limitations all too clearly – that he was not a man to marry or to permit to dominate her life, and that behind his womanizing lay a total inability to endure the normal bonds, responsibilities, pleasures, problems, of a family. As a realist, she would not permit herself the luxury of thinking she could ever change him. Not that she really wished to, for she knew that if she did, it would inevitably destroy the way of life he had carefully created – which in turn made possible his business ventures. So they stayed lovers, equals, friends and partners.

The more she got to know Paul, the more she saw him as a man with extraordinary powers of concentration and strength of will, and realized that his attitude to women (herself included) was part of something crucial to his nature. It didn't particularly trouble her that he was sexually obsessive, and that 'he simply couldn't keep his hands off any woman who came near him'. She claims that as she had never had a jealous nature sexual jealousy wasn't really an issue between them.

But she sensed that he was a very strange character indeed – dominating, clever, independent, but lacking one crucial ingredient to his nature. 'I suppose that one would have to say that part of him had simply never grown up.' Part of him remained the selfish, spoiled only child who had been indulged by George and Sarah. (Hence much of his trouble with his children and his family.) 'But he was utterly determined over anything he wanted, and would never delegate to anyone, because no one was really up to him.'

As far as Penelope was concerned, it suited her to keep her independence, especially as she sensed that at the moment Paul was more in love with her than she was with him, and that once this changed she would lose him. After her divorce she bought a house in Kensington, which he often visited when he came to London, and since she was an accomplished interior decorator, he employed her to decorate the state rooms of the oil tankers he was building.

He excused himself for not proposing marriage by saying that a fortune-teller in New Orleans once said that if he married for a sixth time he would die. (This was probably untrue. He often quoted fortune-tellers to confirm or excuse any line of conduct.)

But he also told her, 'Pen, you'll always be my Number

One.' This time he was not lying, and until he died she remained virtually the only person close to him who was not intimidated by his character, his reputation or his money – which was why he trusted her.

One area where the oddities of Paul Getty's character were particularly evident was in his role as an art collector. With his increased wealth he was starting to take collecting seriously. He had recently bought the so-called 'ranch-house' at Malibu – a stone – built summer residence in a prime location overlooking the Pacific Ocean – and used it as a setting for the valuable French eighteenth-century furniture he'd bought at bargain prices just before the war.

Since then he had picked up further bargains – particularly the Rembrandt portrait of the merchant Marten Looten, which he bought from a frightened Dutch businessman on the eve of war for $65,000, and the superb Ardabil carpet, which he had previously acquired at the bargain price of $68,000 from the sharpest of international dealers, Lord Duveen, when his lordship was on his deathbed. On an off-day at Sotheby's he had also picked up for $200 a painting known as the *The Madonna of Loreto*, which he convinced himself was at least partially painted by Raphael.

In artistic matters, his overwhelming motive continued to be to find a bargain – which stopped him from ever becoming a genuine collector. Even Penelope admits that 'Paul was really too mean ever to allow himself to buy a great painting.'

More to the point, his lack of emotional response made him somewhat like a very clever child who knows a lot but lacks a mature aesthetic response to anything. This was particularly apparent in the small book he put together on his favourite subject – eighteenth-century France. With some of its information evidently lifted straight from encyclopedias, much of it might have been written by a fact-obsessed twelve-year-old – but as a guide to Paul Getty's mind, it is most revealing.

Almost everything within this book relates to money. Various important pieces in his own collection are described – but always in terms of market prices, estimated value, and exactly how much he had spent on them.

This can be fascinating. Who but Paul Getty would have worked out the contemporary cost of making a *boulle* table and concluded that a French nobleman would have paid slightly more for it in real terms in 1760 than the cost of 'a top quality saloon car' in the 1950s?

Similarly he could become absorbed in the minutiae of connoisseurship – over the precise pigment used in one or other of his paintings, for example.

What he appeared unable to do was trust his emotional response to any work of art, in case his feelings ran away with him, so that what he really needed was somebody whose taste he trusted to advise him as he built up his collection. In September 1953 he did meet such a person. During a trip to Italy with another of his current mistresses, the effusive English art journalist Ethel le Vane, he accidentally met, in a corridor of the Excelsior Hotel in Florence, one of the greatest connoisseurs of Italian painting, Bernard Berenson, who, without realizing who Paul was, invited him to tea at the holy of artistic holies, his villa I Tatti on the hill at Settignano, close to France.

It was a strange occasion. On Paul's side was the profound reverence with which he treated the great connoisseur, who possessed in such abundance qualities he was so aware of lacking – artistic judgement, true discrimination, taste and knowledge. And on Berenson's side was a total unawareness of the fact that this strange American with the talkative girlfriend was rapidly becoming his country's richest billionaire.

How much in life is timing! Twenty years earlier, Berenson would not have missed anyone as rich as Getty and he and Joe Duveen between them would have flattered him with their attention, aroused his latent enthusiasm for the pictures they could sell him, and quite probably have ended by helping him create a great collection.

Instead the moment passed. Getty promised to make photographs of some of his marble statuary; and Berenson expressed the hope that they might meet again, but they never did. Berenson was old and disillusioned – not least with himself. Getty was terrified of wasting money and/or being swindled; and not until after he was dead would he give others the pleasure and responsibility of spending just a part of his enormous fortune on works of art appropriate to his collection.

In the meantime, classical sculpture seems to have appealed to him. As a trained geologist, he felt comfortable with marble, and his recent purchase of some pieces of Roman statuary, combined with this autumn visit to Italy, brought some very strange, and, as it turned out, quite far-reaching consequences.

It was one of the Roman pieces he had bought from the collection of Lord Lansdowne, a Roman statue of Hercules, which inspired him to pay a visit to the place where it had supposedly been discovered – Hadrian's Villa at Tivoli outside Rome. Even with the scanty ruins that remain, the villa is a haunted, atmospheric site, and Paul, who was nothing if not suggestible, seems to have been overcome by an awareness of the presence of its one-time owner, the most artistically creative and enigmatic of all the Roman emperors, Hadrian.

The sense of *déjà vu* is fairly common. But to a very rich, self-made man, there is an additional incentive to believe in reincarnation – because of the explanation it can offer for his otherwise inexplicable success. As E. L. Doctorow has the self-made Henry Ford remark to the self-made Pierpont Morgan in his celebrated novel *Ragtime* – 'I explain my genius this way – some of us have just lived more times than others.'

Paul, who appears to have felt this very strongly, may also have been influenced by the reason Henry Miller gives for the same belief – 'Sex is one of the nine good reasons for believing in reincarnation ... the other eight are unimportant.'

What is clear is that his visit to Hadrian's Villa came at an impressionable moment when the sudden uprush of his wealth and far-flung enterprises found a sort of echo in what he had already learned of Hadrian's activities. Just as the ageing Hadrian had stayed at the villa and continued to initiate enterprises and great events in the furthest corners of the Roman Empire, so Paul had been making great things happen in the distant reaches of the Getty Empire. Hadrian had been the richest man on earth, and Paul was fast becoming much the same himself. He also liked to think he had a stoical Roman attitude to life, and felt that he even looked not unlike a Roman emperor. Finally, for the true snob – and snobs came little snobbier than Paul Getty – what pedigree could conceivably approach direct descent from a Roman Emperor?

The more that Paul thought about it – and he seems to have thought about it quite a lot – the more did he pick up similarities, echoes, resonances, between the long-dead Emperor Hadrian and himself.

'I would very much like to think that I was a reincarnation of Hadrian's spirit, and I would like to emulate him as closely as I can,' he confided to a female friend in London.

CHAPTER NINE

FATHERHOOD

FOR A MAN who thought so much of dynasties, Paul Getty was a strangely absent father. Had he not been quite so totally immersed in the vast expansion of his fortune, one wonders if he might have found a little time for his four children who were growing up so far away from him. Probably not. It was not lack of time so much as that he clearly saw his children as a threat to the two things that meant most to him – making money and the serious pursuit of pleasure.

Nevertheless, very occasionally he did make contact with them, possibly from curiosity, like a Trappist sniffing at the pleasures of the flesh – only to recoil from the temptation. Describing these occasions in his diaries, he always presents himself as such a loving and devoted parent to his children that it is hard to realize that he almost never saw them. Young Ronald is described as 'bright and lovable', George is 'very mature, with an excellent mind and personality', and young Paul and Gordon are invariably referred to as 'my two dear sons'.

The most intriguing of Getty's extremely rare adventures into active fatherhood occurred on Christmas Eve, 1939, with war in Europe just declared, and provides the sole occasion in their entire childhood when the four 'beloved' sons actually found themselves in one room together. He had just scurried home to Los Angeles from Naples, having left his new bride, Teddy, to face the war alone in Italy. For once he must have felt the need for the consolations of a family, and he called up his ex-wife Ann to let him take young Paul and Gordon out to a toy shop, where they saw a penguin dressed as Donald Duck and he bought them Christmas presents. Fini and Ronald had come to live in Los Angeles just before the war. And so on Christmas Day 'all four of my beloved sons' as he insisted on describing them – fifteen-year-old George, ten-year-old Ronald, and young Paul and Gordon, seven and six respectively – were brought to the house on South Kingsley Drive to bring Christmas greetings to their eighty-seven-year-old grand-mother, Sarah.

Getty must have arranged this out of filial deference rather than paternal affection, for it sounds an uncomfortable occasion – the very deaf and lame old lady, the four unknown boys who shared her blood and were so awkward in each other's company, and the presence of this mysterious rich father with the down-turned mouth who must have seemed an almost total stranger.

But again he made it sound like a happy party for a most united family when he wrote in his diary of the 'lovely tree in mother's sitting room' and the 'heaps' of Christmas presents. 'Mother enjoyed it like a youngster,' he assures us. He seems to have stayed long enough to greet his offspring and kiss his ancient mother on the cheek before departing like the ghost of Christmas.

As Sarah's health deteriorated after this, and she died two years later, this exercise in Christmas togetherness was not repeated, and it remained the only contact there would be between the young Gettys during boyhood, despite the fact that they were all living at the time in California, and that on them would ultimately rest the future of the largest fortune in America.

What made Paul Getty such a disquieting, and ultimately such a disastrous, father was the way in which he almost totally cut off from all his sons in their childhood and adolescence and then, when it suited him, re-established relationships as if nothing

untoward had happened, attempting to groom them to perpetuate what he always liked to call 'the Getty dynasty'.

It couldn't work, for by then the damage had been done.
The boys had missed their father when they needed him, none
of them really knew him, and each had been damaged in a different way. Almost inevitably, all the boys were jealous and suspicious of each other, so that the 'dynasty', instead of helping to
support its members, actually produced fearful antagonisms
between them. Jealousy, bitterness and non-stop litigation would
all stem from the problems Paul Getty bequeathed his sons
when he gave them a phantom billionaire as a father.

The firstborn, George Getty II, should have suffered least.
He was far too young to have known his father when he abandoned poor Jeanette in 1927, and she remarried fairly swiftly – a
well-to-do, kindly, Los Angeles stockbroker, Bill Jones, who
treated young George as a son, sending him to private school in
Los Angeles and then to Princeton, where he planned to
study law.

During his childhood George's contact with his father was
minimal, but Jeanette took him regularly to call on Grandma
Getty, who had always had a soft spot for her firstborn grandson.
Not only did the child bear the precious name of her own
lamented husband, but George Getty Senior had left him that
$300,000 in his will. Shrewdly invested by his stepfather, this
sum of money was increasing, and, together with the growing
income from the Sarah C. Getty Trust, guaranteed that George
would always be comfortably off, quite apart from anything he
earned.

This situation should have suited George, who had inherited little of his father's drive or business genius, and who was
made for the undemanding life of an unambitious Californian
attorney of independent means. But it was not to be. With his
name and his position, George's fate was sealed from the start.
He was destined for the company his grandfather and namesake
founded, and in 1942, when George was just eighteen and in

his first year at Princeton, his father claimed him for the role he had to play in life.

George was just about to join the US Army, intending to return to Princeton when the war was over, but now, for the first time in his life, his father took an interest in him, taking him to visit the old Athens oilfield, scene of several of his own successes in his distant youth. Here he made it clear to George that his future lay irrevocably in the oil industry, and that one day he could expect to head the family business.

How could George refuse? But first he had to serve for four years in the Army, as an infantry officer to start with, then in the war-crimes prosecution team. Demobilized in 1946, he finally decided that instead of completing university he would join his father.

George made a conscientious businessman and, as his father's heir apparent, rose with unsurprising swiftness in the management hierarchy of the Getty companies. After serving creditably as his father's representative in the Neutral Zone of Arabia, he returned to California to become vice-president of Tide Water Oil at the age of thirty-one. Success was beckoning, and his life should now have been extremely sweet.

But as a businessman George was already suffering one fatal flaw. As a child he seems to have picked up from his mother a sense of fear and awe for the absent figure of his father which he never lost. Even as a grown man he never overcame it, and the more responsibility he gained as Paul Getty's heir apparent, the more his fear of his father served to undermine him. In the end it helped to kill him.

But George's problems were as nothing when compared with the handicaps his father heaped upon his unfortunate half-brother, the 'bright and lovable' Ronald. Being half German, Ronald was inevitably the odd one out from the family from the start.

Soon after his father had obtained his dearly bought divorce

from Ronald's mother, Fini, back in 1932, mother and son settled in Switzerland. Fini herself never remarried, and until the
outbreak of the war in 1939, she and Ronald were looked after
by the boy's German grandfather, Dr Otto Helmle, who since
the divorce had become one of Getty's bitterest opponents.

During this period, Dr Helmle had other matters on his
mind. As a prominent Catholic, he was secretary of the German
Centre Party, precursor of the post-war Christian Democrats,
and in 1933 had actually refused the post of Minister for
Economics in Hitler's first government as Chancellor. Later, as
his opposition to the Nazis grew, he felt happy in the knowledge that his daughter and grandson were safely in Switzerland
where he could easily visit them from Karlsruhe. So as a child
Ronald grew up in Switzerland, speaking German, believing he
was Swiss, and more or less oblivious of the the existence of his
real father.

By 1939, Dr Helmle had been banned from all political
activity along with his friend and fellow party member, Konrad
Adenaeur, and was actually imprisoned for a period, losing all
his money in the process. (In 1944, he was lucky to escape arrest
a second time – for involvement in the plot against the Führer.)
At the time of his imprisonment he sent Fini and his ten-year-
old grandson to the the safety of Los Angeles, where for the first
time Ronald learned about his father.

'Even then,' he says, 'I didn't know him, as I hardly ever saw
him. Occasionally my mother used to take me to visit my
grandmother Sarah, but all I remember about her was that she
seemed kind and was in a wheelchair, and was so extremely deaf
that communication was impossible. My father was running the
aircraft factory in Tulsa at the time so I never saw him. Occasionally a cheque would arrive from him for my birthday, once
he sent me a pair of roller skates, and that was about it. I can't
say I thought about him very much, although I realized that
there was something lacking in my life, particularly when I
saw other kids going off to ball games with their fathers and I
never did.'

It was only gradually that Ronald learned that on top of everything else he missed out on from the absence of a father, he was suffering a more serious handicap. His half-brothers, George and young Paul and Gordon, were all incuded in the Sarah C. Getty Trust, and as such were destined to become great heirs to the ever-growing fortune of the Gettys. Ronald was not.

What made the situation so unjust was that the reason for this glaring inequality was not his fault. Excluding the infant Ronald from the Sarah C. Getty Trust had been his father's chosen way of getting even with Dr Helmle over the divorce – including the money it had cost him for the settlement, and the way the delays had prevented him marrying Ann Rork before his third son, Paul, was born. And as if to underline the arbitrary nature of the exclusion, while Ronald was excluded from the trust, any children he might have were specifically included.

To be absolutely fair to Getty, back in 1936 when the trust was established for the benefit of his children and unborn grandchildren, the capital involved was relatively small; and since he was smarting over what he saw as Helmle's victory, he felt that rich Dr Helmle should therefore have the privilege of providing for his grandson.

What neither of them had foreseen was that Helmle would lose all his money to the Nazis, while Getty would proceed to build the greatest fortune in America.

After the war, Fini and Ronald started to return to Germany or Switzerland each summer, so that, as Ronald says, 'Europe was always very much home to me, and Los Angeles a sort of interval in my life. I naturally thought myself more European than American.'

Not until 1951, when Ronald was twenty-two and in his final year of business studies at the University of Southern California, did his father see fit to contact him. As with George, he wanted him to take his place in his rapidly expanding business empire. And as Ronald puts it, 'I was pleased that he asked me to work for him, but I can't say it was a particularly emotional reunion.'

A training course followed with Getty Oil, and in 1953 Ronald joined the Getty-owned Tide Water Oil's marketing department, where he was so successful that three years later he was running the department with a salary of $40,000 a year.

But at Tide Water he inevitably came into increasing contact with the young vice-president, his half-brother George, and a feud began, with jealousy and bitterness on either side. Despite his success, George would always feel insecure before his father, and resented having this half-brother in his company just in case he attracted more than his fair share of their father's affection. Ronald, on the other hand, was becoming increasing aware of the massive handicap his father had inflicted on him by excluding him alone of his sons from the Sarah C. Getty Trust. It was an awareness which would grow like a cancer in the years ahead, until it all but destroyed him.

In comparison with the problems Paul Getty thrust on to George and Ronald, life seemed infinitely easier for Paul and Gordon, the two boys whom he had fathered so casually on that former child prodigy, Ann Rork. As he was increasingly away in Europe and the Middle East during the 1950s, he saw even less of them during their adolescence than he had of George and Ronald, leaving them exposed to the undivided force of their mother's dominating personality.

When her marriage ended with that 'noisome' – and profitable – divorce at Reno back in 1936, Ann had rapidly embarked upon a marital career in which three further wealthy husbands, interspersed with various lovers, took the unlamented place of Paul Getty. First on the scene was Douglas Wilson, an eminently forgettable millionaire from Memphis, Tennessee, by whom she had one daughter, Paul and Gordon's beautiful but put-upon half-sister, Donna.

Wilson was succeeded by Garret 'Joe' McEnerney II, a San Francisco attorney, and it was the break-up of this marriage that left Ann – or 'Mrs Mack' as she was called – in possession of a comfortable, creeper-hung house at 3788 Clay Street in Presidio Heights, close to the smartest part of San Francisco.

During this period, Getty himself was giving the boys nothing but his name and child support. There is a unique entry in his diary in the middle of the war recording just one visit that he paid them. Gordon recited him a poem he had written 'on the good qualities of negroes' – but instead of saying what he thought of Gordon or his poem, Getty, fact-obsessed as ever, simply recorded that 'Paul is eleven years old and weighs 86 pounds, while Gordon is ten and weighs 76 pounds.'

'My sons – all of them – are great rewards,' he added – so great that he saw neither Paul nor Gordon for the next twelve years. And a year later, when twelve-year-old Paul wrote Papa a letter, Getty sent it back unanswered with the spelling mistakes carefully corrected.

Paul was still bitter over this years later. 'I never got over that,' he said. 'I wanted to be judged as a human being, and I could never get that from him.'

Since the boys had virtually no contact with their father, they had no idea of the vast expansion of his fortune. According to Judge William Newsom, a friend and contemporary of both boys at San Francisco's St Ignatius High School, 'They knew they had a rich, even very rich father, but as he had almost no influence upon their lives one didn't hear much about him.' Judge Newsom describes life at Clay Street at this time as 'financially comfortable, not prodigal, with money no great issue either way. Neither Paul nor Gordon seemed particularly concerned about money or the lack of it – nor did they seem to dwell on expectations.'

But if their absent father left a gap in Paul and Gordon's lives, Mrs Mack seemed more than capable of filling it. Hers was a powerful presence, and she was clearly the dominant influence on both her boys as they grew to manhood in this unconventional one-parent family in the midst of post-war San Francisco.

Now in her mid to late thirties, a sexy, bustling woman with fine eyes and auburn hair, Mrs Mack was almost everything that

Jean Paul Getty wasn't – theatrical, easy-going and exuberant. Still very much the one-time would-be movie queen, she was a lively woman with, according to her daughter, 'a very high I.Q.' She was consciously artistic, with considerable taste in literature and music. She was clearly a woman of resource, who when short of money could always rustle up a little extra on her own account through property speculation in Marin County.

With such a mother – and no father on the scene to cramp their style – the boys should have had an idyllic adolescence – and in many ways they did.

A natural bohemian, Mrs Mack believed in freedom, and left the boys largely to their own devices. But she was also a highly social creature, and the gregariousness which had so infuriated Jean Paul Getty made her encourage both her boys to entertain their friends at home. (Being three years younger than Gordon, the boys' half-sister, Donna Wilson, was inevitably over-shadowed in this male-dominated household. A very pretty girl, she was also very shy and tended to be overlooked, playing little part in her brothers' lives until considerably later.)

Mrs Mack was the most hospitable of mothers, and by the boys' mid teens, the house on Clay Street had become an open house for Paul's school-friends. Part of the attraction was undoubtedly Mrs Mack herself – who Was one of those mythic mothers who enjoy a wide rapport with all her children's friends. Some were probably in love with her, while others recall her as a sort of rakehell aunt. Judge Newsom compares her with Graham Greene's outrageous Aunt Augusta in his comic novel *Travels with My Aunt* – but the usual reaction from old habitués of '3788', is that 'Mrs Mack was Auntie Marne to the life'.

Tolerant by disposition, Mrs Mack raised no objection to the boys and their friends drinking at home as they grew older, on the basis, as Donna put it, that 'it was better to have them getting drunk where you knew where they were, than somewhere else where you didn't.'

At a time when few other middle-class parents were quite so liberated on the subject, this added greatly to the popularity of the Getty household, and of Mrs Mack herself, who was partial to a drink and would 'sit down and have a beer with us herself' as one of her sons' friends fondly remembers. Soon the house on Clay Street was referred to as 'the 3788 Club' – or simply 'Thirty-seven, Eighty-eight'.

The members of '3788' formed a fascinated following round the Gettys, with young Paul very much the leader of the pack, which was inevitably called 'the Getty Gang'. Having inherited much of his mother's Irish charm and sociability, he played up to his audience, making them laugh at his stories and his exploits, and dressing the part of the would-be tearaway and playboy.

But there was more to the attractions of 3788 than Ann and alcohol, and the house became something of a cultural beacon in middle-class, post-war San Francisco. Music was of growing importance to the family – particularly to Gordon, whose collection of operatic records was already vast and steadily increasing – as was his knowledge of opera and the greatest operatic singers.

Several of them – including such legendary figures as the soprano Licia Albanese and the lyric tenor Tagliavini – gave recitals at the house when visiting San Francisco, and the boys' love of opera would develop in the years ahead, so that even in their periods of deepest disagreement, they would remain united as members of the esoteric cult of dedicated opera buffs.

As a household, Clay Street seemed a perfect setting for the boys to develop as intelligent and original human beings, and at first sight, Paul appeared to get the best of it, living his spoiled, highly social life, aided and abetted by his doting mother. Like her he drank a lot. (Sometimes beer with kippers for breakfast to her dry martinis.) Popular with his friends and attractive to the girls, a charmed life seemed to lie ahead of him.

With Gordon things were rather different. Both boys were handsome but in very different ways. With his pointed face and lively manner, Paul looked rather like an adolescent satyr, but as Gordon approached his full height of six feet two, he increasingly resembled a large edition of the youthful Schubert. As Donna puts it, 'Paul exuded sex, whereas Gordon didn't exude anything very much,' and Paul was inevitably his mother's favourite. According to Bill Newsom she 'thought him the wittiest, cleverest handsomest boy in California'.

Paul's reaction to his mother's spoiling was to make the most of it and cheerfully get on with life. But when Gordon failed to receive the same attention from his mother, he tended to withdraw into himself, building a wall of self-sufficiency which soon became a key part of his character.

By reacting against his mother's easy-going ways, Gordon appeared as something of a puritan, and in contrast to his mother and his brother, he never was a drinker. Paul had a succession of glamorous motor cars, including a Cord and a Dodge convertible, which he drove stylishly and rather fast. Gordon chose calmer vehicles – a solid Oldsmobile and a still more solid Buick, which he drove with great deliberation.

But while life at Clay Street seemed particularly relaxed, the absence of a father-figure probably affected both boys more than their friends appreciated. In Gordon's case it left him no parental alternative to his mother, and when he found he couldn't cope with Mrs Mack's shenanigans or drunkenness or lovers, he tended to create a private, separate life away from home. Before going off to university, he actually moved into the easy-going Irish household of his old schoolfriend, Bill Newsom, making a sort of father-figure out of Newsom Senior. By then Gordon was a clever, inner-directed loner whose true home was music, poetry, and economic theory. These would see him through the troubles and distractions of the years ahead.

Unlike the self-sufficient Gordon, who felt no need for organized religion, Paul, at sixteen, underwent a serious conversion with the Jesuits of St Ignatius. And although at first sight Paul's life seemed more enviable than Gordon's, he was in fact more vulnerable than his brother. If he modelled himself on anyone it was probably on handsome Edgar Peixoto, a charmingly failed lawyer, who was one of his mother's many suitors. 'A stylish, most intelligent man whom drink had sadly overtaken', is how one of Paul's friends remembers him. Bill Newsom, recalling Peixoto's conversation and his phenomenal memory for Norman Douglas's most ribald limericks, says, 'Most of us thought Edgar was a hero.' Paul certainly did – but Gordon didn't.

Paul's character seems to have contained many contradictions. His wildness hid a certain melancholy, and behind the chronic need for friends lay considerable insecurity. Where Gordon loved the certainties of chess and economic theory, Paul was already drawn to the excesses of high romantic literature. He was a great reader, and was soon collecting books, having started with a first edition of *The Great Gatsby*. He relished the *fin-de-siècle* decadence of Wilde and Corvo, but his prize discovery was that overblown diabolist, Aleister Crowley. The self-styled 'Prince of Darkness and Great Beast 666', who flourished on a daily intake of heroin that would have floored half a dozen lesser men, Crowley came to be regarded as something of a forerunner of the 'psychedelic generation' of the sixties; for Paul to have picked upon him now is a hint of how his mind was working and the way his interests would develop.

Paul had finished high school and was about to go to the University of San Francisco when the Korean war broke out in 1950. His mother suggested using her influence with a general she knew to stop him being drafted, but he wouldn't let her. Instead he went to Korea, made corporal, but otherwise showed little aptitude for soldiering, serving out his time in an office at the Seoul headquarters. A year later Gordon also broke off his studies in economics at Berkeley to join the Artillery, took a commission, but didn't like the Army any more than Paul and spent his service at the base camp of Fort Ord.

When he returned from Korea, Paul was already in love with pretty Gail Harris, the only child of Federal Judge George Harris. Unlike the Gettys, who were very much newcomers to the city, the Harrises were third-generation San Franciscans, and the Judge, a Truman appointee, was a leading figure in the community. But for all Paul's wildness, the Judge and his wife, Aileen, became very fond of him, and he in turn was sufficiently in love with Gail to give up drinking. When Paul and Gail decided to get married, the only person not in favour was Mrs Mack.

Hating to lose her favourite son, she argued forcibly that at twenty-three he was far too young and wild and immature for marriage. But despite her warnings and objections the Harrises supported the young lovers, who finally married, quietly, in Woodside's Our Lady of the Wayside Chapel in January 1956.

The bridegroom's father, who was then in England, would, true to form, have ignored the marriage, but prompted by Penelope Kitson he sent a telegram of congratulation signed, 'Your loving Father' – though not a present.

Gordon by now seemed firmly married to poetry, economic theory and music – above all music. He possessed a baritone voice to match his size, and dreamed of studying at the conservatory and one day finding worldwide fame and fortune as an opera singer.

Up to this point in their lives neither brother had paid the faintest attention to the oil business, to their half-brothers George and Ronald, or to their unknown father, who was drawing wealth in such unimaginable quantities from beneath the sand in one of the hottest, driest, most uncomfortable spots on earth.

PART TWO

CHAPTER TEN

THE RICHEST LIVING AMERICAN

I N OCTOBER 1957 Paul Getty finally emerged from the capitalist closet in which he had been living in relative obscurity for so long. *Fortune* magazine, after several months' research among America's super rich, including Rockefellers, Morgans, Hunts, and Fords, publicly proclaimed Jean Paul Getty, an 'expatriate businessman living in Paris', the 'richest living American'.

Photographs taken of him at the time give the impression of a nocturnal creature suddenly flushed out of hiding and exposed to the cruel light of day. The secret game he had been quietly engaged in since his father died was no longer secret, his wealth no longer private, and a number of important things began to change for Getty – and for those around him.

The great fortune and the business interests he had been creating could no longer remain the discreet affair which he had been conducting for so long by long-distance telephone from hotel bedrooms, with the records carried in his head or stowed away in shoe boxes. Henceforth it became increasingly like other major fortunes, and although he did his best to keep his style of life unchanged, it was now that he inevitably became a public figure, subject to all the pressures on the very rich – publicity, begging letters, speculation, envy, fawning ballyhoo; and from now on his features started becoming known as well.

He pretended to regret the loss of his previous 'gratifying' anonymity, remembering how in the past reporters covering events at which he was present had generally overlooked him. 'For all I know,' he said, 'they took me for a waiter.' But no longer. 'After managing to avoid the limelight all my life,' he wrote, 'to my acute discomfort I became a curiosity, a sort of financial freak overnight.'

In fact he was vain enough to start relishing the notoriety. But according to his secretary, Barbara Wallace, 'It was now that things started going wrong.'

Ann Rork Getty had been right when she accused her former husband of having had 'no interest in his sons until they were old enough to take their places in his precious dynasty'. Indeed his lack of interest in his offspring was positively superhuman. How could anyone, one asks, remain so impervious to his own flesh and blood as to ignore them totally for years on end, never writing to them, never inquiring if they were intelligent, half-witted, handsome, keen on women, keen on animals, musical or criminally insane. But Getty never had inquired. He genuinely was not interested, and until they were old enough to be of use had never bothered with them.

For his son Paul Junior it must have been tempting to respond with a similar lack of interest. But as he needed to support not only Gail, but his first-born son, Jean Paul Getty III, born in November 1956, he decided at around this time to try the family business for a job – and contacted his half-brother George, now vice-president of the Getty-owned Tidewater Oil, with headquarters in Los Angeles. (The company had recently changed its name from Tide Water.)

Apart from a shared father, the two half-brothers had nothing else in common. They didn't know each other and would never come to like each other. But George did offer Paul a job – pumping gasoline in a Tidewater service station in the smart white trousers, neat white hat, and shiny black bow-tie of a Tidewater pump attendant.

Soon Gordon, who had nothing very much to do, would

join him, and after a while both brothers were seconded for training at Tidewater headquarters. But there was still virtually no contact with their distant father until the spring of 1958, when out of the blue he telephoned Paul to summon him to Paris. He was to have a chance to prove himself at last – in the Getty Oil installation in the Neutral Zone of Arabia.

Paul answered that as he had a wife and baby son, he would naturally want to take them with him.

'Fine,' said his father. 'Bring them to Paris first so I can meet them.'

Which explains how Paul and Gail and the baby all arrived for lunch with the head of the family on an early summer day at the Hôtel Georges V in Paris. It also explains how something happened which would have far-reaching consequences for the Getty family. The group around the table started to get on rather well together.

Gail, who had never met her father-in-law before, had been expecting 'an extremely grumpy man'. Instead he greeted his son with, 'Paul, no one told me that your wife was pretty,' and proceeded to charm her as only he could charm a pretty woman. The old misanthrope was equally delighted with his grandson – 'a bright, red-haired little rascal' with 'a remarkable ability for making his grandpa obey his commands', as he wrote with untypical enthusiasm in that evening's diary.

Even now this exercise in family bonding might have ended there and then, but for events in Paris at the time. A violent demonstration had begun against de Gaulle's Algerian policy – and the barricades were going up uncomfortably close to the Hôtel Georges V.

Getty was not a man for violent revolution – and in some alarm decided to decamp to Brussels with his new-found family. And there for the next few weeks they stayed, living in unaccustomed luxury at the Grand Hotel, and going every morning to the newly opened Brussels Exhibition. Here they would breakfast, first, at the Canadian Pavilion off waffles with maple syrup, followed by a trip to the Soviet Pavilion for what Gail still remembers as 'the most delicious caviare I've ever tasted'. Getty, as a man of habit, started to enjoy himself.

A pleasurable holiday with younger members of his family was something Paul Getty had not experienced before. In Gail he had the perfect daughter-in-law, who found his stories fascinating, and would listen to him, more or less entranced, for hours on end.

The 'red-haired little rascal', seventeen-month-old Jean Paul Getty III, continued as a source of permanent delight; and Paul Junior began to captivate his father, as none of his other sons had ever done before. By the time the holiday in Brussels ended, Getty had come to an important decision, not just for Paul and Gail, but for all the Getty family.

Although everything had been arranged for the arrival of Paul and his family in the Neutral Zone, Getty had changed his mind. As he said, life in a trailer in the heat of the Arabian desert was not the thing for a newly married couple with a baby. Gordon was still unmarried, and could easily take his brother's place – which was what occurred a few weeks later, when he was summarily dispatched to the Getty Oil installation in Arabia.

But the truth of the matter was that 'Big Paul', as the family sometimes called him, had grown attached to what he called 'my little family', and had no intention of losing them if he could help it.

Since Paul had rapidly become his favourite son, it was time for him to have the fatted calf. And as it happened, there was the ideal post within the Getty empire waiting for him. The more the old man thought of it, the more he liked it.

As part of the expansion of its refinery capacity in Europe, Getty Oil had recently acquired the small Italian Golfo Oil Company, with a refinery at Gaeta outside Naples. It had an office in Milan but Getty planned to expand it, change its name to Getty Oil Italiana, and move its headquarters down to Rome. Who better to install as general manager than his son Paul?

In fact Paul, with his love of travelling and books and leisure, was an unsuitable young man to place in charge of anything, particularly as he'd had no experience of management. But none of this counted with his father. Paul was his son and any son of his should find running a modest operation such as Golfo Oil a picnic.

It was in his new-found grand-paternal mode that the old tycoon continued to show his 'little family' such untypical affection. From Paris he actually drove them to Milan himself – in easy stages and extremely slowly – in his ancient Cadillac; and once in Milan, he insisted on installing them in an apartment in the centre of the city – close to the Golfo office in Piazza Eleonora Duse. The fateful connection of the next generation of the Getty family with Italy had started.

Not that any of them could possibly have guessed the crucial role which Italy would henceforth play in all their lives – particularly as their first reaction to Milan was by and large unfavourable. The pleasures of Milan take time and patience to discover, and the youthful Gettys hated the climate, didn't like the food and couldn't understand the language.

Also it was clear that Paul would never make a businessman. But he applied himself, attempted to understand the complications of the oil business, and when his father told him, 'always wear a dark suit', duly purchased one.

It was during this honeymoon period between the father and the reunited son that Paul made a gesture which touched the old man more deeply than one might have thought.

Twenty-five years earlier, when twenty-one-year-old Ann Rork (as she still was) gave birth to her premature son aboard ship off Genoa, there'd been a muddle over naming him. When the ship stopped at the next port of call, the infant had been small enough to be taken ashore in a hat-box and was officially registered by the Italian notary in La Spezia. The proud father had wanted the child named after him – Jean Paul Getty Junior – but the notary misheard him, and promptly named the child 'Eugenio' instead.

'Eugenio', meaning 'healthy offspring', was a popular name in positive-thinking, Fascist Italy, but back in America it was less acceptable and inevitably became 'Eugene'. Paul hated it, never used it, and now that he was back in Italy took the occasion to change his name officially to the form his father had intended. Eugene Paul was now no more. Jean Paul Getty Junior took over.

While the renamed Jean Paul Getty Junior was basking in the unusual rays of fatherly approval, his siblings were having an altogether tougher time of it. Plump George, although officially singled out as his father's principal heir and successor, and appointed vice-president of the Getty-owned Tidewater Company, was more than ever haunted by his father – and by those letters which began 'My Dearest George' and ended up 'Your Ever-loving Father'. Getty Senior never ceased his eagle-eyed surveillance of every corner of his empire, and his letters criticized in minutest detail the mistakes and failings of his conscientious but cruelly frustrated eldest son.

George was now in his mid thirties, father of three lively daughters, and something of a pillar of polite Los Angeles society. But as someone said of him, he would have 'made a splendid manager of a small-town, Midwest hardware store' and found command of a major oil company, with a father sniping from the sidelines, something of a nightmare.

Ronald's lot was equally uncomfortable. A journey with his father to the Neutral Zone in 1956 had failed to bring them any closer, and although his fluency in French and German fitted him to be manager of the Getty-owned Veedol company in Hamburg, where he was a considerable success, relations with his father were as cool as ever. (They were not helped by George's habit of penning unbrotherly notes about him to his father and by Ronald sending similar letters about George's failings in return.)

The truth was that Getty was still harbouring resentment for the trouble he had had from Dr Helmle all those years before; and when Ronald married pretty Karin Seibl in Lübeck, Germany, in 1964, the billionaire would see no reason to break the habit of not acknowledging any of his children's weddings.

Even the sunny Gordon had his troubles when he took Paul's place in the manager's office in the Getty installation in the Neutral Zone. Acting on father's orders, he refused to pay the customary bribe to the local Emir; but then insisted on supporting a female member of his staff against the Emir's jurisdiction. She had been discovered having an affair with one of the Emir's subjects – an offence for which the penalty was death by stoning. By refusing to accept this, Gordon had to suffer house arrest from the Saudis when it was discovered that he had helped the woman flee the country.

It was an episode reflecting well on Gordon as a human being, but it failed to impress his father as a businessman, who felt that the girl had known the rules, and should have paid the price. Besides, he was now on good terms with the Saudi king, and wanted to remain so. So Gordon was rapidly recalled and sent to manage what was now the Spartan Trailer Company in Tulsa. When he tired of this, he quietly returned to Berkeley to finish his degree in English.

Getty was clearly not a sympathetic father, but the most unflattering picture of him in this role comes from that summer-time of 1958 when he was making so much sentimental mileage out of his 'little family' in Milan.

It was at this time that his twelve-year-old son Timmy was undergoing further surgery in a New York hospital, which was meant to mark the end of a long period of agony. Half blind, and with his forehead disfigured by the removal of a large tumour, he was about to endure cosmetic surgery to remove his scars.

While Timmy waited for his operation, he would telephone his father every day, begging him to return to America to be with him. He would also send heart-rending little messages. 'I want your love Daddy and I want to see you.'

But Getty's heart did not rend easily, and as always business came before his children; every day he would patiently explain to Timmy that he loved him too, but that Daddy's work prevented him returning to America just yet.

The operation took place on 14 August. Getty was in Switzerland at the time, on a long-standing invitation to visit Baron Thyssen Bornemisza, the industrialist and art collector, who was almost as rich as Getty, and whose great collection infinitely surpassed anything he could ever aspire to.

He was flattered to be invited by such a very grand collector, and even had he been prepared to risk his life in a transatlantic flight to New York, it would have been unthinkable to cancel such a visit. He enjoyed great houses, was predictably impressed by the Thyssen pictures, and had actually returned from the Thyssen villa to his hotel in Lugano when a hysterical Teddy finally reached him on the telephone in the early hours of Monday, 18 August. Beside herself with grief, she sobbed out the news to him. Timmy, their own beloved son, had not survived the operation.

Teddy needed consolation, and in his own dry way Getty attempted to console her. Normally grief and human feeling failed to reach him, for he had long been able to retreat into the cool inhuman world of business, but this time something about his child's death caught him. Faced with death, he was always vulnerable, and totally alone. When the call to Teddy ended, it was still too early to think of working, and knowing he could not get back to sleep he took out his diary.

'Darling Timmy died two hours ago, my best and bravest son, a truly noble human being,' he began, but he could not continue.

'Words are useless,' he concluded, and shut his diary.

Fortunately he still had Gail and Paul Junior and baby Paul, conveniently installed in the second floor apartment in the middle of Milan, to take his mind off Timmy's death. And since he was often in the city, running his affairs from a suite in the Hotel Principe e Savoia, he enjoyed seeing them and sometimes took them away from the heat of the city at weekends to smart hotels like the Villa d'Este on Lake Como.

But Paul and Gail and baby Paul apart, there was a further reason for his steadily increasing interest in things Italian. It was not solely the affairs of Golfo Oil which were bringing him so often to his favourite peninsula, but a married woman of a certain age with one of the most magical houses in that magical country.

He had met her in Paris through his social arbiter and friend, the rich Commandant Weiller. She was a stately blonde, *tipo* Ingrid Bergman, married to a gloomy Frenchman who, being French, was naturally unfaithful to her. And she, being glamorous and very grand and Russian, was plainly ready for a passionate affair.

Thus began Getty's long and uncomfortable relationship with thirty-six-year-old Mary Teissier. She was elegant, and a little mad, something generally put down to her having had a grandfather who was second cousin to Tsar Nicholas II of Russia. Her husband, Lucien, had a house in Versailles where they spent the summer, but he also owned the Villa San Michele, on the slopes of Fiesole, close to Florence. Some said the villa was designed by Michelangelo. The gardens were exquisite. The rooms were furnished with museum pieces. From the cloistered dining-room an unrivalled view of Florence lay below. And Teissier had turned his villa into an exclusive small hotel for the very rich. Whenever Mary Teissier was there, Getty's name began appearing on the guest-list.

She had much that appealed to Paul Getty – lineage, style, human warmth and a considerable knowledge of the world. The fact that she was also jealous, improvident, and congenitally unpunctual, as only a relation of a Tsar could be, merely added to her attractions.

It was because of all of this – and because of her status as a married woman with a demanding husband – that the courtship of Mary Teissier took considerably longer than Getty habitually expended on the pursuit and bedding of a simple mistress. Love was mentioned. So was marriage. As he travelled between Milan and Naples, Getty made frequent visits to the Villa San Michele. But 1959 began with Mary Teissier still more or less attached to her grey-faced husband.

Now that *Fortune* magazine had robbed him of his precious anonymity, Paul Getty's days as a vagabond billionaire were numbered. He still loved living in hotels – where he could eat frugally off the hotel menu, save money by washing his own underwear in the wash-hand basin (his excuse being that laundry washing powder damaged his skin), and guiltlessly enjoy the women he had always listed – by name, colouring and city – in his black address book.

But ever since those few uncomfortable days in Paris, his personal safety and security had begun to worry him. So did reporters and would-be fortune-seekers. He clearly needed an established European base from where he could run his empire, enjoy his privacy, and savour his women and his valuable possessions.

Originally he thought of France – but the memory of barricades outside the Hôtel Georges V obsessed him. France might well be on the edge of bloody revolution. And, much as he loved it, Italy was little better. One place alone still beckoned him with memories of gentle meadows, gracious country houses, a deferential populace, and a well-fed aristocracy: the haven of gentility and peace, with the world's fattest, most secure financial institutions – England.

Getty was rising sixty-six, and his wealth was steadily accruing at an effortless half a million dollars daily, when the most capable member of his entourage, Penelope Kitson, introduced him to George Granville Sutherland-Leveson-Gower, 5th Duke of Sutherland.

Although the largest landowner in Scotland, His Grace, who had never been particularly bright, had somehow contrived to be short of money and was finding it awkward to maintain Sutton Place, the Tudor mansion he had purchased forty years before from the self-made press lord Viscount Harmsworth. (Before feeling sorry for the Duke, one should remember that he currently owned a Mayfair mansion next to Claridges, a somewhat smaller stately home in Surrey, plus Dunrobin Castle, Golspie House and the curiously named House of Tongue in Sutherland.)

Getty, with that truffle-hound-like nose for sniffing out a bargain, offered the needy duke some £60,000 for his now unwanted Tudor hideaway – approximately two hours' income from the Neutral Zone and exactly half what the Duke had paid Harmsworth for the place forty years before. Sutherland accepted.

Much work and money would be needed to make Sutton Place fit for even a self-denying billionaire to live in. And practical Penelope would spend many months selecting curtains, carpets and furniture and taking charge of builders, plumbers, electricians and upholsterers on his behalf. He also bought a seventy-foot table from the castle his old friend, the American press lord William Randolph Hearst, had owned in Wales, two grand pianos, and several pictures. 'I must not spend any more on pictures,' he wrote in his diary.

But by the spring of 1960, Paul Getty would proudly take possession of something he had never really had before – a home.

CHAPTER ELEVEN

LA DOLCE VITA

ROME IS TRADITIONALLY a dangerous place for romantic foreigners with money, and the city had never seemed more dangerously seductive than at that moment in the autumn of 1958, when the newly named Getty Oil Italiana moved offices from Milan to Rome, and Paul and Gail followed.

They found an apartment in the historic Palazzo Lovatelli in Piazza Campitelli, one of the smallest and most enchanting squares in the oldest quarter of the city. There was a fountain opposite the great baroque church of Santa Maria in Campitelli, and around the corner were the ruins of the theatre of Marcellus, built by Julius Caesar. After Milan it must have seemed like entering a different country in another century, and Piazza Campitelli made the perfect setting for a Roman idyll.

Gail was pregnant for the second time, and there was still so little traffic on the streets that she used to hire a horse-drawn open carriage when she went out shopping. In July 1959 she had a daughter and they called her Aileen after Gail's mother.

Paul had a burgundy-coloured MG sports car, which was much admired by the Italians, and sometimes for weekends they would drive to nearby towns like Tivoli and Palestrina. Rome could have hardly seemed more beautiful, but life was not particularly exciting – most of the young Gettys' social life consisting of occasional dinners with older couples, usually Americans connected with the oil industry.

Paul enjoyed exploring Rome, started learning Italian and continued to collect his books and records. He was twenty-six and in that dangerous state of waiting for something wonderful to happen.

But Rome in fact was not as sleepy as it seemed in Piazza Campitelli. When the Gettys came the great period of the Italian cinema was already drawing to a close, but legendary directors like Visconti, Rossellini, and de Sica were still working in the Rome studios of Cinecittà. The greatest of them all, Fellini, caught the atmosphere of the period with a film which actually appeared that autumn. It was a vivid portrait of the decadence and glitter of Roman society which centred round the Via Veneto. The hero, a journalist (Marcello Mastroianni), while despising the life that he is leading, finds himself unable to escape as he seeks in vain his true identity.

Fellini called his film *La Dolce Vita* – The Sweet Life. And before long, Paul and Gail would be tasting something of *la dolce vita* for themselves.

During that summer, old Paul was busily reliving his love affair with a very different Italy through his continuing romance with golden-haired, demanding Mme Teissier. Early in 1959 she left her husband and the Villa San Michele and became his full responsibility.

Her son Alexis still believes that something more than simply sex and money was involved. 'It was the sense of power that Getty exuded. She was utterly obsessed with him. From the day they met until the day she died there was absolutely no one else.'

Getty was in love with her – as he was with all his women – but this didn't mean that he could possibly be faithful to her, and he secretly enjoyed her jealous rages. He certainly provoked them over his other women – even, at the dinner table – and she was particularly jealous of his friendship with Penelope, which she could neither tolerate nor change nor really understand.

Poor, insecure unhappy Mary Teissier! Her chronic unpunctuality annoyed him. Her drinking shocked him. And her unpredictable Russian temperament ultimately bored him. But there was something about her – possibly her sense of style and those grand Romanov connections – that always kept a certain hold on him. And during these early days of their affair she acted as his guide to the upper reaches of the Italian nobility, which for reasons of romantic snobbery held such enduring fascination for him.

In Rome she pulled every string she knew to get him into that most improbable bastion of Roman snobbery – the exclusive Circolo della Caccia, the Rome hunting club. Patterned on a traditional English hunt, the Circolo was dominated by aristocrats jealous of the one thing Getty secretly admired and envied – their tides and their ancestry. And they in turn enjoyed the chance to blackball this parvenu American who possessed the one thing most of *them* admired and envied – vast amounts of money.

He would have made a curious huntsman, but how he would have loved to have been a member of the most exclusive club in Rome as he entered its discreet headquarters on the Largo Fontana Borghese. His failure to get elected hurt him deeply – and increased his growing discontent with Italy.

As a consolation, when he visited Naples and his new oil refinery at Gaeta, Mary was able to introduce Getty to what passed for the cream of Neapolitan society, including several dukes and princes – no big deal in a country boasting nearly 200 dukes and practically as many princes – but it made him happy. Then she spoiled things by persuading him to buy an island called Gaiola in the Bay of Naples.

Gaiola was tiny, and he bought it sight unseen when Mary mentioned that its previous owners had included the Emperor Tiberius, the Fiat heir, Gianni Agnelli, and the Earl of Warwick. Since she was always short of money, Mary was attracted by the prospect of the $7,000 commission on the deal – but was smart

enough to keep this from her lover. (As she said, he would have
wanted it.)

The day dawned when Getty came to take possession.
Gaiola was beautiful, but had a melancholy atmosphere; and one
look at the thirty yards of sea between it and the mainland was
enough for Paul. He emphatically refused to step aboard the
rowing boat to take him over, and after a hurried meal, he
packed his bags and, Mary's lamentations notwithstanding, never
ventured there again.

As Penelope remarked, 'If you're that rich, what's another
island?'

Besides, by now he had bought a more suitable establishment near Rome – from someone with an even more resounding title than the Earl of Warwick – Prince Ladislao
Odescalchi.

La Posta Vecchia was one of the Prince's former country
houses, and had been a staging-post on the ancient Via Salaria,
near the old Etruscan site of Palo. Although considerably
decayed, as were the Odescalchi, it was an imposing building
with its portico and Roman arches, and, when he bought it,
Paul had plans of living there for part of every year. The indis-
pensable Penelope supervised the décor in the comfortable style
of an English country house which pleased him.

Getty loved the house, but had always been concerned
about his safety and all the publicity about his fortune made
him doubly anxious. Palo was by the sea, and according to his
secretary, Barbara Wallace, he began worrying about being kidnapped there by pirates.

Kidnap was becoming an obsession and, because of this, La
Posta Vecchia never became the centre for the grand Italian life
Getty dreamed of. He ordered bars on bedroom windows, and
the most up-to-date security. He even kept a loaded shotgun in
his bedroom, but even so he rarely stayed for long. In Rome he
felt happiest – and safest – in the old familiar Hotel Flora on the
Via Veneto.

When he had originally bought La Posta Vecchia he had
consulted his Italian lawyer about adopting Italian nationality –

but now it was a subject that he never mentioned. England was increasingly stealing his affections.

It was partly age. He had always felt at home in England, and had even come to tolerate the weather. More important, he felt safe there, and the British upper classes were quite different from those dried-up Romans who believed they had a right to teach a Yankee billionaire a lesson.

Even the publicity about his fortune was in his favour. The British aristocracy has always had a deep respect for money – and as he discovered in his far-off days at Oxford, it was not too hard to get to know them. More than ever, Paul enjoyed meeting almost anybody with a title.

It was on the suggestion of Commandant Paul Louis Weiller that he now recruited Claus von Bülow to his staff. This Danish lawyer, who had worked for a period in Lord Hailsham's chambers, had a reputation as a womanizer and a social figure. Born Claus Borberg, he had adopted the surname von Bülow from his maternal grandfather, a former Danish minister of justice, after his father, Svend Borberg, was imprisoned after the Second World War for collaborating with the Nazis.

Getty appointed Claus his 'chief executive', but since the old man hated delegating anything to anyone, he also acted as a sort of social secretary. Here he was invaluable. Claus really did know almost everyone who mattered – which was particularly useful now, as Paul embarked upon a belated honeymoon with the British upper classes.

Before he had purchased Sutton Place from the Duke of Sutherland, he had already met that most relaxed of noblemen, the Duke of Bedford, and was genuinely delighted when invited as a weekend guest to Woburn. He was equally delighted when the Duke of Rutland invited him to Belvoir Castle (which, Claus told him, gentlemen pronounce 'Beaver'). But his desire to establish his credentials. as a fellow owner of a stately home brought trouble.

It was Claus's idea to combine the coming of age of the daughter of a kinsman of the Duke of Norfolk, Jeanette Constable-Maxwell, with a gala party for the refurbished Sutton Place in June 1960. Paul had met Jeanette and her father, Captain Ian Constable-Maxwell, through the Duke of Rutland, and it seemed generous of this famously ungenerous American to be offering his house for the occasion.

But at some stage things got out of hand, and what began as a twenty-first birthday party rapidly became the monster party of the London season. To the last moment, Claus was busily suggesting even more distinguished guests. So was the Commandant Weiller, and by the night of 2 June the list had swollen to 1,200. It included royal dukes like the Gloucesters, humdrum dukes like the Rutlands and the Bedfords, ship-owning Greeks like Onassis and Niarchos, plus the Douglas Fairbankses, the Duchess of Roxburgh and Mr and Mrs Duncan Sandys (who came in lieu of Diana Sandys's father, Sir Winston Churchill, whose party-going days were over).

Apart from the Rutlands and her immediate family, little Miss Constable-Maxwell knew almost no one. Nor did Getty – who had not seen fit to ask any members of his family.

Worse still, what had been carefully planned as the acme of the social season finally became an outright free-for-all. After much advance publicity the freelance party-going classes were alerted, and, just before midnight, gate-crashers started to arrive in droves. By the standards of the sixties, it was fairly harmless. No one was seriously hurt, the Cellini salt-cellars were *not* stolen as was thought at first, and although a photographer was thrown in the swimming-pool, damages were estimated at a mere £20,000.

The only lasting hurt was to Getty's reputation, which never quite recovered. For although he gained sympathy for what had happened, there was also an impression that the whole affair had been excessive and distinctly vulgar – somewhat on a level with the previous year's Battersea Park party thrown by American impresario Mike Todd – but not such fun.

Certainly the party did little to establish Getty as an honorary member of the British upper classes, nor did it herald an era of feudal extravagance for the latest lord of Sutton Place. On the contrary, while it may have seemed that he had now ascended to the dizziest reaches of high living, he was in fact as firmly rooted in economy as ever.

It was the same old puritan response to self-indulgence. Deep down he must have known that neither George nor Sarah would have wasted money on a party such as this – still less upon a house as opulent as Sutton Place. Once more he was forced to justify himself before those ghostly keepers of his conscience – which meant that from the moment that he took possession, everything about his life at Sutton Place became a challenge to save money and avoid unnecessary expense. Indeed, Sutton Place called forth the highest flights from Getty, in his long career as lifelong virtuoso in the subtle art of saving money.

It was typical of him to have discovered a young female lawyer to help him with this sovereign task. Robina Lund, the twenty-five-year-old daughter of Sir Thomas Lund, the President of the Law Society, had recently qualified as a solicitor when Getty met her with her parents. Contrary to rumours, she insists that – not for his want of trying – she never did become his mistress, but remained his friend, admirer, legal counsellor and 'honorary daughter'. She was certainly a shrewd adviser, and she helped him achieve the magical fiscal situation of being legally resident in Britain while regarded by the taxman as domiciled in his native but now never visited USA.

In addition to this memorable achievement, she also helped him make another massive saving which presumably assuaged whatever guilt he felt at living in unseemly splendour. This was over the actual ownership of Sutton Place. For although he had made the original deal with Sutherland, the house was actually purchased not by him, but by a subsidiary of Getty Oil called Sutton Place Properties, of which Miss Lund was a director. Sutton Place was then designated Getty Oil's official European headquarters.

Thus, in effect, Paul could live at Sutton Place scot-free, with his home charged to the company, and the company in turn could charge the cost against its tax as part of its operating expenses.

Nor were the minor costs of daily living overlooked. Getty was always careful to explain to anybody interested that at Sutton Place a dry Martini was actually costing him a quarter of the price he would be paying at the Ritz. He was also very much aware that his few servants and the gardeners cost approximately a third of what he would have paid in California. Ordinary guests tended to get ordinary fare, like simple cottage pie, and office costs were kept in check by re-using envelopes wherever possible, recycling elastic bands and being careful with the use of printed writing paper. In the dining room, small electric fires were used to save on central heating.

Having spent his life avoiding giving anything to anyone, he saw no reason now to change his mind, and it was only right that his deep Obsession with economy finally brought its own poetic retribution. As he had learned when staying as a guest in the stately homes of his beloved British aristocracy, there has always been an unstated but effective rule that just as guests are expected to put their own postage stamps on letters, so they are naturally expected to insist on paying for their personal telephone calls. But after a while he realized that this was not happening at Sutton Place, and that some of his guests were making expensive calls to Australia and the States.

It seems that this upset him deeply, partly from meanness, but also because he felt that, since he was American and rich, he was being taken for a ride, and his guests were treating him as they'd not have dreamt of behaving with, say, the Duke of Westminster.

This was the origin of Getty's greatest social blunder – the installation of his famous pay-phone for his guests at Sutton Place. It was quite logical but that was not the point. He should have realized that as a billionaire, and an American one at that, he could simply not afford to seem as stingy as an English duke.

★

One of the interesting might-have-beens in the Getty saga is what would have happened had that lunch party at the Hôtel Georges V not occurred, and if Paul had gone as planned to the Neutral Zone, with Gordon being made manager of Golfo Oil, later Getty Oil Italiana, instead.

Gordon, with his passion for music, would have loved Milan and its opera house. Being unmarried and susceptible, he would probably have married an Italian. And then, when Paul and Gail returned to California – as they undoubtedly would have done after the heat and horrible discomfort of the Neutral Zone – it would have been Gordon and not Paul who might well have started the Italian branch of the Getty family – with a very different outcome for the future.

Instead, by 1962, having left his father over the trouble in the Neutral Zone, Gordon was safely back in San Francisco and was standing in a bar called La Rocca's Corner when he met tall, auburn-haired Ann Gilbert, daughter of a walnut farmer from Wheatland in the Sacramento Valley. He was twenty-eight and she was twenty-three. They fell in love. In 1964 they married. And over the next six years they produced four sons, Peter, Andrew, John and William. Thus, while his brother Paul was busily creating Roman Gettys, Gordon's boys grew up as true Americans.

Even in his days at Clay Street, Gordon had always been in search of the simple pleasures of a settled home. In total contrast to his father, he was naturally uxorious, and his marriage proved that rarity among the Gettys – a stable and happy relationship.

One of the reasons was probably that Gordon and Ann were largely complementary to each other. Ann had a strong puritan element, having been brought up according to the precepts of fundamentalist Baptist Christianity, but she was also worldly, very practical and thoroughly determined to enjoy the good life after enduring the opposite for so long on a walnut farm in the Sacramento Valley.

In many ways Gordon remained harder to fathom than his wife. Perhaps as a defence against his father, he continued to appear a sort of lost professor trying to remember where he was. 'I am not entirely of this century,' he admitted on one occasion, and Penelope's verdict on him was more or less typical of how most of his father's friends at Sutton Place regarded him. 'Gordon,' she said, 'is potty but in a highly intelligent way.'

Gordon's pottiness was deceptive. He was to prove extremely down-to-earth where his family was concerned – and was determined that his sons should never suffer what he himself had endured in his own childhood. He was also the most indulgent and generous of husbands, to the point that Ann was often said to wear the trousers.

But beneath his undoubted kindness and the protective camouflage of the mad professor, Gordon could be extremely sharp and surprisingly persistent where his interests and those of his immediate family were concerned – as his father now discovered. For as well as producing further male heirs to the enormous fortune in the Sarah C. Getty Trust, Gordon's marriage had a more immediate – and for his father, less agreeable – result. As a married man with a young wife who herself saw little point in needless self-denial, Gordon soon discovered he was short of money – which struck him, as it struck his wife, as utterly absurd.

He had a father known to be his nation's richest citizen, dollars were gushing ceaselessly into the trust specifically established by his grandmother for her grandchildren's benefit, and yet he and his wife were currently subsisting in a small motel and wondering where their next few thousand dollars were to come from.

It is often claimed that Ann was the cause of what ensued, but Gordon's friend Judge Newsom firmly insists that it was he, not Ann, who encouraged Gordon to commence the lawsuit to compel his father to disgorge at least a little of the money locked away in Grandma Getty's trust to benefit the grandchildren. The outcome was predictable – uproar from stately Sutton Place.

For although the amiable Gordon tried to describe his lawsuit as a 'friendly' legal action simply intended to clarify an obscure financial situation, it was the equivalent of placing ground glass in the old man's coffee, or barbed wire in his double bed. Worse – for by questioning the legality of the Sarah C. Getty Trust, Gordon was not just threatening the future of the Getty fortune. He was getting at his father at the crucial point where he would always be acutely vulnerable.

For years the Sarah C. Getty Trust had been at the centre of the weird emotional-financial game his father had been playing as he built his fortune. By existing to receive the accumulated conscience money he had been paying to his parents' memory, the trust had also become a wonderfully tax-efficient method of protecting and enlarging the fortune itself.

'Whatever they say about J. Paul Getty,' says Judge Newsom, 'he was pretty good at one thing – accruing and preserving capital.' And the way he did it was to use the Sarah C. Getty Trust to hold his accumulated capital and thus avoid taxation. It has been claimed that for many years Getty never paid more than $500 a year in tax. Over the years building up the corpus of the Sarah C. Getty Trust had become his absolute obsession.

Since he controlled the Trust, he was able to ensure that it never paid a cash dividend to the beneficiaries, i.e. himself and his children. Since a cash dividend was income, it would have been subject to taxation. Instead he always paid a stock dividend, which increased the beneficiary's holding in the Trust, but was not considered income and so remained untaxable.

For a miserly man like Getty this was a perfect method to create a private golden mountain. His surplus wealth would make it grow. The taxman couldn't touch it. And nobody threatened it – until Gordon went to law to ask for some of the money in the trust which Grandma Getty had clearly intended him to have.

One can see how deeply threatened Getty must have been. For the real danger to his whole magnificent creation was not the payment of a relatively small cash dividend from the trust to Gordon to keep him happy. It was more complicated – and more dangerous – than that. As one of the income beneficiaries of the trust, Gordon was entitled to 6.666 per cent recurring of his father's income from the trust – and he was claiming retrospectively that, in order to pay him this, his father should have paid himself dividends in cash, not stock, since the Trust was founded back in 1936.

If Gordon could establish this in court, the Sarah C. Getty Trust would fall apart, as the tax-free basis of its dividends unravelled.

Gordon and his legal adviser, Bill Newsom, were as aware of this as Getty himself, and were counting on the threat to make the old man see a little sense and find a way of disbursing some badly needed income to the income beneficiaries. But Paul Getty was not a man to submit to threats – and particularly not over something as important as his mother's trust, from someone as unimportant as his youngest son.

The result was a bitter, complicated legal battle which dragged on, with intermissions and explosions, for the next seven years – at the end of which, by a judgement of the California Supreme Court, Gordon lost.

This was largely because his father had engaged the most powerful legal hotshot of the day, the formidable trial lawyer Moses Lasky. Also, if Bill Newsom is correct, at the last moment the judge himself recoiled from the enormity of submitting the great Sarah C. Getty Trust to the potentially lethal machinations of the tax-man.

After his father's death, when he himself became one of the greatest beneficiaries of the trust, Gordon would have reason to be grateful for this judgement. In the meantime, during the seven years the case had lasted, it had produced much tension in the family, and a number of surprises which were going to affect its future.

In the first place, during the legal process Gordon had been able to persuade his father to pay out certain sums of money from the trust to him and to his brothers, Paul Junior and George. Despite this, George had dutifully sided with his father – to the point of writing outraged letters to Gordon on the lines of 'How could you do this to our own dear father.' Little love was already lost between the two half-brothers – and this trouble over the Sarah Getty Trust widened the rift which continued to the following generation.

But the strange thing was that, such is the perversity of human nature, and in spite of George's loyalty, it was Gordon, not George, who ended up in favour with his father.

Ann played a part in this. 'See here, Mr Getty [as she always called him], let's have an end to this', she is supposed to have said to her father-in-law when things were getting particularly hard for Gordon. And the billionaire, who never said no to a woman, is said to have agreed to give a grudging semblance of forgiveness to her husband.

More to the point, perhaps, the way in which Gordon had maintained his case impressed him. Of all his sons it was the vague and otherworldly Gordon who had shown the courage and determination to oppose him. It was an important omen for the future – and Getty almost certainly respected him for it.

He still insisted that he couldn't understand Gordon's economic theories, still less his music, but they started seeing more of one another. He got on well with Ann and liked the children. Then, as a sign of ultimate acceptance, Gordon was appointed a trustee of the museum and, ultimate accolade, in 1972 was reinstated as a trustee of the very body he had tried so hard to break – the vast, the ever-growing and the still unassailable Sarah Getty Trust.

CHAPTER TWELVE

NEW BEGINNINGS

MEANWHILE, IN ROME, life was looking up for Paul Getty's favourite family, who had now moved on from Piazza Campitelli to a family house on the Via Appia. By 1962 they were six in number – two more children, Mark and Ariadne, having been born in 1960 and 1962 respectively.

With the children born so close together, they formed a tight-knit family; the eldest, red-haired Paul, particularly adored his father. He remained his grandfather's favourite too, and was a bright, unusually affectionate small boy.

But although the family seemed so united, Paul and Gail were very much innocents abroad and the unreality of Rome started to affect them. It is hard to describe the atmosphere of the Italian capital in the early sixties. It was very much a pagan city. Today's traffic and pollution hadn't started, and something about the city's beauty and antiquity gave the sense that life in Rome was richer, sexier, and more instantly enjoyable than in any other city in the world. Like most things in the Eternal City this was largely illusory, but the fact remains that Rome at this period seemed extraordinarily exciting – particularly for young, good-looking foreigners with money.

Apart from Rome itself there was another reason for the feeling in the air. Attracted by the reputation of the Italian movie industry, and the weakness of the Italian lira, in the spring of 1962 20th Century Fox had just begun production of one of the most expensive, crisis-riddled film epics of all time – *Cleopatra*. Further productions followed, including Clint Eastwood's Italian-made 'Spaghetti Westerns', all of which brought actors, writers, US dollars, and a touch of glamour to the night life of the city. Paul and Gail found their social life improving.

An American friend remembers them from the summer of 1962. 'There were parties almost every night. It seemed that none of us had any worries, and Paul and Gail appeared the most carefree of all. Paul was elegant and slim and very bright, and Gail seemed particularly pretty with her short hair and great vitality. They made the perfect couple, and I remember thinking how enviable they were – and how lovely it would be to be so rich and married with four nice children. Looking back they both seemed just a shade too perfect.'

Which, of course, they were – but they did enjoy themselves. They could afford sufficient help to look after the children, and made a host of friends, including the writer William Styron and the film director John Huston. Paul and Mario Lanza spent a lot of time together working out a way to bring American baseball to Italy, while Gail loved dancing at clubs like Lollobrigida's on the Appia Antica, or the famous Ottanta Quattro in the Via Margutta.

Gradually they found that they were leading almost separate lives, and differences in their characters began to show. Gail was gregarious, loved parties, and was high on energy. Paul was different. Part of him wished to be a glamorous playboy, but as Gail says, 'he didn't realize how glamorous he was, and anyhow was much too shy to do anything very much about it.' His other side was extremely serious and hankered after books and learning.

Life in Rome had done nothing to resolve the two sides of his personality. He had begun to hate his work with Getty Oil Italiana, he was responsible for a large young family in a foreign city, and he had the feeling that something in his life was seriously adrift. He told Gail that what he really wanted was to be an oceanographer.

As this seemed impossible, he became discontented. He was drinking and became increasingly reclusive. Often, when he and Gail were going out, he would change his mind at the last minute and decide to stay at home reading. Whenever possible he avoided driving. He had always been an introvert at heart, and was showing signs of opting out from the life around him.

This left Gail to enjoy the dancing and the parties on her own. As she admits, 'I really wasn't the maltreated wife, Saint Gail, who stayed at home while Paul was out swinging around. To be honest it was rather the reverse.'

'One of the qualities Fellini's *La Dolce Vita* failed to encompass was monogamy, and it was probably impossible for the marriage to have lasted in the midst of so much worldly glamour. So-called open marriages rarely do – particularly if there are differences of personality between the partners. Inevitably Gail fell in love with someone else. And just as inevitably – being the character she was – she decided that she had to go.

Lang Jeffries was almost entirely Paul's antithesis – and Paul, who knew and liked him, was surprised as well as rather shocked when Gail confessed she was in love with him and wished to live with him.

A rugged, all-American former actor from Los Angeles, Jeffries had been married to the film star Rhonda Fleming. He was a great sportsman – golfer, yachtsman, tennis player – and he had come to Rome to make low-budget Roman television epics which, as Gail says, 'he didn't take too seriously'.

Paul and Aileen inevitably resented him, but Mark and Ariadne came to like him, for, if nothing else, Lang was dependable.

Paul was genuinely upset that Gail wished to leave him, but they had a pact that they would never lie to one another. Paul had had love affairs himself, so couldn't argue when she said she was in love. They were still fond of one another, and made the sort of pact affectionate couples often do when their marriage dies upon them.

Gail would have the children and set up home with Lang in a new apartment. Paul would also move. (Gail in fact would find a flat for him.) And as she was breaking up the marriage, she felt she had no financial claim on him, so there was no question of alimony. Nor at this point was there any talk of remarriage. Paul begged her not to think of getting a divorce, and she agreed. They would all remain in Rome, stay friends, and Paul of course would see the children as and when he wanted.

It seemed the best solution – if a very Roman one. 'We were absurdly civilized,' says Gail. 'It might have been better if we'd not been.'

Left to himself, it was now that Paul Junior decided to enjoy himself, and despite his shyness and his love of privacy, he seems to have had a great success with women. Von Bülow loyally describes him now as 'incredibly handsome and sexy', and probably overstates the number of his Roman conquests when he says that 'he slept with more beautiful women than his father'. (Perhaps the claim depends on how one interprets 'beautiful'.)

On the other hand, there may be something in the implication that Paul was secretly competing with the old man's exploits as a womanizer. It was very much a game for him, and friends who knew him now insist that his love affairs were always tactful and discreet – 'not blatant and exhibitionist like so many visiting Americans with their women'.

Nevertheless the Getty name would prove a great advantage when it came to stars like Brigitte Bardot, who was in Rome making *Le Repos du Guerrier* (English title, *Love on a Pillow*) in 1962.

At this period in Rome, Paul was drifting. He found no pleasure in his work for Getty Oil Italiana, and had little of his father's self-control deriving from the need to make a lot of money. Paul knew quite well that, work or not, he would finally inherit his due portion of the Sarah C. Getty Trust, and was currently marching to an old Italian tune. It was entitled *Dolce far niente* – sweetly doing nothing.

In Rome there had always been an accepted role for rich young men like him to play. Nothing vicious or particularly depraved. The young *signore* desires to enjoy himself before shouldering life's burdens, which come soon enough. He wishes to relax, drive slowly round the city, meet interesting people and be gracious in return, collect books, eat well, drive down to Positano or up to Santa Margherita, lie in the sun with someone pretty, drink, get laid, and then next day begin again. *Dolce far niente.*

Happiness. Like everyone in Rome Paul simply wanted to be happy. So did Gail, but in Paul's case the search for happiness would lead him to the love which would all but ruin his life.

Talitha – pronounced Tah-lee-tah – Pol was as pretty as she sounded, with doll-like face, an eager, sexy nature, and a sense of happiness that spread to those around her. She was that perilous rarity, an enchantress, and only in retrospect does one see the danger enchantresses can bring to others – and ultimately to themselves. For those who fall beneath their spell expect too much, indulge them to excess, then blame them when the spell is broken.

Although she lived in London, Talitha was Dutch. Her father, Willem Pol, a handsome painter, had married pretty Adine Mees, from a well-to-do Amsterdam family, in 1936. Three years later, they found themselves in Java on a painting expedition as war began in Europe, and the German invasion of their homeland kept them in Indonesia.

In September 1940 the Pols were still in Java when Talitha was born, and rather than bring her back to Europe they moved on to Bali – where they were captured and interned when the Japanese arrived in 1943. In captivity their conditions were appalling. Willem was parted from his wife and baby daughter, and although they were reunited after the Japanese surrender, Adine never fully recovered from her sufferings. She died in 1948.

When Willem remarried, three years later, it was to the child of a celebrated British painter of an older generation – Poppet, daughter of Augustus John. They bought a simple London terrace house in Chilworth Street in Paddington, but spent their holidays in a cottage in what was then the sleepy village of Ramatuelle, near St Tropez in the South of France.

Having no children of her own, Poppet acted as a mother to Talitha, who particularly needed affection after the horrors of the prison camp. Talitha grew to love the South of France, and she and Poppet and her father were extremely close.

Like many spoiled pretty girls, Talitha longed to be a film star and was actually in Rome in 1963 as an extra in a five-second crowd scene in the all-providing *Cleopatra*. On this brief visit she did not meet Paul Getty Junior, and afterwards, apart from carnal propositions from various producers, her career in films seemed over. Not that this worried her unduly. With her looks and her family connections she could enjoy a lively social life in London, and then get married.

For an enchantress like Talitha this shouldn't have been difficult. As a friend of hers remembers, 'She had a penchant for attracting clever older men, but actually preferred the company of younger smarter ones.' Some of them were very smart indeed. Lord Lambton knew her, Lord Kennet thought her 'an absolute knockout', and Lord Christopher Thynne fell in love with her. But the last also remembers 'how difficult Talitha was to keep as a girlfriend because she was a most tremendous flirt, or rather an overflirt, and I never knew where I was with her'. Nor, it seems, did any of her lovers.

For she was not as carefree as she seemed, and still bore the mental scars from her childhood in the prison camp. Lord Christopher tells of how he once jokingly made the sign of the evil eye at her by pointing two outstretched fingers at her face, and how she cowered away. He asked her why, and she told him that his gesture reminded her of how the camp guards used to push their fingers into the children's eyes to hurt them.

Much of her flirting served as a cover for her insecurity. What she needed was someone young and rich and handsome to look after her – someone exactly like the now unattached Paul Junior. All that was needed was the catalyst to make this happen.

In Gothic tales there is often a doom carrier who emerges from the shadows, plays his fateful part, and then departs on his separate unhappy destiny. With Talitha and Paul, this role was played by Claus von Bülow. After Jean Paul Getty's death in 1976, von Bülow would leave England for America and marry the heiress, Sunny von Anersberg, who had inherited a seven hundred million dollar fortune from her father, the American utilities multi-millionaire, George Crawford. And there is an eerie symmetry in the way von Bülow, who would one day find himself accused of trying to murder his glamorous rich wife, was already pointing Paul and Talitha to an equally harrowing disaster.

Von Bülow was living in a grand apartment in Belgravia, and inevitably knew Talitha. Shortly after New Year, 1965, he invited her to dinner. Like many at the time, Talitha was fascinated by Rudolf Nureyev, who had just defected and was starting his career in London with the Royal Ballet. She had already met him at Lee Radziwill's house in Henley-on-Thames, and von Bülow told her he was coming and promised to place her next to him at dinner.

But the temperamental Cossack never came, and von Bülow sat Talitha next to Paul instead. Paul was in England visiting his father, and had not expected to encounter anyone so pretty and amusing in London.

★

Next morning, at the house at Chilworth Street, Talitha complained of a cold and told her father she would lie in late. Willem, having heard her returning in the small hours, guessed it was probably a hangover, and left her to sleep it off.

But later that morning, Poppet Pol returned from a shopping expedition to discover a young man on the doorstep with a bulky cardboard box of flowers. He asked where Talitha Pol lived, and when she asked him who he was he introduced himself.

He was invited in, and having charmed the parents, Paul Getty Junior invited Talitha to Sutton Place to meet his father.

Surprisingly she failed to impress him, for the ancient amorist possessed a prudish side which disapproved of modern girls in mini-skirts. But if Talitha and old Paul failed to hit it off, this did not stop her sensing the attractions of his son. When Lord Christopher saw her a few days later he knew at once his hopes were over. Soon afterwards, Talitha and Paul Junior flew to Rome together.

This was the last the Pols would see of them till early summer, when they came to stay at Ramatuelle. Willem found Paul 'more likeable' than ever – easy to talk to, erudite, and still a little shy.

At this point there was still no talk of marriage. But everywhere he went with Talitha people remarked on what a handsome, happy pair they made together.

Arrangiarsi – a particularly Italian word for a particular Roman speciality – literally, 'to arrange oneself'.

In the spring of 1966, life was arranging itself around the Roman Gettys with the deceptive ease which is another speciality of the city. The sun was shining, Gail had settled down with Lang in a large flat in a modern quarter of the city, and Paul and Talitha were living happily together in a penthouse apartment of some luxury next to the Carlo Pontis in. Piazza Aracoeli.

At the very centre of ancient Rome, the venerable church of the Aracoeli, the altar of heaven, derived its name from the altar which the Emperor Augustus supposedly erected in a temple on the site after seeing a vision of a virgin and a child.

Thus, as well as being in a highly fashionable location, Paul and Talitha were living in one of the most historic parts of ancient Rome. They were also near the city's famous 'Wedding Cake' – the great white marble monument to the first King of united Italy, Victor Emmanuel; and close at hand was the balcony from which the elder Getty's one-time hero, Mussolini, had harangued the Roman multitude in Piazza Venezia.

But that was in the past. For the present, now that everyone seemed happy with the current dispensation, it was time to sort the situation out as fairly and as fast as possible.

Despite their earlier agreement, Paul and Gail had finally divorced, but since it was so amicable and Gail got nothing, they decided to invite their mutual friend Bill Newsom to help arrange the details of the children's settlement. A successful lawyer in San Francisco, he had been at St Ignatius with Paul and Gordon. Everybody liked and trusted Bill and he knew the law. Invite him over.

So William Newsom arrived in Rome. He had always been extremely fond of Paul – but he was also wary of him. He responded to his charm, his cleverness, his wit, all of which were reminiscent of his mother Ann's – but he also remembered something of his wild side from the past.

But here in Rome Paul was happily in love – and Paul in happy mood was the most irresistible of mortals. (When the black mood descended, things were different.) So Bill Newsom found it relatively easy to arrange the details of a settlement for the children.

As Gail was not requesting alimony for herself, Paul readily agreed to pay approximately a third of his after-tax income as child support. In 1965 this meant a third of $54,000 plus medical and educational expenses. It was also agreed that above $54,000 there should be a sliding scale so that if Paul's income rose above a million dollars, 5 per cent a year of it should be paid annually into trusts of which Paul, Gail, and Bill Newsom would be trustees.

An additional clause was inserted in the settlement. In order to protect the children from fortune hunters while they were still young, it was decreed that any of the children would be disinherited from the benefits of the trust if they married before the age of twenty-two.

It all seemed generous and straightforward – not that this would stop the agreement causing trouble in the future. But like everyone that summer, Paul simply wanted everybody to be happy.

Bill Newsom felt the same, and as he boarded his plane at Fiumicino for San Francisco, he was hopeful for the future of his friends.

It seemed that everything was working out, and the perfect weather, continuing through August and September, made this a celebratory Italian summer for the Gettys. Wishing to have somewhere far from Rome where they could take the children, Gail and Lang discovered a Tuscan house called La Fuserna in the tiny village of Orgia, to the south of Siena. The house was absurdly cheap but needed renovating, while the village was still miraculously unspoilt, the countryside spectacular, and everyone who stayed there loved it. For the children this would become their favourite home – the place where they would spend their holidays, play with the children in the village, and hunt for mushrooms in the nearby woods in autumn.

Meanwhile in Rome even old Paul appeared in his nearest to a sunny mood when he arrived at the Hotel Flora with Mary Teissier.

He once wrote of the Emperor Hadrian that 'the great traveller had come to a time of life when the inconveniences of travel made him loath to take long journeys'. Now, in his early seventies, he felt the same. He was increasingly scared of travel, and coming to Italy at all had been an emotional ordeal. Since he wouldn't fly, and wouldn't risk the Channel ferries, his answer was to board the Queen Elizabeth at Southampton at the start of its transatlantic voyage, then disembark at Cherbourg. Even he admitted that a transatlantic liner was unlikely to be shipwrecked in the English Channel.

But once in Rome, he felt safe in the haven of his beloved Hotel Flora, and began his tour of the sights that he had always loved. Again he had that strange sensation of *déjà vu*, of having seen everything centuries before as he strolled through the Roman forum.

But the sense of returning to the past was at its most intense when he visited his favourite building – the great rotunda of the Roman Pantheon, which was rebuilt in its present form by the Emperor Hadrian in AD 120. He seemed to take a personal pride in it and in its survival, and on seeing the building yet again he explained to Mary something that only he could possibly have thought of.

Had it ever struck her, he inquired, that the Pantheon was so well built that during the whole time of its existence it had never needed fire insurance? Just think of how much money that had saved, he added. 'Had it been kept insured since the day it was built 2,000 years ago, the total insurance premiums with compound interest would add up to more money than there is in the world today.'

It was a sombre thought – and grounds for self-congratulation. But at the same time, as he looked at the building, he realized that Hadrian had missed a splendid opportunity to immortalize his name. The emperor had been too modest in giving credit for the building to its original founder, the consul Marcus Agrippa, whose name he placed in massive letters on the pediment.

This grave mistake he resolved he would not repeat when he came to build another Roman villa to perpetuate his own memory. He had been considering doing this for some time, and not until 1968 would the work begin. But he had now decided to create a museum near the ranch-house site at Malibu, which would house his furniture collection, items of marble statuary, and the pictures he was buying.

There had already been discussions on the form of the museum, but against some contradictory advice, he had decided on exactly what he wanted. Some years before, on a trip to Naples, he had visited the site of the fabled villa of the Roman multi-millionaire Calpurnius Piso, which had been buried in volcanic ash when Vesuvius erupted and destroyed Pompeii and Herculaneum.

Detail obsessed as ever, Getty had taken the trouble to find out all about it. It had been excavated in the 1760s for the King of Naples by a German archaeologist, and Getty had studied his report – together with the plans of the villa, the treasures with which it had been crammed, and the mass of records on papyrus preserved in the volcanic dust, which had given the place its name – the Villa dei Papiri.

He had been most impressed by it, and since he had convinced himself that he had been the Emperor Hadrian, the Villa dei Papiri took on a particular significance. Hadrian had been a friend of Piso's and had often visited his villa – which meant that Getty himself must have been there.

It had once been part of Hadrian's imperial power to order the construction of temples and great public buildings in the furthest reaches of his empire. Desiring to 'emulate his spirit', Getty would now repeat these earlier activities, and recreate this villa which he knew so well in a distant spot he also knew – facing the Pacific on the shore at Malibu.

It could be made identical with Piso's villa – the same decoration on the walls, the same plants and shrubs, even copies of the original bronze statues in the gardens. Since he was now as rich as any Roman Emperor, he could make sure that it was filled with even more prestigious treasures than Piso's. And he could finally correct the error he had made when he built the

Pantheon. His name, and his alone, would be recorded in this villa which he would build in California.

While Getty was still in Rome, the America. As paterfamilias, Getty was becoming positively benign, and accompanied Gordon to an unusual family occasion – the recording of a full-scale opera in the Naples opera house which Paul Junior was backing to the tune of $20,000.

The budget did not stretch to one of the Verdi operas Gordon would have liked, and his brother had chosen one of Mozart's lesser-known operas, *Il Re Pastore* – The Shepherd King. It is the story of a lost inheritance and the rediscovery of a king disguised as a shepherd boy in the sunlit world of classical mythology. As the old man and his two sons heard the ravishing Lucia Popp sing the lead part in one of the happiest of Mozart's operas, the music may for once have matched the mood with which they faced the future.

CHAPTER THIRTEEN

ROMAN WEDDINGS

I N DECEMBER 1966, as if to underline the part that Rome was playing in the fortunes of the Gettys, Paul and Talitha married in the very place where Gail had wed Lang Jeffries a few months earlier, and Jean Paul Getty had married Teddy Lynch in 1939 – the city hall, the Campidoglio, crowning the Roman Capitol, the central point of ancient Rome itself.

It was a spectacular setting for a marriage, with its views across the ruined Roman Forum, and the nearby Palace of the Senators of Rome. The ancient equestrian bronze statue of the Emperor Marcus Aurelius still rode the plinth designed for him by Michelangelo, and the antique statues of Castor and Pollux, guardians of Rome, flanked the steps descending to the city. The wedding photographs show Talitha in mink-trimmed bridal mini-skirt, holding a lily, and looking like the sixties flower-child she was, between two smiling adults, Paul and Penelope.

Paul at thirty-four was better-looking than he'd ever been, and the smile gave just a hint of the shy charm people still remember. Penelope, in her beautifully tailored coat, was standing proxy for the bridegroom's father, who was too busy making money to attend. (According to one story, he told a visiting oil tycoon that he didn't know about the wedding.)

Not that Getty Senior would be greatly missed – at the ceremony or at the ensuing bridal lunch at the Casa Valadier restaurant, in the Borghese Gardens. Still less was he missed at the big, all-night reception held in the apartment of a sculptor friend. It was a memorable affair, one of several 'parties of the year'.

Next morning the bridal pair rose early and departed for an extended honeymoon in Marrakesh.

Of course the old man had known all about the wedding, but he had disapproved of everything to do with it. For by now he had fallen out of love with handsome Paul Junior – which, combined with escalating troubles with the Naples refinery, placed a further strain upon his love affair with Italy.

Behind Getty's changed attitude towards his once-favourite son lay rumours he had been hearing concerning him and Talitha. Both, it seemed, had recently become hippies, and had joined the counter-culture of the sixties with extremely worrying dedication.

By being in Europe, Paul Junior had in fact originally missed out on the hippie cult when it started in his native San Francisco. But it might have been devised with him in mind; and now, like the man in Molière who suddenly discovers he has always spoken prose, Paul discovered he had always been one of nature's hippies. The Eastern-born Talitha encouraged him, and flower power, self-fulfilment and the drug-hazed lure of the magnetic East had entered both their lives with a vengeance.

A sort of gentrified hippiedom was the perfect way of life for a couple like Paul and Talitha. With its cult of non-violent anarchy, self-expression, and rejection of Western materialism, the hippie movement was particularly adapted to the easy rich with nothing very much to do. Almost overnight nobody in Rome had been cooler and more hip than Paul and Talitha, but not even charming Paul could manage to combine the hippie ethic with the oil industry. Nothing seemed more soul-destroying than the activity from which his family derived its money, nothing more crucifying than to have to work in a dark suit in the offices of Getty Oil Italiana. So the offices of Getty Oil Italiana rarely saw him any longer.

Nor did Gail and the children see much more of him, although they were all still living in Rome at the time. One afternoon the family had been enjoying an English film at the Fiammetta cinema and noticed a bearded hippie enter, wearing long hair and small John Lennon glasses. Only young Paul recognized him as his father.

Soon after this, Paul and Talitha had gone to Thailand, where they had conducted their first serious experiments with drugs. Back in England someone at Sutton Place made sure that the old man saw a magazine with pictures of his son, bearded, long-haired and dressed in what the caption called 'a tie-dyed green velvet outfit that would have made any hippie green with envy'.

Old Paul was not impressed, for unlike his son he was emphatically not a natural hippie, and although the Emperor Hadrian had worn a beard from the age of thirty-two, old Paul always had a powerful dislike of facial hair.

At Sutton Place there was also no dearth of information over what was happening in Rome, and in particular over the affairs of Getty Oil Italiana. Angry words were shouted down the telephone.

'Any idiot can be a businessman,' said Paul Junior – which was rather like the Prince of Wales informing Her Majesty that any fool could be a monarch.

It was shortly after this that his father's latest mistress, the notorious Duchess of Argyll, had calmly announced at lunch at Sutton Place that she had heard that Paul Getty Junior was on heroin. Getty had been deeply – indeed painfully – shocked. He had a genuine horror of drug addiction, and it was now that he broke off relations with his son until he promised to desist. Paul Junior wouldn't promise – and it wasn't long before he was tendering his resignation as general manager of Getty Oil Italiana – which his father, as head of the company, accepted.

This left Paul without a job – but not without his income, which that year approached $100,000, from Grandma Getty's trust.

It was early summer. The tourists were already in the city, and the penthouse flat was airless in the Roman evenings. Now that Paul was jobless, were the newly-weds feeling a touch of that Roman sickness known as *accidie* – the boredom that afflicted monks and courtesans?

'*Carpe diem*,' says the inscription that recurs throughout the city on its monuments and public buildings.

'*Carpe diem* – Seize the day.'

They did.

Le Palais Da Zahir (mixed French and Arabic for 'the Pleasure Palace') had belonged to a French property developer called Monsieur Aigret, who had bought it twenty years before as a speculation and couldn't sell it. It had been standing empty ever since, in the picturesque ancient quarter of Marrakesh known as Sidi Mimoun.

Enterprising Bill Willis – fashionable, high-camp, American interior decorator – had shown it to Paul and Talitha while they were there on honeymoon, and they had fallen in love with it and bought it for $10,000. Since then Bill had been restoring it for them with typical panache, repairing ancient woodwork and mosaics, finding them decorative objects, furniture and carpets in profusion, and having tiles specially baked in Fez to replace antique tiles which were missing.

Paul had known handsome Bill when he still owned the small antique shop at the top of the Spanish Steps in Rome. Bill had always had an instinct for the very rich, which is a prerequisite for success in his profession, and he was most successful. (Since then he has done over villas for Alain Delon, Yves St Laurent, and the sister of the King of Morocco.)

When Da Zahir was finished, John Richardson (distinguished biographer of Picasso) found it sinister, but most of the other visitors thought it fun and loved it.

It had a blue front door (blue against the evil eye), four separate courtyards (in one of which Talitha planted roses), spectacular views of the Atlas mountains from the roof, and an air of timeless beauty and decay, which was part of the charm of old-world Marrakesh before they built the ring-road and the modern airport.

'*Tout lasse, tout casse, tout passe*' – and nowhere more seductively than here in Marrakesh, 'the most southerly town of civilized history', as Sacheverell Sitwell once described it.

Since the wartime days when Allied statesmen like Churchill and Eisenhower came here to enjoy the climate and the scenery, the town had become fashionable as a staging post on the hippie trail to the East. With Paul and Talitha in residence, Da Zahir was becoming part of the trail itself.

'The house was a dream, like so much round Talitha and Paul,' says a visitor remembering that summer. 'It was always *en grande fête*, always a perpetual party with fascinating and amusing people and something wonderful occurring. It might be jugglers and fortune tellers or musicians. One evening a Moroccan general turned up just like that with his private troupe of dancers. Thanks to Talitha, the food was quite delicious – when it came.'

As hosts Talitha and Paul were not wildly rich, certainly not in the class of hyperwealth of millionaire American expatriates like Peggy Guggenheim or Barbara Hutton. But they possessed the Getty name, with its promise of imminent riches, which was somehow more exciting than the ponderous reality of total wealth.

Even then this somehow marked them out from all their guests. Not that their guests were poor themselves or boring. *Au contraire*, they included literary geniuses like Gore Vidal, serious celebrities like Mick Jagger, and cosmopolites as socially impressive as Prince Dado Ruspoli.

But as son of one of the richest human beings in the world, Paul was starting to project a touch of the revered apartness once dispensed by minor European royalty. Two centuries earlier, he might have been a dauphin to a Bourbon king. Now he and

Talitha were becoming members of a lonely superclass with rules and tastes and *mores* of its own.

Talitha's unsuspecting parents arrived at Da Zahir on a fortnight's holiday late that autumn. Finding the gardens lit by camphor flares, huge fires of olive logs blazing at each end of high-beamed rooms, jasmine and wood-smoke flavouring the air, and delicious meals consumed at night on priceless rugs beneath the stars, their first impressions were predictable – *Arabian Nights*, no less, they murmured to each other.

But they also felt uneasy from the start about Talitha and Paul, who frequently seemed moody. Also about the number of freeloading guests, whose presence could infuriate their son-in-law, so much so that the Pols heard him shout to Talitha to kick them out. When this happened Talitha became depressed.

Then it rained – heavily – and despite the tasteful work of Mr Willis, the roof leaked. And finally it dawned upon the Pols that there were reasons other than rain and guests for Paul and Talitha's moodiness. As Poppet put it, she and Willem realized that the diet in Da Zahir was not confined to orange juice and charbroiled baby lamb and onion tart.

The local cakes from Mr Very Good the Baker had curious ingredients, as had the home-made jam with the lingering aftertaste which everyone apparently enjoyed. In Poppet it produced heightened colours and everything moving in slow motion. Willem said he would have preferred two double Scotches. Poppet soon discovered to her cost that as well as drowsiness, drugs could induce extreme loquacity in others.

One night at dinner she was seated next to a nice young man with long blond hair who fell asleep between courses, resting his head upon her shoulder. When he awoke, he started begging her to let him take her with him on a trip, explaining that, although LSD was wonderful, you needed somebody beside you until you grew used to it.

★

Despite so many charming people, the drug scene of Da Zahir failed to captivate the Pols, and when they left for France soon afterwards, they were uneasy for the future of the Getty marriage.

Their unease lifted somewhat when a son was born to Talitha in Rome on 30 May 1968 – but the given names worried them: Tara Gabriel Galaxy Gramaphone Getty.

'Rich kid with daft name', as a newspaper in Paul's home town San Francisco put it.

Then Talitha and Paul were off on their travels again – 'Come East, young lovers, the journey not the arrival matters' – taking with them baby Tara G. G. G. plus scatty English nanny, bound for Indonesia and Bali to rediscover people and places Talitha remembered from her shattered childhood.

But the Pols' old house in Bali had been destroyed. The nanny's culinary skills stretched no further than scrambled egg, and while Tara was developing a lifetime aversion to it, Paul and Talitha were forming a taste for something more exotic. What Paul wanted more than ever now was happiness – along with love and peace and the heightened self-awareness only drugs could bring. So did Talitha. But her letters to the Pols began to hint that she was not entirely happy. Heroin was giving her a sense of mounting persecution and unease – and spots on her face which also worried her. By now both she and Paul were totally addicted.

When the Pols visited them in Rome they were shocked at the change they saw in both of them. Even Poppet knew enough to realize that the ingredients of Mr Very Good's cookies were not the cause.

The enchantress's spell was broken. Privately Talitha told her father that she couldn't cope and was frightened and wanted to return to London. For Tara's sake she felt she must escape from drugs and hippiedom and Italy.

Soon after this a friend of Talitha's, passing through Rome, called at the apartment in Piazza Aracoeli on the off-chance of seeing her. Not realizing that Talitha was back in London, and finding the house wide open, she entered and walked up the stairs to look for her. No one was about, but hearing music from the top of the house, she went to investigate. Instead of Talitha, she discovered Paul recumbent on cushions on the floor, smoking opium. Lost in another world, he did not notice her.

With the marriage breaking up, neither spouse was being faithful, and there was now another woman on the scene – Victoria Holdsworth, former model and one-time wife of Lionel Brooke, the last white rajah of Sarawak. Victoria was young and very beautiful, and since she had been brought for a holiday to Marrakesh, Paul had been seeing her a lot, so that she dates the beginning of their long and intermittent love affair to this period. But although Paul was infatuated with Victoria and grew to depend on her, he also stayed deeply and possessively in love with Talitha.

One of the benefits of wealth is that you can always shelve your problems, keep your lover, buy an unhappy wife a house in another country, and thus solve everything and nothing.

Thus too a sort of compromise was reached. Paul would go to London with Talitha, where they would buy a house together so that she could set up home with Tara, start her life afresh and undergo a cure for heroin addiction. Paul meanwhile would continue living in Rome with Victoria, but also visit Talitha and Tara as often as he could in London. Talitha promised she would visit him in Rome with Tara. In this way life could cheerfully continue. No one would be hurt. Everybody would be happy.

In its day, Queen's House on Chelsea's Cheyne Walk must have been one of the loveliest houses in London. Built beside the

Thames in 1707 and sometimes erroneously attributed to both Wren and Vanbrugh, it had been modernized by Lutyens in the 1930s, and was still one of the most desirable residences in this most desirable quarter of the city when Talitha and Paul first saw it.

(Its new owner, hoping to exorcise its ghosts, has returned it to its original name of Tudor House, but throughout this period it was always known as Queen's House.)

It possessed a forty-foot-long drawing-room with original eighteenth-century panelling and splendid views across the river, a fine old garden once part of the original Chelsea Manor, magnificent gates by an anonymous Surrey ironmaster, and one of the prettiest dining rooms in London.

But for Paul its immediate attraction was that for several years in the 1860s it had been home to one of his heroes, the poet and Pre-Raphaelite painter, Dante Gabriel Rossetti. The Pre-Raphaelite Brotherhood, which Rossetti founded with the painters Millais and Holman Hunt, held a special place in the hearts and minds of the hippie generation of the sixties, who saw them as Victorian precursors of much that they believed in – romantic idealism, a carefree and non-judgemental attitude to sex, and, in Rossetti's case, a strong element of drug-induced hallucination which they detected in his painting.

Queen's House was one of the shrines of the Brotherhood, for it was here that Rossetti came to live in 1862, after the mysterious death a few months earlier of his favourite model, whose features haunt many of his paintings, his auburn-haired, drug-addicted wife, Lizzie Siddal, who had consumed an overdose of laudanum in his presence.

Rossetti's story fascinated Paul. For whatever the reasons behind Lizzie's death, it had clearly marked the painter down like a sudden stroke of high romantic doom. He was at the height of his powers as an artist, but from the moment he entered Queen's House, Rossetti's guilt and grief for his dead wife started to obsess him. Already addicted to chloral, one of the Victorians' preferred narcotics, he relied on it increasingly to calm his nerves and alleviate his sadness, drinking it in quite alarming quantities, despite attempts by friends like the poet Swinburne and the novelist George Meredith to stop him. Under the influence of drugs he became increasingly reclusive, his health gave way, and he died at the age of fifty-four in 1882.

Paul was excited by the strong associations between Queen's House and the Pre-Raphaelites and seemed unconcerned by the gloomy nature of the story – and by any parallels it might hold for him. On the contrary, after feeling so much in common with the Pre-Raphaelites and having purchased the house, he was anxious to restore it as much as possible to what it must have been in the years when the painter lived there.

By a strange coincidence Poppet and Willem Pol also knew the house, but in a guise very different from the gloomy haunt of Rossetti during his 'chloralized years' of the 1860s.

Lutyens's modernizations had banished the murk and cobwebs of the past, and the house had been owned in the 1930s by the Queen's stockbroker, urbane Hugo Pitman, who was a friend of Ian Fleming's and a patron of Augustus John. Poppet could remember going to the house on several occasions as a child and seeing her father's pictures hanging on the walls. She even remembered meeting Queen Elizabeth (the present Queen Mother) there. Pitman was always rumoured to have been in love with the Queen, and Poppet's memories of drinking champagne in Queen's House with a real queen made the house seem very special.

Because of this she was shocked to see decorators putting dark paint on to eighteenth-century panelling, hanging sombre-coloured curtains, and installing modern central heating. The Queen's House she remembered was a place of gaiety and light with open fires in the rooms, and she felt unhappy as the house took on an atmosphere of curious ill-omen, which it must have had when Rossetti lived there.

★

Once Talitha and Tara were in residence, none of this seemed to matter any longer. Talitha loved the house, and her return to London soon became a great success, as her London social life began again. She was not as deeply addicted to heroin as Paul; alcohol had been a greater problem. She had little difficulty giving up the drug for periods and by the summer of 1970 she seemed completely cured of heroin and hippiedom and Rome. She also seemed cured of Paul, and had even got on friendly terms with his father. The old man was still refusing to speak to him, but occasionally took Talitha out to dinner.

Inevitably she found herself a new young lover, and she had finally got to know her old hero, Nureyev – and was said to have been the only woman he was ever physically in love with. Soon the trips to Rome with Tara tailed off. By the spring of 1971 she plucked up courage to inform her husband that she wanted a divorce.

It is a measure of his lack of contact with reality that Paul was genuinely shocked. He insisted he was still in love with her, and the prospect of losing her made her doubly precious. So he begged her to return to Rome at once to talk things over. At first she was reluctant, but her lawyers told her it would strengthen her position over a divorce if she could show that she had tried for a reconciliation. So on the morning of 9 July she caught the morning plane to Rome.

That evening she visited Paul in their old apartment, but the meeting ended badly and she returned to spend the night at the Dutch embassy in Rome (conveniently, her aunt Lot Boon was married to the Dutch Ambassador), promising to return to continue the discussion next evening.

On her second night in Rome, Talitha returned to Piazza Aracoeli at around nine thirty. The atmosphere was calmer than the night before, for Paul had made it clear that he definitely wanted her back and was even prepared to change his way of life if that was necessary. He would give up both his drugs and his mistress if she promised to return to him.

If anyone knows for sure what happened then, it's Paul.

Somehow he persuaded Talitha to stay, and finally she fell asleep in the terrace room on the roof of the apartment, with its views of the Roman Capitol where she had married Paul just five years earlier.

Some time after ten o'clock next morning Paul awoke. Talitha did not.

CHAPTER FOURTEEN

CASUALTIES

JEAN PAUL GETTY himself had been in Rome shortly before Talitha's visit, and invited Gail and the children for a few days' holiday at La Posta Vecchia. She and her family still enjoyed the old man's favour, and she particularly recalls a luncheon at the house in honour of rival oil-man Dr Armand Hammer, head of Occidental Oil, who was also visiting the city.

Even now old Paul took an old man's pleasure in provoking jealousy among his women. Placing Gail beside him, he had whispered, 'Just watch this!' – knowing that the presence at table of his latest mistress, the voluptuous Mrs Rosabella Burch, would inevitably upset the insecure Mary Teissier. But in fact Rosabella provided a more engrossing spectacle by flirting outrageously throughout the meal with the aged but patently entranced Dr Hammer.

During this short stay in Rome Getty had still refused to contact Paul, and returned to England at the end of June without seeing him. However, he insisted that Gail and the children should stay on for a few days longer if they wished. They did, and because of this had just got back to Orgia when Gail received a call from her distraught ex-husband late in the afternoon of 11 July. He told her what had happened and how Talitha had been taken to Rome's Villa del Rosario Clinic in deepest coma. There they had tried to resuscitate her – unsuccessfully – and shortly after midday she had died without regaining consciousness.

He sounded so desperate that Gail decided to drive to Rome at once to be with him. She found him overwhelmed with grief and terrible remorse. He couldn't face returning to Piazza Aracoeli, so she suggested that he went to La Posta Vecchia instead. He agreed and, as he seemed inconsolable, she stayed with him.

Everyone mourned Talitha, and not least Gail and the children. As she says, 'Talitha played no part in the break-up of our marriage, and we'd grown extremely fond of her.' The funeral was held in Amsterdam, where Talitha was buried in a simple grave beside her mother. Those present included Paul, the Pols, a few close members of the family, and Talitha's old admirer Lord Lambton, who had flown in from London with three of her one-time girlfriends.

The Pols were numbed with grief, Willem in particular. Shortly afterwards he had a heart attack, from which he never fully recovered. But it was Paul who appeared most riven at the funeral. With Talitha gone, he realized he loved her more than ever. Stricken with remorse and guilt, he could not forgive himself for what had happened and for having been incapable of saving her.

But what exactly *had* occurred that night in Piazza Aracoeli? Since Paul himself refused to say, the sequence of events was never clarified and the facts behind Talitha's death remain a mystery.

According to the death certificate signed by doctors at the clinic, death was due to cardiac arrest and high levels of alcohol and barbiturates were discovered in the blood. As Talitha was known to be a heavy drinker who sometimes took barbiturates to offset the effect of alcohol, there is no reason to doubt the facts recorded on the certificate. Barbiturates and alcohol taken together in large quantities can be a lethal combination which could certainly have accounted for her death.

The point was that, as a heroin addict, Paul was in a vulnerable position and could not risk saying anything himself about the circumstances of Talitha's death. Possession of narcotics was an indictable offence in Italy, often carrying a penalty of imprisonment, and things would almost certainly have turned extremely nasty for him if the police had initiated an official inquiry and his addiction had been revealed.

To avoid this and stay safely out of Rome until the situation cleared, he opted for a period in Bangkok – which he had loved when he visited it with Talitha in happier times. In Thailand drugs were available if he needed them, and he would have peace and quiet to recover from her death and decide about the future. To keep him company Gail persuaded one of his oldest Roman friends, the Runyonesque ex-restaurateur Jerry Cierchio (famous proprietor of Jerry's Club on the Via Veneto) to go with him. If anyone could stop Paul brooding, it was Jerry, and during their two-month absence Paul did his best to come to terms with what had happened.

But once back in Italy it was clear that he would never forgive himself. Paul was obsessed with it. Sometimes his grief became unbearable, making him rely on drugs more heavily than ever – which fuelled his anxieties and sense of guilt, until they formed a vicious circle.

The children were affected too, and Gail had to cope with them on her own – as well as with two-and-a-half-year-old Tara. For when the child's future was discussed, she had said at once, 'Tara's place is with his family here in Rome.'

Simultaneously she had had to deal with Paul, who relied upon her more than ever for advice, and whose state of mind was not improved by growing rumours that the true cause of Talitha's death had been not barbiturates but an overdose of heroin taken in his presence.

There was no evidence to support this, and it was, *ipso facto*, unlikely that having finally got off heroin herself, and then made Paul's addiction such an issue over their separation, Talitha would have suddenly succumbed to the drug on her second night in Rome. It was equally unlikely that, had she really died from heroin, the doctors at the clinic would have missed the evidence. It has been asserted that an autopsy conducted eight months after Talitha's death revealed traces of heroin in the body. If this is true it still does not prove that heroin was the cause of death. The combination of alcohol and barbiturates would still have been a more likely cause. Also in a former heroin addict like Talitha, traces of the drug could have been deposited a considerable period before she died.

For a while nothing happened, but as Paul was a fairly well-known addict, rumours continued. He spent Christmas with Gail and the children. Then in the new year came reports that, following widespread speculation, an examining magistrate would finally conduct a full inquiry into the nature of Talitha's death. He would, of course, wish to interview her husband, Paul Getty Junior.

The inquiry was fixed for the beginning of March. In the second week of February, Paul flew to London, never to return to Italy.

It would have taken a braver man than Paul to have stayed in Rome and faced the Italian drugs squad to clear his name before an official Italian inquiry. In the first place, he would have had to face simultaneous trial by the Italian media, with world press and television eager for the story. Every item from his private life would have been sensationalized – along with details of his most intimate relationships – with Talitha, with Victoria, and with Gail and the children. Innocent friends would inevitably have been involved.

But the real danger was that any inquiry would inevitably expose details of his own addiction. Irrespective of what had happened to Talitha, this would soon lead on to a court case with the likelihood of prison at the end of it.

The judge issued a request for Paul 'to come here voluntarily and give what help he can to the inquiry'. Hardly surprisingly he got no answer, and although for a time Paul was dreading extradition back to Italy, his fears proved groundless. It would have been unusual for the Italians to have asked for extradition of a witness in a case involving foreigners whose own government was not demanding action.

So the inquiry into Talitha's death was inconclusive and the file stayed open, but Paul could never return to Italy. With his children still in Rome, this meant that their already slender contacts with their father all but ended.

More serious perhaps, by evading the inquiry Paul deprived himself of any chance of explanation – or of public expiation – for his wife's demise. The most unlikely accusations – that she had taken a massive overdose of heroin, that Paul had actually provided it, even that he had helped inject her, were never answered, and whatever actually took place on that July night in the apartment in Piazza Aracoeli would have to rest between his conscience and himself.

With all this hanging over him, Paul returned to the house he owned beside the river where a century earlier his hero, Dante Gabriel Rossetti, had come to brood over the death of beautiful Lizzie Siddal. This was the house where Talitha had also lived until recently, and which Paul had so carefully restored to the state it had been in when Rossetti lived there. Now it seemed he had succeeded all too well, and, thanks to an eerie trick of fate, he found himself reliving the whole grim saga of Rossetti's downfall.

This was probably an important factor in Paul's subsequent behaviour. Heroin addicts are often imitative, finding security and satisfaction in mirroring the life-style of another addict. In Paul's case he might almost have been Rossetti, and there was a disturbing symmetry in the way he seemed to duplicate his actions. This very house had seen Rossetti become increasingly reclusive, haunted by remorse, and relying on ever greater quantities of alcohol and chloral, until his health was virtually destroyed. Paul's behaviour was identical, except that he had more effective twentieth-century soporifics.

But the cause of his misery was so similar to Rossetti's that the words employed by Hall Caine, Rossetti's first biographer, to describe his plight could have applied to him: 'Above all it was my impression that Rossetti had never ceased to reproach himself for his wife's death as an event that had been due in some degree to failure of duty on his part or perhaps to something graver.'

For somebody like Paul, England, unlike both Italy and the United States, possessed one great advantage – its official policy towards narcotics. In England, addiction was regarded as a medical rather than a social problem, and addicts who registered with a doctor could legally receive their drugs on medical prescription. In theory the dose should steadily diminish, as the aim of the 'treatment' was principally therapeutic.

Thus, for Paul, London was something of a haven and he discovered a doctor who was happy to call on him at Queen's House in his Bentley.

With Paul in residence, the house became as idiosyncratic as it had been in Rossetti's day. Rossetti had kept a menagerie (including his famous wombat) in the garden but Paul had a number of stuffed animals in the house itself. In his bedroom was a more puzzling memento – a wooden model of a flying-boat. This was in fact a model of the legendary *Spruce Goose*, the huge wooden flying-boat obsessively constructed by another son of an oil tycoon who made himself a notorious recluse, Howard Hughes. Paul did the same now, as he shut himself away and made the house a shrine to Talitha's memory and a ghetto for his own oblivion.

Everything to do with Talitha was lovingly preserved, including her clothes and letters, her photographs and the portrait painted by her father.

On the face of it, his was a deeply tragic situation – bereaved, addicted, cut off from those he loved and from his beloved Italy. But one can also see the dreadful consolation that it offered someone of Paul's increasingly reclusive temperament – and why it kept its hold on him so long. Here, in the very house where a romantic poet had destroyed himself with drugs while mourning his beautiful dead wife, he could do the same, joining a hazardous tradition of narcotic self-destruction. He and the ghost of Dante Gabriel Rossetti could come together in their grief around the memory of the beautiful departed.

Paul's days must have dragged interminably and at times his depressions were appalling, but he was strong and single-minded and felt that this was what fate intended. He was punishing himself for what had happened. Believing himself valueless, he could find little of value in his own surroundings. Thus, for all his wealth, his world became a tiny segment of a very private hell. He played his opera records, watched interminable TV, drank much, ate little, and when life became unbearable, he always had what seemed to be the perfect antidote.

At times he tried to kick the habit, but this was something wealthy addicts always find a problem. On the few occasions when he couldn't find money for drugs, the Getty name was good for credit.

Although he was often lonely, he was not alone. Victoria helped to keep him company, and he soon built up a very private group of friends. Gradually, some of the members of the counter-culture of the sixties who had been his friends and guests in Marrakesh joined his circle. These were people he could trust, and who understood his situation. Mick Jagger and his then wife, Bianca, lived just a few doors away in Cheyne Walk and often saw him. So did the Marianne Faithful and hopelessly addicted gallery owner Robert Fraser. But as far as his future was concerned, his most important visitor was another neighbour, the knowledgeable Old Etonian with the small antique shop round the corner, who had been a friend of Talitha's.

During the sixties, Christopher Gibbs was a well-known figure in Chelsea. Handsome, stylish, and extremely well connected – his father was a banker and his uncle governor of Rhodesia – he was a most unusual character. Having attended university in France and studied archaeology in Jerusalem, he became something of a trend-setter for the sixties with his parties and the Arabic furniture and carpets he dealt in. His flat, a short walk along Cheyne Walk from Paul's house, had been used as the setting for one of the theme films of the sixties, Antonioni's *Blow Up*. But his most famous role was probably his friendship with the young Mick Jagger. It was Gibbs who discovered Stargrove, the Jaggers' splendid Victorian country house in Berkshire, and helped them furnish it. Gibbs was often with them in Marrakesh, where he introduced them to his friends the Gettys.

At the time Paul had lent him £1,200 for a small house in the Atlas mountains. Gibbs still owned it, and was grateful. Now that Paul needed company and friends that he could trust, he was anxious to repay the debt. Besides, he genuinely liked Paul and like most of his friends felt desperately sorry for him.

During this period, one member of the family appeared entirely immune to what was going on – the ageing patriarch at Sutton Place. At seventy-eight old Paul was still as firmly in command of Getty Oil as ever, and richer than he'd ever been. With Neutral Zone production at its peak in 1971, his personal fortune climbed to $290 million, with the Sarah C. Getty Trust ahead of it at $850 million.

Getty himself had single-handedly fought off a number of attacks upon his empire, and had saved his tanker fleet despite declining American demand, so that when the Arab–Israeli war began in 1973, Getty Oil would be well placed to profit from the worldwide oil shortage.

Typically, when told about Talitha's death, he showed no flicker of emotion. It seemed to be the same with the news about Paul Junior. 'No Getty can be a drug addict,' he said firmly, and although his son was living barely thirty miles away in London, he adamantly refused to see him. From time to time Paul would try to reach his father on the telephone, begging Penelope to use her influence. She always got the same reply: 'When he stops taking drugs we'll talk, but not till then.'

Twelve days after Talitha's death, echoing the way his father had treated him, Getty virtually struck Paul from his will – leaving him $500.

But behind the show of strength, the lord of Sutton Place was vulnerable. He had never been as big a man as he had wanted; but he now looked rather small, with shoulders hunched, and liver spots mottling his cheeks. Suddenly, despite his money and the women round him, he seemed very much alone.

His policy of abandoning his sons in infancy, and then recalling them to take their places in the business when they came of age, simply hadn't worked. There was no closeness or affection, nor had there been much understanding between them. He still resented them, still angrily attacked them when he felt that they were threatening his own unique position.

Timmy apart – and he had loved Timmy only after he was dead – the one exception for a while had been his precious Paul. Gail still says how sad it is that Paul Jr. never realized until too late how much his father loved him. Possibly he did, but when Paul fell from grace, this simply made the old man's heart set harder.

'The only way we can preserve what we have created is through our children', he had written recently like the old Victorian he really was at heart. Had he thought about this earlier, he might have been more careful in the way he had treated these four beings on whom so much depended.

In many ways the unkindest cut of all had been the one he dealt his half-German second son, tall unhappy Ronald. Had Ronald possessed a little of the charm of his half-brother Paul things might have been different. But Ronald wasn't easy. He had a stubborn streak that had made Getty say occasionally, 'Ronnie's the son that's most like me', but the truth was that the older Ronald got, the more he reminded Getty of his German grandfather, his old enemy, Dr Helmle. And it was the vendetta with Dr Helmle which was at the root of all the trouble.

Ronald's exclusion from the Sarah C. Getty Trust had been

a cruel injustice, which made him feel discriminated against by the other members of the family. During the ups and downs of their relationship, Getty had sometimes given his son his faithful promise to rectify the situation, and include him in the Sarah C. Getty Trust. But he never had. Perhaps he was concerned that by adding to the number of beneficiaries, he would have made the trust vulnerable to his eternal enemy, the tax-man. Perhaps when it came to it he simply didn't want to include Ronald and was still seeking his revenge on long dead Dr Helmle by victimizing his grandson.

One effect this had was to make Ronald feel that he had no future in the family business, and in 1964, Shortly after his marriage, he left Germany and his position in the Getty-owned Veedol company and returned to California. He was intent on making large amounts of money on his own account to prove his independence and show what he thought of his father. Unfortunately he chose Hollywood, and swiftly showed that, for all his alleged similarities to his father, he lacked Big Paul's obsessional capacity to learn every detail of whatever business he embarked on.

He had inherited nearly $2 million from Grannie Getty – who had always thought that he was badly treated – and allied himself with two Hollywood producers to produce a number of low-budget films like *Flare Up* starring Raquel Welch, *Zeppelin* and *Sheilah*. But although these films are still shown on TV, they failed to make his reputation or his fortune.

'I'll have the money, and they'll have the know-how,' said Ronald, referring to his co-producers.

'And by the end they'll still have the know-how *and* they'll have your money,' replied his father – who as usual when it came to business was remarkably perceptive.

Gordon was completely different; and recently, despite their law-suit and their differences in character – which were considerable – Getty had come to feel a grudging admiration for his absent-minded son.

Gordon had courage and was clever. Probably too clever, that was his trouble. He had tried his economic theories on his father who, by and large, couldn't understand them. Nor could Getty appreciate Gordon's music. Occasionally at Sutton Place the great voice would go booming down the corridors.

'Gordon practising,' Getty would say, almost benevolently.

But he rarely failed to add that Gordon wasn't practical. On occasions, though, Gordon could surprise him, for sometimes his wild ideas actually worked – as when he suggested that the heating system in the Pierre Hotel could double up for air-conditioning in summer, thus saving several million dollars upgrading the whole system in the hotel. Gordon was also an admirable family man, and he had followed his father's example by producing only sons. Old Paul was proud of them.

To show that the lawsuit was forgiven, he bestowed on Gordon the highest accolade in the Getty firmament – the all-powerful position of trustee of the Sarah C. Getty Trust. But try as he might, he could never see Gordon taking a more active role in the oil business.

In contrast, the eldest son and heir-apparent, George, Vice-president of Tidewater Oil, was deeply conscious of family tradition. Like most bad parents, Getty was inconsistent with his sons, favouring one against another, and thus creating jealousy just as he did among his women. George was the most jealous of them all. He was a great carrier of tales against his siblings, trying to curry favour with his father – first against Ronald, then against Gordon during his law-suit, even saying that Gordon was not a Getty but the child of Ann Rork's third husband, Joe McEnerney, which was ludicrous.

But as Vice-president of Tidewater, George had truly suffered. His father had always had an instinct for the weaknesses of others, and rarely spotted them without attacking. He'd been unforgiving when Tidewater's oil exploration bids had failed one by one – particularly those in Pakistan and the Sahara – and shut down the company's exploration section without consulting George. Similarly he had personally sold off part of Tide Water's unprofitable marketing network in the western USA over George's head in a $300 million deal with Philips Petroleum's John Houchin, at the Hotel Flora, on the last occasion he had been in Rome. George had been incensed.

'My father's the president in charge of success and I'm the vice-president in charge of failure,' he lamented – a fairly accurate assessment of the situation.

George's personal life had also deteriorated since he had broken with his former wife, Gloria, in 1967. In the ensuing divorce proceedings Gloria claimed that George had been distant, cold, aloof, unfeeling – all the things the wives had said about his father.

For a period George had thought himself in love with Lord Beaverbrook's granddaughter, Lady Jean Campbell. She had met him at dinner at Sutton Place and found him 'very strange, very unrelaxed, and always referring to his father during conversation as "Mr Getty" '. She thought this odd, and tried persuading him to call him 'Father', even 'Dad', but it was always 'Mr Getty'.

'I realized then that George was scared stiff, absolutely terrified of Mr Getty and of what Mr Getty thought of him.'

In 1971 George remarried – not to Lady Jean, who preferred Norman Mailer – but to Jacqueline Riordan, a San Francisco heiress who had inherited $30 million from her previous husband, an Irish-American financier who had made a fortune from a dubious pension scheme in Switzerland and who had perished when a mud-slide engulfed him in his bedroom. (Jacqueline somehow managed to escape.)

The old man had been fond of Gloria, who'd been a good wife to George and mother to his three daughters, and felt saddened by the divorce. But he couldn't help approving of a new wife who had so much money. 'It's not so much a marriage as a merger,' he began to say with satisfaction. But once the merger was effected Jacqueline soon became its senior partner, using her power unmercifully against poor George once she had reached the same conclusion as Lady Jean about his attitude towards his father.

George in fact was secretly becoming frightened of almost everything by now – his enemies, his wife, his ex-wife, the Tide Water executives, life itself.

To counter this he did his best to earn respect from those around him as a prominent social figure, fund-raising for the Los Angeles Philharmonic, sitting on the board of the Bank of America, even breeding horses just as the Queen of England did – in short, turning himself into the sort of character he could respect. It didn't work. Papa was always there to rule his life, and making no attempt at all to hide the fact that he despised him.

Not surprisingly, George was drinking by now – more or less secretly, but to excess. By the beginning of 1973 he was taking sedatives and speed and probably injecting something inadvisable. On the night of 6 June he had another bitter row with Jacqueline, once again over Mr Getty. Their rows were almost always over Mr Getty. At the end of the row he flipped, all the frustrations, hatreds, impotence and rage surfacing in one great wave of anger, and he panicked.

He locked himself in the bedroom of their valuable house in beautiful Bel Air and started shouting. He drank. He swallowed a lot of Nembutal. He tried to stab himself with a barbecue fork, but failed to pierce his stomach. Then he fell into a coma.

Finally friends broke down the door and got him out and called an ambulance, but there was a muddle now about the hospital. No one could permit Tidewater's Vice-president to be taken, in what was thought to be a drunken stupor, to the common casualty department of the nearby UCLA hospital. So they took him to a more discreet hospital instead, which took twenty minutes longer.

To save his name they lost his life. For ironically, George wasn't drunk, but was suffering from a potent overdose of all the drugs he'd swallowed. By the time they reached the hospital,

George, beloved eldest son and heir-apparent to the richest and coldest man in America, was dead.

'His father killed him,' said his widow, when journalists came to see her.

In London it was early evening when the news of George's death reached Barbara Wallace, who telephoned Penelope. Penelope knew that Getty was having dinner with the Duchess of Argyll at her house in Mayfair. But one of her daughters said, 'You must go to him and break the news to him. He'll need you.'

So she did.

When she told him George was dead, Getty was transfixed with grief, poleaxed, stricken, unable to weep or speak, such was his anguish. For this was one of those extremely rare occasions when the structure of his life – his fortune, his ambition, his constant activities, his women and his powers of concentration – were all useless, blown away, leaving the lonely child who had grieved for his dog Jip, for his dear Papa and darling Mama, and for Timmy, 'bravest and best of all my sons'. Now George had joined them in the line-up of this old man's misery.

On the way back to Sutton Place he wouldn't speak to anyone, and next morning still refused to talk of George. But he had a portrait photograph of him hung in the hall of Sutton Place, with purple round it, purple being the imperial colour of the emperors of Rome and also of mourning.

Shortly afterwards he agreed to speak to journalists, one of whom repeated the widow's original remark.

'She says his father killed him. Have you any comment, Mr Getty?'

'None,' he answered.

CHAPTER FIFTEEN

KIDNAP AND RANSOM

THE AREA BETWEEN Corso Vittorio Emmanuele and the Tiber has many of Rome's great renaissance palaces, for this is where papal families like the Borgias, Farnese, and Riario once resided – and these narrow streets have seen more mayhem in their time than any other quarter of the city. At night they still seem faintly sinister, but by the small hours there is rarely any sign of life, apart from the Roman cats and the occasional night-watchman on his rounds. So no one could have missed the young Paul Getty as he walked down the Via della Mascherone towards the mask-like fountain of a girl spouting water from her mouth, after which the little street is named.

He was a red-haired beanpole of a boy, and after a night out he often wandered home like this to the apartment he was sharing with two young painters in Trastevere on the far side of the river. Today it would seem a stupid thing to do, but Rome was a safer city then, and when an elderly white Fiat drew up beside him with a squeal of brakes, he was not particularly alarmed.

'Excuse me, *signore*. Are you Paul Getty?' called out the driver.

'Yes,' he said, 'I am.'

With which two men jumped out, grabbed him, and despite his struggles forced him into the back of the car, which swiftly drove away. As the clocks of Rome were striking 3 a.m. on the

morning of 10 July 1973, the next disaster to afflict the Getty
family had started.

Since the death of Talitha, and Paul's flight to London, Gail's
chief preoccupation had been to hold her family together, and
although her marriage to Lang Jeffries had ended two years
earlier, she felt she was succeeding. She was thirty-seven that
April.

She and the children all loved Italy. They went to the house
at Orgia for weekends and holidays, and in Rome were now
living in a modern apartment in the middle-class area of Parioli.
In those days living was so cheap for foreigners with dollars that
she could live comfortably, but she was far from rich, and child
support from Paul in London tended to be erratic. She drove an
Opel station-wagon, had many local friends, most of them Italian, and lived an essentially private life around her children.

Wishing them to enjoy a European education, she sent them
not to the American School in Rome, but to solid old St George's
on the Via Salaria, which still claimed in its prospectus 'to provide
a sound, all-round British style education for English-speaking
children between the ages of eight and eighteen'.

But like much in Rome in the early seventies, St George's
was affected by the new-wave culture which was hitting Italy.
The three younger children made the most of their time there,
but Paul, the eldest, rebelled. He was more seriously affected by
the divorce and by Talitha's death than the others, and proved
harder to control without a father.

By 1973, when he was just sixteen, he had effectively given
up on regular education. When Lang was around he had never
got on well with him, resenting his presence in his father's place.
Now, being highly independent, he had set his heart on painting
and educating himself by reading what he wanted. He was serious enough about this for Gail to agree to let him share the
Trastevere studio with two older friends of the family, Marcello
Crisi and Philip Woollam.

As she says, 'Paul was doing his *vie bohème* thing, and in Paris no one would have noticed.' But Rome was different. With the *dolce vita* dead and gone, Rome in the early seventies had lapsed back into something like an old provincial city, where the cult of the Italian family was still very much intact, so that leaving a sixteen-year-old like Paul to his own devices could later on be made to seem distinctly shocking.

In fact Paul kept in close touch with all his family in Rome. As he had little money, he was smart enough to get his local *trattoria* to accept his paintings occasionally in return for meals, but most days still saw Gail driving over to the flat with food for him and his flatmates. When she didn't, he usually came home to eat and see his siblings. They were devoted to him, so that although Paul was living on his own, the Getty Family Italiana managed to remain a most united family.

Paul was a strange mixture. Gail described him as 'extraordinarily precocious, more like a boy of twenty than sixteen'. After the divorce, his reaction against Lang had made him increasingly idolize his father and the hippie life-style he embodied. Aged eleven, he had been invited for a fortnight to Marrakesh, which naturally struck him as the most glamorous place on earth. He became very fond of Talitha, and her death when he was fourteen came as something of a blow, as did his father's flight to London.

Gail recalls that 'around that time, Paul became very quiet, very locked-in', and it was because of this that she had encouraged him to paint and mix with others. He still spent his summer holidays with the family at La Fuserna, and had grown to love the people and the romantic countryside south of Siena. Mark, his younger brother, was devoted to him and tells of how they once got lost exploring the woods above the house. As darkness fell and they failed to return, Gail was beside herself with worry, but it was Paul in his role as elder brother who kept his nerve and brought them home in safety.

One friend of Paul's who came to stay in Tuscany each summer was Adam Alvarez, son of the writer Al Alvarez. Adam remembers Paul as 'surprisingly straightforward and nothing like the wild character the press created after the kidnap. But his life was complicated by what had happened in his family. He missed his father and he often seemed unhappy.'

Back in Rome he changed, for in Rome the Getty name could give him what he undoubtedly enjoyed – the status of a minor celebrity. Someone in the press had called him 'the Golden Hippie' and he had earned some easy money modelling nude for a magazine. The nickname was repeated when the police grabbed him on the fringe of a student demonstration and made him spend a night in prison – bringing less agreeable publicity. This seems to have put him on the side of the oppressed, for he was soon adopting a powerful line against the rich, rather as his father used to. 'The rich are the real poor of the earth. Their malnutrition is of the spirit. One should pity them,' he said – which sounded better in Italian, and was picked up in the foreign press and duly found its way to Sutton Place, where his grandfather read the piece but made no comment.

But the old man was unlikely to forget the previous summer when Paul had come to visit him in brightly coloured jeans and sneakers. Grandpapa didn't approve of jeans or sneakers and the visit hadn't been repeated.

It was in early 1973 that Paul began dating Martine Zacher, a pretty German divorcée with a year-old baby daughter. She was a very liberated woman, eight years his senior, who acted in a small alternative theatre. He became fond of her, but saw no reason to be faithful. Since becoming known as the Golden Hippie, he was surprised at how many girls made themselves available.

Thus in Rome Paul had enjoyed an enviable existence – going to discothèques (where in fact nothing very much occurred), chasing girls, smoking hash and playing at being a dedicated artist. Since he was very young his mother felt that, given time, he would finally grow up and leave all this behind him. Far from condemning him, she believed that, as she put it, 'rebelling against convention can be a sign of originality, and an indication that someone might be special'.

But according to Bill Newsom, Paul was behaving as he did because he 'worshipped his father and was trying to outdo him as a hippie', this despite the fact that he rarely saw him, and had had little contact with him since he went to London.

'We communicate by occasional postcards and mysterious telegrams,' said young Paul in an interview with *Rolling Stone* magazine.

On the night of the kidnap, Mark was away in San Francisco with his maternal grandparents, and Aileen was off with friends, leaving Gail with Ariadne and Tara at La Fuserna. But that Sunday morning, something made her feel uneasy and she decided, on the spur of the moment, to drive back to Rome. When she rang Paul, one of his flatmates told her he had not returned.

This worried her, but there was no further news of him until that evening, when the phone rang and someone with a southern Italian accent asked politely if she were the Signora Getty.

When she said, 'Yes', he answered, like someone from the cleaners telling her her clothes were ready, 'We have your son, Paul Getty.'

'What do you mean?' she said impatiently. 'He's here in Rome.'

'No, *signora*. He is with us. We are kidnappers and have him captive. He is safe, but we will require much money to release him.'

She stammered that she had no money.

'Then please prepare to ask for it from your father-in-law. He has all the money in the world.'

It was then she understood her caller wasn't joking.

'Where is my son?' she asked angrily.

'I tell you he is with us. He is in good health and he'll stay that way as long as you do as you are told and arrange about the money. But don't go to the police. Just wait to hear from us.'

With which the man rang off – and Gail collapsed.

When she recovered, it was as if her world had suddenly collapsed as well. She had never felt thoroughly frightened before, but she now experienced real terror, blanking out all other feelings, and leaving her weak and shaking. All her thoughts of Paul were suddenly of the vulnerable child she remembered, with his private weaknesses and fears. He had been a shy, extremely loving child, and she could not stop thinking how frightened he must be and how easy it would be for his kidnappers to hurt him.

She had always felt at ease with people, particularly Italians, and she loved Italy. But Italy was suddenly a foreign land.

'I felt utterly alone, and I had to find out what in God's name I should do.'

Her first reaction was to ring her parents in America, who did their best to reassure her and said she must certainly contact the police, which she did, telephoning the Carabinieri station in the nearby Piazza Euclide. Then she called her ex-husband, Paul, in London.

They had recently been drawing closer to each other. Paul was on his own but seemed more in charge of his life than at any time since Talitha's death. Gail had spent part of May with him at Cheyne Walk – since when few days had passed without them speaking to each other on the telephone.

So when she broke the news of what had happened, they shared the sense of shock and horror for their child. Both were in tears, and since Paul seemed even more upset than her, Gail found herself trying to console him. It was only when she said he must contact his father to raise money for the ransom that he seemed to move away.

'I can't,' he said. 'We never speak to one another.'

'Then I'll have to speak to him myself,' she said. But before she could the Carabinieri had arrived.

The Arma dei Carabinieri pride themselves on being a tough,

hard-headed *corps d'élite* who help hold Italy together in spite of the most corrupt governing class in Europe. What they lack in imagination they make up for in cynicism and knowledge of the world – and are rarely over-sympathetic to what they see as rich, indulgent foreigners living in their midst.

Three local officers were commanded by one Colonello Gallo – Colonel Cockerel – 'who looked and behaved exactly like a rooster'. They were soon joined by officers from Carabinieri headquarters who grilled her for the next five hours – chiefly about her and her son's private lives. She repeated the words of the telephone call verbatim, but they made little attempt to hide their doubts about the kidnapping – and about young Paul himself.

'We know your son, *signora*. He is probably with a girl or with his hippie friends. He will almost certainly turn up.'

The Carabinieri left at around 11 p.m. and it was agreed that because of the Getty name, and the danger to the other children, the press were not to be informed. But someone did inform them and it wasn't Gail. Within twenty minutes the Italian press was on the line, followed by ABC New York, NBC Chicago, and finally CBS from London.

By then there was no point in Gail denying the kidnapping, and next morning it was the front-page story of Rome's daily paper, *Il Messaggero*. The story followed the line the officers had taken during Gail's interrogation.

Under banner headlines, 'Joke or Kidnap', most of the article concentrated on the character and lifestyle of the 'Golden Hippie', and suggested that quite probably Paul, 'famous for his wild hippie life-style', had gone off with a girlfriend, or some of his wilder acquaintances. There was no reference to Gail's conversation with the kidnappers or to a demand for a ransom. As far as *Il Messaggero* was concerned, Paul had simply 'disappeared'.

But the article changed the situation. In the first place, it would take some time for the element of doubt over the kidnap to go away – and endless complications would ensue until it did. More serious still, since the Getty name was always news, the chance of dealing with the kidnap quietly behind the scenes was over from the start.

Gail's flat in Parioli instantly came under siege from journalists and television crews desperate for a story, making her effectively a prisoner with Aileen, Ariadne and Tara – for as well as being trapped by the media, she also had to stay within reach of the telephone waiting for the kidnappers to call.

Although it is often seen as the great Italian crime *par excellence*, kidnap was rare in Italy until the early seventies when Luciano Liggio, the Milan-based *capo dei capi* of the Sicilian Mafia, developed it as a means of raising capital for the Sicilians' rapidly developing international drugs cartel. It was then that it began to flourish, and the Sicilians had many imitators. The smartest were probably the students in the Red Brigades, who kidnapped and murdered ex-premier Aldo Moro in 1978 with terrible efficiency, just as the crudest were undoubtedly the Calabrians from the South of Italy.

The Calabrian Mafia, the N'drangeta, was an ancient, loosely linked federation of *mafioso* families from this poorest part of Italy, who for centuries had been making money from protection rackets on the local peasantry. Recently some of the younger, more ambitious members had been contemplating kidnap as a quicker source of profit.

Paul's captors were a gang of petty criminals from Calabria with tenuous connections with the N'drangeta. Gail believes that someone in the *trattoria* where he sold his pictures fingered him to them. Until now there'd always been an unspoken rule among *mafiosi* against harming or involving foreigners, but Paul was so vulnerable – and everybody knew his grandfather was so extremely rich – that the thought of kidnap must have seemed a foolproof source of easy money.

The planning apparently took some months. There was no problem trailing him, as he had absolutely no awareness of his danger. Seizing him was just as easy, and once they had him in their car his captors held a chloroform-soaked pad across his face, then drove him through the night, still gagged and blind-folded and more or less unconscious, till they reached the deso-late countryside they knew in the toe of Italy.

Here they kept him captive, much as they kept their animals – generally in cattle-huts or shelters in the woods. To begin with they were not so much cruel to him as callous, as Southerners tend to be with animals. He was chained by the ankle, but since his captors all wore masks, they removed his blindfold except when they were on the move.

For one so young he did his best to keep his dignity. When he complained about the dirt, they took him to wash in nearby streams. He had nothing to read, but they gave him a radio – on which he heard reports about the 'mystery' of his kidnapping. They fed him cold spaghetti and tinned tuna-fish and water. They told him that as long as he did as he was told he would not be hurt and his ordeal would soon be over.

At this stage his captors seemed highly confident – and were clearly counting on a speedy deal to make their fortunes. Since the boy's grandfather was so rich, they were certain there would be no problem finding the money for the ransom.

'*Ci sentiremo*' – 'You'll be hearing from us' – were the kidnap-per's final words to Gail before ringing off, and she stayed like a lover by the telephone waiting for the call to come. But kidnap is a form of torture and they let her stew. For ten long days and sleepless nights she had no hint of whether her son was alive or dead or what had happened to him.

Not that she sat by her telephone in silence. She was plagued throughout the day by telephone calls – supportive calls, abusive calls, and even obscene calls, none of which made life easier.

She had still been unable to make contact with Big Paul at

Sutton Place, as he was never available and never rang her back. Nor did she hear from Ann and Gordon in America. Thinking herself totally abandoned by the Gettys and left to face the music on her own, she had never felt so lonely in her life, and as day dragged after day, with the promised call from the kidnappers never coming, she became convinced that something unspeakable had happened.

At night she could not sleep for fear of the nightmares that pursued her. Did the silence mean the kidnappers had killed him? What if they never rang? What if she simply never saw her son again?

But finally they did communicate with her – not by telephone, but through the post, in a colourful, artistically-done collage of letters cut from magazines, briefly setting out the kidnappers' demands for a ransom. They were asking for ten *miliardi* of lire, roughly 17 million dollars, a considerable sum even by Getty standards, which could come from one source only, the eighty-one-year-old family patriarch back in Sutton Place.

Shortly after this, Gail received a second letter – this time from Paul himself. It had been posted in Rome, and her heart missed a beat when she recognized his writing on the envelope. The letter started by telling her what she knew already, that he had been kidnapped, but gave no clues as to his whereabouts or the identity of his captors. He simply wrote that he was safe and well, and added a fresh warning against going to the police.

Clearly writing at the kidnappers' behest, he concluded by begging her to speak as soon as possible to his grandfather about the ransom. If his captors failed to receive the money swiftly and in full he would be 'badly treated'.

The letter ended with a line that made her blood run cold.

'Pay up, I beg you, pay up as soon as possible if you wish me well. If you delay it is very dangerous for me. I love you. Paul.'

★

Paul Junior still refused to talk to his father about the ransom, and although Gail continued ringing Sutton Place, Getty Senior was never available. This puzzled her. Big Paul had always been extremely charming to her in the past, but now it was clear that he wished to have no contact with her.

By now he had, in fact, made his attitude to paying ransom money all too clear in a statement issued to the press. Jean Paul Getty was standing firm on what he claimed to be a matter of principle. As he put it in his statement: 'I have fourteen grand-children, and if I pay a penny of ransom, I'll have fourteen kid-napped grandchildren.'

As a public statement warning off other potential kidnap-pers this was fair enough. There was presumably a chance, however minimal, that payment of a ransom for one child might conceivably encourage somebody to kidnap another, and the statement also squared with the law in Italy, where the payment of a ransom to kidnappers is theoretically against the law.

But all of this was hypothetical. In Italy it has always proved impossible to forbid the payment of ransom money to release a loved one, just as the reality was that Getty's eldest grandson and namesake, Jean Paul Getty III, was actually in the hands of crim-inals and at that very moment in danger of his life.

As everybody knew, his grandfather – and he alone – could pay virtually any ransom demand and barely notice. So could he seriously intend to leave his grandson in captivity? What if the boy became sick or was tortured? Would he still stick firmly by his principles, and high-mindedly refuse to save him?

Getty made it clear that his reasons for doing so had less to do with principle than with his personal feelings on the matter. In the first place there was his puritan disapproval of his so-called 'hippie' grandson. He had heard enough about him to believe that he was like his father, and he wanted nothing to do with either until they changed their ways.

He also blamed the boy for getting kidnapped in the first place, and thereby involving him, his grandfather, with the

At eighty-three, Paul Getty had had three face-lifts, the last of which had failed, making him look inordinately old.

Getty with his mistress, Mary Teissier. 'She was utterly obsessed with him. From the day they met until the day he died there was absolutely no one else.'

Paul II and his wife Talitha on the jungly patio of their house, Le Palais Da Zahir (the Pleasure Palace) in Marrakesh.

On the hippie trail. Paul II at a peace demonstration in Rome in 1969.

Paul III shortly after his kidnap in 1973. His lost right ear was later rebuilt with cartilage taken from one of his ribs.

John Paul Getty III with his wife Martine and children Balthazar and Anna in London, 1976.

J. Paul Getty in
the dining room
of Sutton Place,
circa 1960.

In the film, J. Paul Getty (Kevin Spacey) reconnects with his son John Paul Getty II (Andrew Buchan), his wife Gail Getty (Michelle Williams) and grandson John 'Paul' Getty III (Charlie Shotwell).

Sixteen-year-old Paul Getty (Charlie Plummer) is kidnapped in Rome.

The kidnappers call Gail and demand $17 million for Paul's return.

Getty sends his advisor Fletcher Chace (Mark Wahlberg) to assess the situation.

A desperate Gail pleads for the kidnappers to set her son free.

The captors grow increasingly angry that the ransom has not been paid.

Getty informs the press that he will not pay the ransom for his grandson.

Fletcher Chace urges Getty to pay the ransom.

dreaded Mafia. For the truth was that the old man had been terrified of kidnap even before Paul disappeared. This was why he had never stayed for long at La Posta Vecchia (where he had kept the loaded shotgun in his bedroom), and at Sutton Place was already taking serious advice from his personal security expert, Colonel Leon Turrou.

For several years Turrou, a Frenchman and former CIA agent, had studied the techniques of kidnap prevention and had written a book on the classic case of the 1930s, the kidnapping of the Lindbergh baby in America. A scared old billionaire like Paul Getty was an ideal client, and by now the Colonel had placed him in a state of semi-siege at Sutton Place, with armed guards in the house, lethal Alsatians in the grounds, and the latest in surveillance technology almost everywhere. Impressive locks and a bulletproof steel plate were fitted to his bedroom door, and armed guards with unsmiling faces drove before and after his Cadillac on the few occasions when he ventured out.

His grandson's kidnap made things that much worse, and so terrified was the old man that he became scared to answer the telephone, firmly refusing to use it to discuss anything remotely connected with the kidnap just in case the Mafia got through to him. As Gail put it, 'He seemed to think that they might come up and grab him through the telephone.'

Perhaps he did, although his fear of the telephone probably had a simpler explanation. In Paris eight months earlier, the Israeli secret service, the Mossad, had actually used the telephone in an attempt to assassinate Mahmoud Hamshari, the PLO representative in France. A small Semtex device with an electronic sensor had been planted in Hamshari's apartment, and when the Israelis reached him on the telephone, they were able to transmit a signal down the line to activate the bomb which nearly killed him.

At the time the case made a stir among intelligence professionals; as one of them, Turrou would certainly have known about it, and it was just the sort of tale to have captured Paul

Getty's imagination. Certainly, throughout the period of his grandson's kidnap, he took exceptional precautions with anyone he spoke to on the telephone, and for anything related to the kidnap would generally get Penelope to speak on his behalf.

Not that he ever talked about the kidnap if he could help it. As he had shown when Timmy died, he couldn't cope with unhappiness or grief, nor would he permit anyone to question his decisions. As Penelope put it, 'With the kidnapping it was quite frightening to see how totally the shutters descended on the subject.'

Three weeks had passed since Paul had disappeared, yet nothing had been done to further his release. Apart from the two letters there had been no further contact with the kidnappers either. The Carabinieri had drawn a total blank on their identity, Paul Getty Senior was standing absolutely firm against paying them a cent, and Paul Getty Junior was insisting there was nothing he could do.

In Rome everything continued to devolve on Gail, who was living through a more and more appalling nightmare. Time dragged interminably, for as she says, 'In a kidnap situation, every hour is twice as long as an ordinary hour.' Apart from a few friends there was no one else she could turn to. The only members of the family who came near her were old Willem and Poppet Pol, who had flown to Rome from the South of France on hearing of the kidnap and had now returned to Ramatuelle with five-year-old Tara. She was sad to see him go, but she was also grateful, as it would have been hard to cope with a five-year-old while doing her best to keep Aileen and Ariadne happy.

That wasn't easy either, as she was feeling anything but calm herself. She was powerless and desperately anxious, yet she knew she had to keep her wits about her to deal with the kidnappers when and if they did decide to call. All she could do was go on sitting by that telephone until they rang – which finally they did when least expected, late in the evening of 30 July.

She recognized the voice of the man who had telephoned

originally, and this time he introduced himself. To identify himself in future, he would give himself a code name she could easily remember – the word *Cinquanta* – Fifty.

As before, he sounded oddly respectful, using the third person singular and calling her *'signora'*; but when she broke the news that no money was forthcoming for the ransom, he exploded – first with anger then with disbelief. He could not believe that anyone as rich as Paul Getty utterly refused to pay, and accused her of a trick. She tried explaining the old man's reasons – naturally without success. As an Italian, Cinquanta simply couldn't comprehend anyone behaving like that.

'Who is this so-called grandfather?' he shouted. 'How can he leave his own flesh and blood in the plight that your poor son is in? Here is the richest man in America, and you tell me he refuses to find just ten *miliardi* for his grandson's safety. *Signora*, you take me for a fool. What you say is just not possible.'

Gail could hardly say that she agreed with him, but she did her best to calm him down, saying that she needed time, and begging him to be as kind as possible to Paul. He said he would, but told her to contact the rest of the family to get the money.

Most families draw closer in a crisis and support each other during a disaster, but not the Gettys. With his limitless money and his close connections with Italy, the old man could certainly have got the boy released quite swiftly had he wished. Gail believes that 'had Big Paul dealt with the kidnap as he dealt with a business deal in his prime, Paul would have been free within twenty-four hours.'

But not only was Big Paul refusing to do so: by cutting off from Gail completely and retreating into his fortress at Sutton Place, he had effectively paralysed the family as well, since none of them wanted to offend him. As he was not on speaking terms with Paul Junior, and Gordon and Ronald were both in America, one of the richest families in the world was rendered incapable of helping a grandson of sixteen who was in peril of his life.

Nor was any support forthcoming for Gail herself at a time when she was sick with anxiety, harassed by the press, and trying desperately to keep the rest of her family afloat while she dealt with the kidnappers. By now she had started to receive countless letters of support and sympathy from unknown people round the world, but not a word from any member of the family.

It was then that she saw the Getty family for what it was – remote, unreachable, closed off from human contact. It all went back to Big Paul himself, who had always used his money as a substitute for human feeling. She felt that being a Getty was like becoming part of a mathematical progression; as the family empire had grown more complex and remote, those within it found it impossible to maintain normal relationships with any-one outside. Like Big Paul, they too became frightened, always needing to protect themselves and their precious money from outsiders.

It was only now that she realized how different they all were from her parents and her own supportive family, and that some-thing human had been lost as the great financial empire had expanded. How lifeless and devoid of love it had become. And Big Paul was the most loveless and lifeless of them all.

August started with a heat wave. Italy had gone on holiday and it was as if those responsible for finding young Paul Getty had gone on holiday as well. It was possibly the heat. But nothing at all was happening. Officially it was the task of the Carabinieri to deal with the crime and rescue Paul, but as they were having not the faintest glimmer of success they had fallen back on the eas-ier option of claiming that the kidnap was a hoax.

According to their theory, Paul and his so-called 'hippie friends' had simply staged the whole affair to extract money from the family. There was not a shred of evidence to support this; it was inconceivable that Paul would torture his mother in this way, and his subsequent sufferings totally disproved it.

But as a theory it was a convenient way of saving face for

incompetent policemen. Face, *figura*, is particularly important for the Carabinieri, as for most Italians, and they could claim, as claim they did, that the reason they were getting nowhere was not because of their incompetence, but because there had been no kidnap in the first place.

The hoax idea was also attractive to the general public. Romans love rumours, particularly cynical ones about the rich, and even more about rich foreigners. So the story gathered credence in the press and was soon reported back to Britain, where it inevitably reached the patriarch of Sutton Place. Given his attitude towards the ransom – and his grandson – it clearly suited him to believe it too.

'D'you think the boy and his mother cooked this up together for the money?' he is said to have asked his personal assistant, Norris Bramlett.

The reaction to the story at Cheyne Walk was not dissimilar. As usual in the face of unhappiness and worry, Paul Junior had become more reclusive, resorting increasingly to drink and drugs, so that Gail was finding it more and more difficult to get through to him by telephone. Now the suggestion that his son was simply indulging in a massive practical joke ended his anxiety, and gave him and the family a perfect alibi. Not only did it excuse them for doing nothing; it also reassured them with the thought that, far from being kidnapped, that 'rascal' Paul was hiding somewhere with his friends in perfect safety.

But as he was actually still chained up like an animal in a hovel in the wilds of Calabria with a group of increasingly edgy criminals trying to extort a ransom for his life, the situation was in fact becoming dangerous. Apart from antagonizing his captors still further, the hoax rumour meant that if they were to get their money, they would need to do something to prove beyond the shadow of a doubt that the kidnap was genuine.

By the fourth week of the kidnap there was still no movement, and Gail was desperate. Since her angry conversation with

Cinquanta, she had heard no more from him. This endless waiting was the chief component of her misery. Throughout the day
she was still waiting by the telephone for news – and when
none came she began imagining all the horrors which could
have befallen her son – an accident, illness, violence from his
captors, anything was possible. The greatest torture was the total
lack of information.

By the second week of that stifling August, she could bear
it no longer. She had to get news from Paul, and it was then that
her lawyer, Giovanni Jacovoni, suggested she should make a
direct appeal to the kidnappers on Italian television.

She was wary of doing this, as her experiences with the
Italian media were far from happy. In the first few days of the
kidnap she had tried being helpful to reporters, but when there
was nothing to report, they became hungry for fresh stories and
turned on her instead, criticizing her attitude towards her son,
her role as a mother, and her situation as a member of the richest family on earth.

'They felt that somebody must be to blame for what had
happened, and since there was no one else around, they picked
on me.'

It was bad enough being blamed for being a Getty; she was
also the victim of the cultural differences between Anglo-Saxons
and Italians. As an American, she was a great believer in maintaining the stiffest of stiff upper lips in public – if only out of
pride and to avoid upsetting everyone in the family, especially
her parents and Mark, who was still with them back in San
Francisco.

As she put it, 'I was damned if I was going to show my grief
publicly, and share it with a couple of million newspaper
readers.'

But this was not what the Italian media wanted. When
disaster hits an Italian family, there has to be a sorrowing mother,
mater dolorosa, with eyes turned hopelessly to heaven and body
racked with anguish. When Gail failed to oblige, the media
treated her with deep suspicion.

Because of this, she insisted on making her television appeal to Paul's kidnappers on her own, direct to camera; but the producer, anxious for some real-life drama, brought a reporter with him when he arrived for the recording. Gail objected, but the producer was insistent. Only when he promised her extremely sympathetic questions did she agree. But a few minutes into the interview and the reporter paused, stared her full in the face, then asked her in a voice of doom: '*Signora*, do you think your son is dead?'

For the second time since Paul had disappeared she fainted. She had been refusing to accept this possibility for so long that when someone actually suggested it, something snapped within her. By suppressing so much strain and worry over the last few weeks she had brought herself to breaking point, and needed several days in bed to recover.

But the interview brought results from the kidnappers. Soon after it was broadcast, Cinquanta called again to reassure her that Paul was certainly alive – and well.

'How do I know you're telling me the truth?' she answered.

The kidnapper thought before replying – then told her to ask him certain questions he would put to Paul to which only he could know the answer. He would call her back with the replies, and if they were right she'd know her son had to be alive.

So she began asking questions such as 'What is the picture on the left of the door in Aileen's bedroom?' or 'What is the name of our next-door neighbour's cat?' When Cinquanta called her back that afternoon with the correct answers it was virtually the first crumb of reassurance she had had since Paul's letter.

This was the start of more regular conversations between her and Cinquanta, and to a point she felt they came to understand each other. She had read somewhere that in kidnap situations the negotiators always try to establish a human relationship with someone among the kidnappers. She also had a vague idea of picking up some crucial piece of information from these conversations, but she never did. The most she ever learned about

Cinquanta was that he had a wife and children, and on one occasion she asked him how as an Italian he could be involved in such a cruel crime against a family.

'*Signora,* it's a job like any other,' he answered. And although he continued bringing her Paul's answers to her questions, he never actually forgot his 'job' for long. He kept telling her how urgent it was to start negotiations. Some of his friends were becoming unpleasantly impatient. He also kept repeating something that she couldn't bear to hear – the danger her son was facing if the Getty family continued to regard the kidnap as a hoax and refused to take it seriously.

It was now five weeks since Paul had disappeared, and from things Cinquanta said, Gail was becoming frightened that the kidnappers were about to harm him. She told her father so when she telephoned him in San Francisco, and since Judge Harris was one of the few people Jean Paul Getty respected and would talk to on the subject, the Judge was able to convince him that something must be done.

The old man still insisted he would never pay a ransom, but he did agree to send somebody to Rome to offer Gail professional support and deal with the situation. The man he chose was a former spy who worked for Getty Oil, J. Fletcher Chace.

Chace has been described as 'one of the good ole boys from the good ole CIA', and since retiring he had worked as security adviser to the Getty installations in the Neutral Zone. At six foot four, with very bright blue eyes and craggy profile, he was a handsome man, and Getty, who was impressed by clean-cut men of action, thought him the ideal character to deal with the case. But as far as his grandson Paul was now concerned, Fletcher Chace was probably the worst emissary the old man could have chosen.

★

For by now the situation in Rome had actually become extremely simple. From the moment Paul was kidnapped there had been two alternatives if he was going to return alive – either the police would catch the kidnappers, or the Gettys would have to pay a large sum of money as a ransom. After more than a month of trying, it was clear that the Carabinieri couldn't have solved the case had Paul been held by Donald Duck – which left the family to face the second option. However distasteful it might be, the only point remaining to be settled was to negotiate a price – and get the boy released as soon and painlessly as possible. Anything else was quite irrelevant, and would serve only to extend the agony.

But since Jean Paul Getty utterly refused to pay a ransom, the agony had to be prolonged until he would, and handsome Fletcher Chace prolonged it with a vengeance.

Like many old ex-spies, Chace was a great conspiracy theorist. He was also highly confident of his abilities. When he arrived in Rome on 12 August Gail was relieved to have this assured professional to deal with the case. One of his first priorities was to make contact with the kidnappers in person, so she readily agreed to let him take the call when Cinquanta next telephoned. But Chace spoke no Italian, and his rusty Spanish started by baffling Cinquanta, then annoyed him, and finally convinced him that, for all his warnings, the Getty family still refused to take the kidnap seriously.

Chace was in fact a natural victim for the double-dealing and deceit which was building up around the whole affair. As a former spy he might have realized that the girl he met in his hotel and started sleeping with was actually an agent on the payroll of the Carabinieri and that her task, apart from making Fletcher feel at home, was to feed him the views of those she worked for and find out what he knew himself.

Chace actually knew very little. There had been numerous reports of false sightings of Paul – several from people Gail knew quite well – and as Chace insisted on following each one up personally, this took time. There was one from a plausible young man who claimed to know where Paul was hiding, and who took him to the monastery town of Monte Cassino, where he pocketed the $3,000 Chace offered him and promptly disappeared.

So, far from bringing matters to a head, Chace's arrival on the scene served to complicate the situation which was already getting out of hand, and postpone yet further any chance of serious negotiations. Indeed, by the end of August a distraught and highly frustrated Fletcher Chace was falling back on the Carabinieri's theory of a hoax. Baffled, bad-tempered and thoroughly bewildered, Chace believed he was at the centre of a considerable conspiracy himself – and reported all the details back to Sutton Place, where they strengthened the old man's resolution not to pay a penny.

It was now early September, and to deal with this supposed conspiracy, Chace thought the time had come to baffle the opposition and the Italian press by taking Gail and the children out of circulation. Given the situation, it was actually extremely dangerous to break off contact with a group of jumpy and potentially dangerous kidnappers at a time like this, but Chace was adamant, and insisted on flying Gail and the children back to London, where for ten days he kept them in conditions of maximum security in a carefully prepared 'safe house' at Kingston-upon-Thames.

It was the sort of cloak and dagger operation he enjoyed, but its connection with a kidnapped boy in Calabria was none too clear. Nor did it give Gail the chance that she was counting on for meaningful discussion with her former husband – nor with Big Paul himself at nearby Sutton Place. Paul Junior had been growing even more reclusive, and when she saw him at Cheyne Walk he refused to talk about the kidnap.

So did his father, who was so frightened of the Mafia by now that he insisted any contact with Gail had to be through Chace. Chace made even this an undercover operation, meeting her at secret rendezvous in the park, but although he promised to

convey her frantic pleas to Getty to do something for his grandson, there was never any answer. Big Paul was sticking by his
principles, and was now thoroughly imbued with Chace's version of events, and the tales of the undercover world he told
him. After ten days Gail and her family had had enough and
returned to Rome. Chace remained for several days at Sutton
Place to reassure his master.

By mid-September it was clear that the situation was a disaster
and that none of the people meant to deal with it could cope.
But two things did make Gail's life a little happier. The first was
that she managed to move to a new apartment in the heart of
old Rome, in a livelier area than anonymous Parioli. The new
flat practically overlooked the old Campo dei Fiori market;
both the girls loved it, and she felt less of a prisoner than she had
in Parioli.

The second was that a member of the Getty family arrived
to keep her company – her thirteen-year-old son Mark. Despite
determined efforts by his grandparents to keep him safely in San
Francisco, he had been pining for his family and in the end they
had to let him go. In her new flat and with Mark beside her,
Gail began to feel a little stronger.

This was as well, as relations between Cinquanta and the
kidnappers were worsening dramatically. Cinquanta had already
warned her that, baffled by the silence in the press, members of
the gang were planning something drastic which would prove
they still meant business.

From the way he spoke Gail knew he wasn't bluffing – any
more than he was taken in by her excuses for failing with the
ransom – and he suddenly produced a fresh demand.

'*Signora*, you must come to talk to us yourself. We will deal
with this together. You will be able to see your son, and I will
guarantee your safety.'

She asked for time to think this over. He replied that he
would telephone next day for her decision.

All her instincts told her she should go. Of course she knew the dangers, but by now she was long past caring. For she also knew that she was doing Paul no good in Rome, and that if things were left to Chace and the Carabinieri the kidnap could go on for ever. By meeting Paul's captors face to face, there was at least a hope of bringing the situation to a head and diverting their anger from her son. She was also naturally excited by the chance of seeing him again.

So when Cinquanta telephoned she said she'd come. He seemed relieved and gave precise instructions. She was to drive a car of a certain make with a bumper sticker and a white suitcase on the roof-rack. She should travel so many kilometres down the *autostrada* to a point south of Naples, where a man would be waiting by the roadside at a certain time. He would throw gravel at her windscreen as a signal for her to stop. Someone from the gang would then take over and bring her to the place where Paul was hidden. Once again Cinquanta guaranteed her safety. Gail said she understood and once again agreed to come.

But afterwards pressure rapidly built up against the whole idea. When she told Judge Harris he was alarmed for her safety and told her some of the risks she would be taking. 'What would happen to the other children if they killed you – as they might – and what good would that do Paul?'

Chace, now back in Rome, was even more opposed to the idea, and firmly banned her from going. With so much opposition, Gail changed her mind.

She now believes that this was 'a terrible mistake. For had I gone, it could have brought everybody to their senses and got things moving. Besides, I would have been with Paul, and might have stopped them doing what they did.'

Instead, her last-minute cancellation of the meeting made relations with the kidnappers that much worse. She had no way of telling them she'd changed her mind, and they were furious when she failed to come. Even the normally polite Cinquanta was enraged when he telephoned her later, accusing her of playing tricks like all the others. At one point they were

screaming at each other down the telephone, and the call concluded with Cinquanta saying he had done his best, that harder
men would now take over and that whatever happened wasn't
his responsibility.

As Gail soon discovered, Cinquanta wasn't bluffing, and
Paul's sufferings began in earnest as his captors took their anger
out on him. They began by confiscating his radio, which had
been his one link with the world outside. Fresh chains were
fastened on his legs. A small bird he had made a pet of was killed
before his eyes. Then they told him that, because his grandfather
wouldn't pay to save him, the time had come to do the same to
him. They kept him bound and gagged for several hours, then
played Russian roulette against his forehead with a .45 revolver.

He never knew if the gun was loaded. After it failed to go
off several times he was blindfolded, bound more tightly than
ever and left like this until next morning.

Around this time a fresh event occurred which added to his
misery. As Cinquanta had hinted, some of the original kidnappers sold out their stakes in Paul just as they might have sold on
a piece of real estate or a share in a casino. The new purchasers
ranked higher in the N'drangeta and were particularly anxious
to raise capital to develop the narcotics business on their own
account. They were older and more ruthless men than their
predecessors, and were looking for a quick return on their
investment.

Paul's captors were unusually affable that morning, which
instantly aroused his suspicions. October had come, and with
the colder weather they had been giving him cheap Italian
brandy to keep him warm, but never before in the morning.
When he said it was too early to start drinking, they told him to
take it – it would do him good. Then they told him that his hair
had grown too long and needed cutting.

He tried to argue with them. He liked his hair long, and
didn't want it cut, but they said it was dirty and insisted. He

might have struggled but there were four or five of them, and he had grown weak with captivity and could see that they meant business. So he sat quietly as one of the men sheared clumsily at his long red hair with small blunt scissors. It was the first time he had had a haircut from a barber with a mask, and the man took particular care to clear the hair from each side of his head. When he finished, he dabbed alcohol behind his ears.

It was then Paul guessed what they intended.

Again he might have struggled, but again he knew there was no point. If he attempted to resist them they would only hurt him, and they would end up doing as they wanted.

So when they offered him more brandy he drank it. And when they gave him a rolled-up handkerchief to bite on, he placed it in his mouth and started biting. And while he was still biting he felt somebody behind him grab his right ear between a roughened thumb and finger and hold it tight.

Then came the searing pain as with one swift stroke of a cutthroat razor the whole right ear was severed from his newly shorn head.

On 21 October Cinquanta informed Gail of what had happened but refused to elaborate. At first she refused to believe him, but he insisted it was true and said he would send her photographs to prove it.

Like any mother, she felt sick with horror at the thought of the mutilation of her child. Despite so many warnings, she had never quite believed that Cinquanta and his friends would do it. Now that they had, she tried to stop herself thinking about it all the time. But it was hard to stop brooding over the savagery of such men and the fear and suffering they had cold-bloodedly inflicted on her child.

With this latest touch of horror she began to wonder how much longer this interminable kidnap would continue – and how much longer she and, more important, Paul could take it.

As a result of a call to the police, polaroid snapshots of Paul were discovered in a waste bin at a certain spot in Rome. They had been taken recently outside a cave, and when Gail saw them she was horrified, for they showed an emaciated Paul and the unhealed wound where his ear had been.

Shortly afterwards Cinquanta rang again. He asked if she believed him now, and said he had warned her it would happen. He added that the ear was in the post.

She was too numbed to argue with him then, but later, when the ear failed to arrive, and Cinquanta rang again to ask if she had received it, there were furious exchanges, with Cinquanta insisting that the authorities must have it, and Gail attempting to express something of her rage and horror at what had happened.

By now the disappearance of the ear itself was creating yet another mystery, more misunderstandings, and further excuses for inaction.

The kidnappers had in fact sealed it in a plastic container filled with preserving fluid, which in turn had been placed inside a padded bag and mailed from the main post office at Reggio Calabria to the editorial offices of *Il Messaggero* on 20 October.

If nothing else the arrival of this gruesome package should have ended all talk of hoaxes and added a sense of urgency to the negotiations. It would have done so anywhere but in Italy, but as Gore Vidal happened to observe around this time, 'There is no such thing as a mail service in Rome.' Officially a postal strike was in progress, and Paul's ear, along with countless other parcels for the city, mouldered in a warehouse till the strike was over.

Finally, on 10 November – three weeks after the mutilation – the package was delivered to the offices of *Il Messaggero* in the Via del Corso – and the editor's secretary who opened the parcel fainted.

By now Gail, having lost all faith in the Carabinieri, had enlisted the support of their rivals, the Italian Polizia. Carlo, the head of the Polizia Statale Squadra Mobile – the Rome Flying Squad – had taken on the case and proved an energetic and effective officer. He had helped Gail come to terms with what had happened, and prepared her for the grisly task of identifying the ear, if it ever did arrive. At his suggestion she had studied photographs of Paul to check upon its shape and appearance.

So when Carlo told her it had arrived, and asked her to come to police headquarters, she was more self-possessed than the secretary at *Il Messaggero* had been. She ignored the press photographers waiting for her outside the building, and was quite positive when confronted with the ear. Yes, she recognized it by the freckles and the shape. It certainly belonged to her son.

It was four months now since Paul had been taken, but even now his agony was far from over.

There had been some small advances. Through Judge Harris, who was a prominent San Francisco Catholic, the Vatican had become involved, and Gail had met 'the Pope's Gorilla', the massive Archbishop Casimir Marcinkus from Chicago, who had been very charming and said he might be able to assist her. This was the priest who would later become notorious for his connections with the corrupt financier Sindona, and also with Roberto Calvi, the head of the Banca Ambrosiana, who ended up hanging under Blackfriars Bridge in London. So it was probably as well that Chace refused to let her take advantage of the Archbishop's underworld connections when he told her, 'I know some important people who I'm sure could help you. If you like I'll talk to them about your son.'

The American government was also showing signs of some concern, since Gail had sent a personal message to President Nixon. Thomas Biamonte, a highly competent ex-FBI lawyer of Calabrian extraction who worked in the US Embassy in Rome, was assigned to the case, and speaking the local dialect of Calabria, had made useful contact with the kidnappers on his own account. Largely as a result of this, the kidnappers had dropped their demands from 10 *miliardi*, or $17.4 million, to a

more realistic 2 *miliardi*, approximately $3.2 million. But having
lowered their price, they had also made it very clear that they
were sticking to it.

Back in Sutton Place, Paul's eighty-year-old grandfather was
also holding out. Hoax or no hoax, ear or no ear, principles
were principles, and he still refused to pay a penny.

As winter started in the uplands of Calabria and the injured boy
was dragged to yet another hiding place, his captors issued one
more ultimatum. They were showing signs of losing patience
once again, and said that if there was no deal soon, a second ear
would be on its way to *Il Messaggero*, followed by further por-
tions of the kidnapped boy's anatomy if it failed to get results.

Paul himself was in a wretched state by now. The pain of the
rough-and-ready amputation had continued, and infection had
set in. Cold and malnourishment coupled with nervous shock
from the operation had left him weakened and dispirited. Since
childhood he had suffered from weak lungs, and what had
started as a bad cold rapidly became pneumonia. His captors,
anxious not to lose $3.2 million, began injecting him with such
massive doses of penicillin that he became allergic to it. When
he couldn't take any more antibiotics and his condition continued to deteriorate, they panicked.

As a last resort Cinquanta telephoned Gail to ask her for
advice.

'*Signora*. You must tell me. What can we do for him?' he
wailed, unable to disguise his anxiety for Paul's condition, and
knowing that he and his colleagues could lose everything if his
illness worsened.

This was the point when Gail knew for certain that if the
kidnap lasted any longer, Paul would die. Nothing on earth was
worth that – not Big Paul's precious principles and his fears for
his other grandchildren, nor the fortune of the Gettys nor the
problems over raising so much money.

So she decided that the kidnap had to end. If no one else

would end it, she would. If no one else could save her son, she would save him.

She told Cinquanta to keep Paul as warm as possible and get ready to release him. The ransom would be paid.

Gail's determination effectively transformed the situation. Suddenly her single-mindedness became contagious. She spoke to her father, who argued so forcibly on the telephone to Sutton Place that Big Paul finally gave in and agreed that somehow the money would be found. But even now, the old man was typically insisting that he would pay only the portion of the ransom which would be tax-deductible – the boy's father had to foot the rest.

This caused problems, as Gail could no longer make meaningful contact with Paul Junior, who was making little sense to anyone. But he did finally agree to his father's terms. Since he hadn't got the million dollars which he had to put towards the ransom, Big Paul would lend it to him, at 4 per cent interest, computed annually. But Gail had been led to understand that as a precondition of payment Paul Junior was insisting that she immediately surrender custody of all her children.

Gail thought she could bear anything by now, but this was the cruellest blow of all. She had endured five months of hell to save her son, and at the moment when she almost had him back, it seemed she had to lose him – and the rest of her children.

There was nothing to be done, however, and her feelings were no longer terribly important. All that mattered was the money – and to get her son released as soon as possible. So she wearily agreed, even getting as far as making arrangements to get the children to the airport – only to discover there had been yet another misunderstanding and Paul Junior was denying ever having asked for custody.

This was typical of the atmosphere of drama and distrust which hovered round the kidnap to the very end. But Jean Paul Getty had agreed in principle. That was what counted – even if he would contribute only $2.2 million of the ransom directly. This was all that his accountants told him could be tax-deductible; so he stuck to his demand that his son should pay the rest in regular instalments from his income from the Sarah C. Getty Trust.

Gail was dreading something else occurring up to the very last, but on 6 December Chace received authorization to withdraw the massive sum of 2,000 million lire in used 50,000 and 100,000 lire notes. All had been microfilmed, and the notes filled three large holdalls which he actually took to the US Embassy on the Via Veneto for safe keeping.

Even now there was a muddle caused by fog and snow on the *autostrada* north of Naples, which was in the grip of its worst winter for nearly fifty years. On the first trip with the money, Chace failed to make contact with the kidnappers. Tempers frayed, and Gail was afraid of yet more drama that could prolong the five-month agony. But on 12 December, Chace picked up the three bags from the US Embassy for the second time and drove 250 miles south of Rome to the rendezvous Cinquanta had arranged. Four kilometres to the south of the turn-off to the town of Lagonegro he spotted a man standing by the road, pistol in hand and balaclava helmet obscuring his face. Chace stopped the car, desposited the three bags by the road and returned to Rome. He had been shadowed all the way by members of the Squadra Mobile, disguised as workmen in a van, who had photographed the man in the balaclava.

Although the kidnap was so nearly over, Gail still had to face the cruellest wait of all. Next day she heard nothing, nor the day after, and she became convinced that, having got the money, the kidnappers must have killed her son. From their point of view it would have made a sort of sense to have taken the ransom and destroyed the evidence – Paul included.

By the evening of the 14th she was on the edge of despair,

convinced by now that what she dreaded had happened. Five months of misery had ended with a silent telephone.

But at 10.30 at night the telephone did ring. It was Cinquanta. He was very formal. He could have been someone in a bank, confirming that the money had been paid, and that his colleagues were keeping their side of the bargain and releasing Paul within the next few hours. He would be left on a hillside close to where Chace had left the money. He gave a precise description of the spot, adding that Gail should come there on her own to fetch him.

'Please keep him warm,' she said, mindful of the freezing weather.

'I'll make sure he has a blanket,' said Cinquanta. Those were the last words he spoke to Gail, and she never heard his voice again.

All thought of sleep was over for the night. The police had been tapping Gail's telephone and passed the gist of the conversation on to the Squadra Mobile, who soon arrived at her apartment. She rang Chace, who came at once. By midnight, she and Chace were in the back of a car from the Squadra Mobile with Carlo at the wheel.

For most of the way it was snowing heavily, and dawn was breaking when they reached the hillside. The countryside was white, and in the early light there was no sign of Paul. They called his name to no avail. Gail whistled as she and the children used to whistle to each other at Orgia. Paul would have recognized the call at once, but there was still no answer.

'You must be prepared – they may have killed him,' said Chace, as the men from the Squadra Mobile went on searching the hillside without discovering any sign of Paul. Then they heard one of the men shouting. He had found something at last – an old blanket, and a blindfold. They must have belonged to Paul, and were the first evidence they had that he was still alive. But where was he?

'You know your son,' Carlo said to Gail. 'What would he have done?'

'Headed for home,' she said.

So the Squadra Mobile drove slowly up the *autostrada* searching for Paul, with Gail and Chace in the back of a squad car. They saw nothing, but over the car radio they picked up a report from the police. An unidentified male had been found in the vicinity, and taken to the headquarters of the Carabinieri at Lagonegro.

At the *caserma* of the Carabinieri in Lagonegro, no one would admit at first that Paul was even there – and when someone did, Gail was told she could not see him as he was being interrogated. The reason for this apparent hostility lay in the fact that she was with members of the Squadra Mobile, who have always been at daggers-drawn with the Carabinieri – and the Carabinieri were determined to retain the credit for 'rescuing' Paul Getty.

But Gail had endured too much by now to bother with such niceties.

'I want my son,' she said. 'Let me see my son.' And the sight of this angry and exhausted woman calling for her child made the officials relent, and finally they brought him to her.

He was so thin and ill that she scarcely recognized him as he came shuffling in, wearing clothes the Carabinieri had bought specially for him. He was filthy, he could barely walk, and a bloodstained bandage round his head covered the wound where his ear had been.

Now that the moment they had longed for had arrived, Gail and Paul were both too overcome to speak. They clung to one another, and it was only when she held him in her arms that she knew for certain that the long ordeal was over.

All that mattered was to get Paul safely back to Rome, and before the Carabinieri could object, she and Chace half dragged him to the waiting car outside and started on the journey home.

All she remembers of the journey is that 'Paul and I were both like zombies, and so tense with emotion that we could still barely speak to one another.'

By the time they reached Naples, news of Paul's release was on the radio, and at Rome reporters were waiting for them by the toll booths as they left the *autostrada*. People were waiting in the street to watch as they drove by. Some of them cheered and waved, but Gail could feel nothing but a sense of total unreality, and relief that the horror of the last five months was over. As yet she had no inkling of the damage that these months had done to Paul – and to her, and to all the family.

A friend had already booked both of them into a clinic in Parioli, where they spent the next three days recovering before going off on holiday to Austria. On their arrival at the clinic, the doctors had examined Paul and the results seemed reassuring. He was young and strong. Physically he'd soon recover, and with modern plastic surgery, even his ear could be rebuilt.

'And the psychological effects?' Gail asked.

Time alone would tell, the doctor answered.

That afternoon, Gail remembered the date – 15 December, Big Paul's birthday. He was eighty-one, and she suggested that it might be tactful if Paul telephoned his grandfather to thank him for what he'd done for him and wish him a very happy birthday.

At Sutton Place, the old man was in his study when the call came through and one of his women came to tell him who was on the line.

'It's your grandson, Paul. Do you wish to speak to him?' she asked.

'No,' he answered.

CHAPTER SIXTEEN

THE DYNASTY

B EHIND THE GRIM façade which Jean Paul Getty managed to maintain throughout the kidnap, things were beginning to go wrong at Sutton Place.

This had nothing at all to do with his commercial interests, which had never looked brighter. The worldwide oil shortage following the Arab–Israeli Yom Kippur war of October 1973 had quadrupled the price of oil from $3 to $12 a barrel on the international market, and shares in Getty Oil were rising steadily. During 1975 the old man would increase the company's cash dividend from $1.30 to $2.50 a share, thus incidentally awarding himself a record income for the year of $25,800,000. By then he and the Sarah C. Getty Trust between them would be worth a staggering $2.4 billion.

But this flow of wealth could not prevent an ill-defined but most disturbing feeling which had started to affect him. It was something he had not experienced before, and was as painful as it was unexpected. At the age of eighty-two, one of the richest men in the world was experiencing a sense of failure.

It had started two years earlier, shortly after his eightieth birthday party at the Dorchester Hotel, which had been arranged by the Duchess of Argyll. At the party everything had still been wonderful. When his friend the Duke of Bedford had proposed the toast – 'May the many witty and lovely ladies around him grow even wittier and lovelier' – everyone applauded. President Nixon had sent his daughter, Tricia, especially to represent him;

and at midnight the President himself had telephoned from Washington with birthday greetings to his loyal supporter and generous contributor to the Nixon funds, his good friend, Jean Paul Getty.

But a few months later the unthinkable had occurred. His confidante and friend Penelope Kitson left him. When she told him she intended getting married once again, to businessman Patrick de Laszlo, he had done everything he could to stop her, including using the ultimate Getty sanction – cutting her from his precious will. He was upset to find this made no difference – but was mollified when the marriage failed some months later, and Penelope returned to see him.

'I won't say I' m sorry, dear,' was all he said – and quietly reinstated her into his will and her cottage on the estate. But Penelope's show of independence had upset him, as had reactions to something else that meant a lot to him – the official opening of his museum at Malibu at the beginning of 1974.

Getty's architect, the amiable Englishman Stephen Garrett, had always had his doubts about the whole idea of recreating this Roman villa by the shores of the Pacific, and had tried to warn his patron. But Getty wouldn't listen, and had continued to follow every detail of the construction from 6,000 miles away in Sutton Place. But when it was opened, Getty's precious dream-child was greeted with almost unanimous derision by the press. 'Vulgar', 'tasteless', 'straight out of Disneyland' were among the reactions, and the London *Economist* was particularly snooty. Art historians, it said, would be pushed to decide if Jean Paul Getty's folly was 'merely incongruous or genuinely ludicrous'.

As usual when faced by something that he didn't like, the old man narrowed his already very narrow lips, and said nothing. But coming right on top of widespread criticism of his behaviour over the kidnap, these reactions to his museum genuinely shook him. Later he would write of young Paul's release having been 'the finest and most wonderful birthday present of my life'. Few believed him.

Faced with a similar situation, poorer men had mortgaged homes, borrowed what they could from friends, even gone into bankruptcy in their attempts to find the money for a grand-child's ransom. And it did not entirely pass notice that while Getty had refused to find the money on the grounds of his so-called principles, he had finally overlooked his principles when he had to; also that by delaying payment of the ransom for as long as possible, he had actually forced the kidnappers to drop the asking price from their original figure of $17 million to $3.2 million – a saving of some $13.8 million.

As a businessman this was something he was certainly aware of. And if it meant that to achieve it his once favourite grand-son had been forced to suffer a five-month nightmare with the Mafia, he presumably felt the price worth paying.

But now he must have had his doubts. For the kidnap proved a genuine disaster to the family as well as to Getty himself. The boy's own sufferings had barely started, and in different ways the damage would continue spreading, bringing yet further misery and grief for years to come.

This was not evident at once. After the kidnap, Gail and her son spent two months quietly recuperating in the Austrian moun-tains with Aileen, Mark and Ariadne. The mountains calmed their fears, restored their spirits and they were soon enjoying life again. Years later Aileen would be remembering this holiday as the last time she had been carefree and completely happy. The rest of the family felt much the same, and they returned from Austria believing that the nightmare of the kidnap was over and forgotten.

It was a good sign that the kidnap had made curiously little difference to their feelings for Italy, and once Gail was safely back in her house at Orgia she shrugged off suggestions from her friends that she might possibly be in need of therapy.

Young Paul had been reunited with Martine by now, and it was only when he returned to Rome to be with her, leaving Gail alone at last, that she realized how right her friends had been. 'For suddenly and without warning, I quietly fell apart.'

She was hit by nightmares from the period of the kidnap, followed by uncontrollable fits of weeping. She took to bed in the depths of black depression. Then slowly, painfully, she pulled herself together.

At this stage, Paul appeared less affected by the kidnap than his mother. This was partly the effect of youth and partly because he had the strong-willed Martine to depend on. For the first time in his life, he found himself enjoying a settled relationship with a girlfriend; and that summer, when Martine discovered she was pregnant, he acted in accordance with the bourgeois principles he had previously rejected – and proposed.

It was a happy wedding, held before the mayor of Sovicille, the seat of the local *comune*, with virtually the whole of Orgia attending. Conscious of her condition, Martine wore a simple dress, and it was Paul who really stole the show. His hair had grown again and he made a striking figure in his specially tailored black Mao suit with dark red piping and his new white gymshoes.

Coming so soon after his release, the wedding was inevitably something of a media event, with the Italian press and television out in strength. Far from disliking this, Paul obviously loved to be the centre of attention – so much so that when a photographer from the London *Daily Express* became delayed and missed the wedding, Paul insisted on going through with it again for the photographer.

Those who knew him insist that this was not exactly vanity. In his longing for media attention he was seeking something that he desperately needed – a true identity which he hoped to find in the role of some sort of cult celebrity.

Just before Christmas he and Martine left Italy for Los Angeles, where they planned to live, and it was in the suburbs of Tarzana (named after the hero of the town's founder, Edgar Rice Burroughs, author of the Tarzan novels) that in January 1975 Martine gave birth to a son. Resisting the temptation of naming him Tarzan Getty, they called him Balthazar. Balthazar was one of the three wise men in the Bible, and if the family was going to survive, a little wisdom wouldn't come amiss.

By marrying Martine, Paul had made something of a sacrifice; for by marrying before the age of twenty-two, he had disqualified himself from any income from the trust his father had set up in 1966, after the divorce, to support the children. This age bar was originally inserted to protect Aileen and Ariadne from potential fortune-hunters, but now it ruled out Paul as well.

He made a virtue of despising what he hadn't got, but from now on lack of funds was to be one of Paul's perpetual problems. He found it particularly galling to have the Getty name without the Getty money. He knew that one day he would inherit a fortune from the Sarah C. Getty Trust – but in the meantime he was having quite a problem to survive.

It was around March 1975 that Gail began receiving pressure from Paul Junior to bring the children back to England. Whenever they spoke on the telephone he sounded so depressed and lonely that she was genuinely worried about him.

Sensing that there was little hope of marrying him or bearing his children, Victoria had left him, undergone a cure and married for the second time – to Oliver Musker, an amusing young London-based antique dealer who was in love with her.

It was after her departure that Paul really hit rock bottom. The only person looking after him by now was a former minicab driver called Derek Calcott, who did his best to ensure that there was something in the house for him to eat – generally chocolate chip cookies and chocolate ripple ice-cream, both of which were bad for him but amply satisfied his addict's craving for something sweet. Feeling helpless and abandoned, he was otherwise completely on his own in a house which had become as gloomy and neglected as himself.

He was also out of money. He was financially incapable,

and the relatively small sums he had been receiving from the Sarah C. Getty Trust had been going on the quantities of street drugs he was using in addition to his prescription drugs.

All this had made him wretchedly vulnerable. So-called 'friends' had started taking his possessions, and he had sold off much of what remained – including the red MG from Rome, for which his sister, Donna, gave him $2,000. He could no longer support the children in Italy and was begging Gail to bring them back to Cheyne Walk.

She was in two minds over this. Part of her dreaded leaving Italy, and she was wary of getting too involved with him again. On the other hand she thought that setting up home in Cheyne Walk might be good both for the children and for their father. Since she and Paul were both alone and were still fond of one another, it also made good sense for them to be together.

So Gail flew to London for a few days for the first time since the kidnap – only to find things even worse than she expected. She arrived at the weekend. Paul was alone in the house, and since he was out of money yet again, his dealer had left him without drugs and he was already showing symptoms of acute withdrawal.

That night he was in such desperate straits that she made up a bed in the study to be near him, and stayed with him as the sweating and the writhing started. When he told her that all he wanted was to kick the habit, she promised she would stay and help him.

There was a drug clinic at Elephant and Castle – one of the poorest areas of South London – which offered addicts treatment every Tuesday, so the following Tuesday Gail took him there and he started on methadone instead of heroin and began cutting back on alcohol. Only when she was thoroughly convinced that he was serious about his treatment did she agree to bring the children back to England.

★

It was a bad wrench leaving Italy, and the children hated it. But by now Gail had convinced herself that it was for the best, and the children all seemed glad to be reunited with their father.

It was decided that Tara should remain in France with his grandparents, and the girls were sent to separate boarding-schools – Aileen to Hatchlands, a finishing school for smart young ladies near Godalming in Surrey, and Ariadne to a boarding-school near Lewes.

After creating consternation by announcing – as a practical joke – that she was pregnant, thirteen-year-old Ariadne settled down and accepted the routine of an English female boarding-school. But Aileen found the whole idea of Hatchlands very odd indeed. Like a true Italian, she hated being forced to sleep with the windows open, and always seemed to have a cold. She was taught fencing, contract bridge, and etiquette, all of which struck her as absurd. So did the trouble that was taken over teaching her to curtsey properly to royalty. Bored and resentful, she kept a secret stock of alcohol, truanted to London, and used to concoct horrifying stories to scandalize her more gullible fellow pupils.

Far from turning Aileen into a socially accomplished young lady, a year of Hatchlands was enough to make a rebel out of her for ever.

At the same time, finding a school for Mark proved more of a problem. As it was hard to get him into a major public school at such short notice, a friend of Gail's introduced him to the less oppressive world of Taunton School in rural Somerset. Here he came to feel very much at home, was popular with the other boys, loved the countryside, worked hard enough to get a scholarship to Oxford and became a very self-possessed, reflective human being.

Meanwhile his brother Paul was having problems as a married man of eighteen with an older wife and two young children, Martine's daughter, Anna, as well as Balthazar, to support. Craig Copetas, a journalist from *Rolling Stone* magazine, who saw a lot of him around this time, recalls that 'he was obviously extremely strong, and physically appeared to be scarcely affected by the kidnap'.

But this was deceptive. Beneath the surface, five months of physical and mental torture had played havoc with a personality already at risk, and Gail is convinced that his nervous system was seriously affected by his sufferings. He was finding it impossible to sleep – and when he did, was a constant prey to nightmares and a never-ending sense of dread. But his real problems came from the brandy which the kidnappers had fed him in captivity. He had inherited his addictive nature from his father, and soon it was clear that by starting his dependency on alcohol, the kidnappers had turned Paul Getty into a hopeless alcoholic.

It was not surprising that he found it impossible to settle down or maintain a close relationship with anyone. Martine often couldn't cope with him, particularly when he turned to drugs – legal and illegal – to help him through the day and enjoy a few hours' sleep at night. When he did succeed in sleeping, he would often wake up screaming.

In her practical way, Martine kept her small family together in Los Angeles, making a home for Anna and Balthazar – and for Paul too, when he needed them. When Grandfather Getty offered him a small allowance on condition that he studied at a university, he enrolled at Pepperdine University in Malibu and opted to study Chinese history. But academic life was as difficult for him as married life, and he was rarely in the lecture hall or the marital apartment.

When he could he came to England and, according to Gail, he continued to adore his father and romanticize his life. Although he rarely saw him, he was as eager as ever for his approval, and still hoped to gain it by becoming an important figure in the counter-culture.

This was what really lay behind his continuing obsession with prominent members of the Beat generation. Copetas was able to introduce him to some of the high priests of the movement, like William Burroughs, Allen Ginsberg and Timothy Leary. He remembers Paul trying to impress Burroughs by giving him one of the earliest Polaroid instant cameras. 'It was quite a present in those days. But Burroughs just looked puzzled and embarrassed and obviously hadn't the faintest notion what to do with it.'

As author of *The Naked Lunch*, Burroughs was a hero to young Paul, while, as Copetas put it, 'The only thing that made Paul interesting to Burroughs was that his name was Getty and he'd been kidnapped by the Mafia and had his ear cut off.'

Later that year the trial was held in Lagonegro of seven men accused of varying degrees of involvement in the kidnapping of Jean Paul Getty III. In Italy it is rare for kidnap victims or their families to risk attending trials that involve the Mafia. But Gail and Paul were determined to confront their ex-tormentors.

Worried by the risks they would be taking, Paul Junior insisted that they had advice from the former SAS man he had been using as a security expert himself since the kidnapping. As a professional the SAS man was so worried by the prospect of a Mafia trial in the heart of Mafia-dominated country that he seriously suggested having Gail and Paul flown into Lagonegro from Naples each morning by helicopter. To Gail this seemed excessive, and they settled for staying in Naples for the period of the trial, and travelling to court by car each morning.

Paul was wearing his hair longer now than ever to hide his lost ear, and many commented on how well he looked. But he and Gail found the trial more upsetting than they had expected – particularly having to encounter the sullen faces of the accused staring at them from the iron cage where they were kept inside the court.

They were dangerous-looking characters, but since the kidnappers had always worn their masks, Paul could not recognize any of them. Nor when she heard them speak could Gail recognize the unmistakable voice of Cinquanta. None of the ringleaders seemed to be among them, for as usual in Mafia trials, the godfathers were wherever godfathers go when trouble comes. One of the top suspects was a leading figure in the N'drangeta called Saverio Mammoliti. He was said to have been in charge of the affair, but the police could never catch him, despite the fact that he appeared quite openly to get married in church at the nearby town of Gióia Táuro just before the trial.

Nor was the ransom money ever found, apart from a small amount discovered on one of the accused. This meant that more than 3 million Getty dollars, in carefully marked Italian lire, were currently helping to equip Mafia laboratories producing heroin and cocaine.

The accused, who were found guilty, received between four and ten years' imprisonment in conditions of maximum security. But Gail felt that no punishment could match the cruelty the kidnappers had inflicted on her son. Some years later a member of the gang who was still in prison wrote to her begging her forgiveness and saying that a word from her would help his chances of release. She didn't answer.

Throughout most of 1975 Gail and Paul Junior seemed to get on well together in Cheyne Walk, partly because the house was big enough for both to live relatively separate lives. Gail found the house more beautiful than she remembered, but also faintly sinister – 'a living tomb' she would later call it.

No, she assured one interviewer, she and Paul had not remarried, nor did they intend to do so.

But now that they were back together, she was shocked by how much he had changed, and the damage which his way of life had caused him. Thanks to his regular Tuesday visits to Elephant and Castle, however, he was showing signs of definite improvement, and during that summer he actually enjoyed a fortnight's holiday with Mark, taking him to stay with friends in Ireland. It was the first time he had been away so long from Cheyne Walk since Talitha's death.

★

Throughout this period the ageing Jean Paul Getty had been trying not to think too much about the future. He had spent his lifetime building Getty Oil — but what was to become of it?

'I'm a bad boss,' he admitted gloomily in a moment of rare candour. 'A good boss develops successors. There is nobody to step into my shoes.'

Theoretically the whole purpose of creating the enormous fortune in the Sarah C. Getty Trust had always been to enrich what he liked to call 'the Getty dynasty'. But here again he had been having doubts. What hope could there be for a dynasty riven by disaster and dissent? Penelope told Ralph Hewins that at times the old man was haunted by the thought that 'the Getty dynasty would end with him, and his empire would be divided up, never to reach the same peak again'.

Sometimes he even went so far as to blame himself for what had happened. Having sacrificed his family to success in business, he wondered if the sacrifice was worth it.

To counter such gloomy thoughts, during the summer of 1975 he tried becoming something he had never been before — a loving grandfather' at the centre of a big united family, 'Mr Family himself' as Gail called him. At different times all the grandchildren would be invited to Sutton Place together with their parents.

At one time Gordon and Ann brought the four boys, Peter, Andrew, John and William. On another occasion George's first wife, Gloria, brought her daughters, Anne, Claire and Caroline. And Ronald and his blonde wife, Karin, came with Christopher, Stephanie, Cecile and Christina. Gail and her children were regularly invited to Sutton Place for the weekend.

Naturally they went, for money is a great healer, and Gail found her ex-father-in-law as charming to her as ever. It was as if the kidnap had never happened, and by keeping off the subject, he and his grandson, Paul, began to get on rather well together.

Later the old man seemed surprised at how much he had actually enjoyed this novel exercise in family togetherness, and would write of how these visits had made 1975 'a most reassuring summer for Grandfather J. Paul Getty'.

Trying to convince himself of what he wanted to believe, he added that the warmth of family affection showed that 'despite everything – be it wealth [*sic*], divorce, tragedy or any of the other myriad conditions and tribulations of life – the Getty family *is* a family and will continue to be one'.

Brave words – but they seemed distinctly forced when checked against reality. For the truth was that few families could have been more disunited than the Gettys, and it was impossible to regard them as an American dynasty in the making, like the Kennedys or the Rockefellers. And ironically, the truth was that most of the family disunity had been caused, directly or indirectly, by Jean Paul Getty.

Even at eighty-two he could not resist playing one son off against another. His current favourite, as far as he had one, was the previously despised and frequently ignored Gordon. Gordon had been appointed along with Lansing Hays as a trustee of the Sarah C. Getty Trust, and he and Ann were the only members of the family whom his father had seen fit to invite to London for his eightieth birthday party.

Gordon's show of independence by suing his father in that long and hard-fought battle over his income from the Sarah C. Getty Trust continued to work wonders both for his morale and his personal prestige, and relations started to improve.

From having been, by Getty standards, on the edge of poverty, Gordon was now distinctly affluent. The increased income of Getty Oil was reflected in the earnings from the Sarah C. Getty Trust, and Gordon and his brother Paul Junior apparently received $4,927,514 in the twelve months prior to their father's death.

This meant that Ann and Gordon were free to live the life they wanted, and almost from the start they made it clear that they would not be following the sort of penny-pinching billionaires' existence exemplified by Gordon's father.

Ann had a strong flamboyant streak which Gordon followed, so that when they found themselves a house it was one of the largest, most spectacular private houses in the whole of San Francisco, an Italianate four-storeyed mansion on the peak of Pacific Heights, designed in the early thirties by the prestigious architect Willis Polk.

Like Ann and Gordon it was considerably larger than life. It had a courtyard with Italian-style frescoes, more than a dozen bedrooms, and unrivalled views across the bay from the Golden Gate to Alcatraz. It had been something of a white elephant, and they got it fairly cheaply since it was going to require a lot of money to make it habitable, let alone the sort of house that Ann had set her heart on.

So buying it had been a sort of proclamation of intent. Gordon and Ann were rich, they were at the very top of San Francisco, and they were going to enjoy themselves.

Ronald's life remained considerably less enviable than absent-minded Gordon's during that summer of 1975. Indeed Gordon's growing affluence emphasized further still the gross unfairness of poor Ronald's continued disinheritance. While Gordon was drawing his millions from the Sarah C. Getty Trust, Ronald was paid his bare $3,000.

On top of this, the business he had set such store by – his grandly named Getty Financial Corporation, a conglomerate of property and fast-food restaurants – had yet to show a real profit.

But after that summer's visit to Sutton Place with Karin and the children, Ronald was more hopeful than he'd been for years. Father had mellowed, and he got on better with him than he ever had before. Indeed, he had personally assured him that justice would be done. He had also made him a trustee of the museum at Malibu, and an executor of his will. All this seemed to point to one thing and one thing only – that at his father's death Ronald would be placed where he always should have been, in a position of equality beside his brothers as full beneficiary of the Sarah C. Getty Trust.

The only member of the family not to be invited down to Sutton Place that summer was the old man's namesake and former favourite son, Jean Paul Getty Junior. During the worst moments of the kidnap, Getty had refused to speak to him, and now, as old age took its toll, he still stood firm.

Paul Junior became deeply upset by this and still telephoned Penelope Kitson from time to time begging her to intercede on his behalf. But it was always the same reply: 'Not until he comes off drugs.'

But although his father wouldn't see or speak to him, there was no way Paul Junior could be displaced as a principal beneficiary of the Sarah C. Getty Trust. As a drug addict, he was not considered fit to be a Getty, but financially Jean Paul Getty Junior was already set to be a multi-millionaire.

CHAPTER SEVENTEEN

POSTHUMOUS PLEASURES

I**T WAS ODD** how little consolation Jean Paul Getty actually derived in his old age from the enormous fortune he had spent his life creating. There had always been something curiously unreal about the vast amounts of money he had conjured from the earth, and because he was always so determined to preserve the fortune from extravagance and taxes, it was as if he had never entirely possessed it.

Just as he had never known quite how large it was, so he had always been uneasy when using it except for the business which preoccupied him even now – that of making even further vast amounts of money.

Over the years, money had taken on various aspects for him – money as power, money to make more money, and in a deeper sense, money to justify himself before his parents and his conscience. But there was never cash to be enjoyed as any normal person might have enjoyed it by the simple act of spending. Because of this, it was as if his money cheated him; and since he had made the fortune in his own image, this meant that he was finally cheated by himself.

He couldn't change his nature any more than he could change his face, and here he was, trapped in the person he had carefully created in order to create the fortune. In the past he had made himself an isolated figure in the interests of secrecy and strength – but now his isolation merely left him lonely. His face, which he had trained so carefully to reveal nothing of his feelings, had become a mask incapable of registering anything at all – even the terror of mortality that never left him. He had made himself immune to love and pity – and now at the age of eighty-three he was incapable of feeling love for anyone. As some are colour-blind, so he was people-blind, having schooled himself for years to ignore the distraction of ordinary emotions.

The result had showed when his grandson was kidnapped and the emotional 'shutter' had descended, just as it also showed in his refusal to lift the telephone and tell his drug-addicted son, Paul Junior, to come and see him. Most of all perhaps it showed in his unawareness of the wrong he'd done to his son Ronald.

Since the age of its owner in no way lessens the attractions of a vast amount of money, Getty continued to attract his women. By their eighties most men are ready for a little rest and dignity about such matters, but opportunity and habit kept him at it, relying on injections from his doctor to give him an erection. By his eighties there were women still protesting their agonized desire to marry him.

Some of his women had vanished from his life, like Mary Teissier, who had more or less succumbed to drink and disappointment and retired to the house he had bought her in the South of France. But there were always fresh admirers on the scene, even aristocratic ones like the Duke of Rutland's sister, Lady Ursula d'Abo, who declared her love for Getty in the pages of the *National Enquirer* – which prompted an answering *billet-doux* from the emotional Nicaraguan Rosabella Burch, in an article in the *Sunday Express*, saying that *she* was considering marrying him – 'He's such a dear man and so amusing.'

But another old Getty habit was that of playing off his women against each other, and watching them fighting for his ancient favours. He would sit now viewing television in the evening, lost in thought and pointedly ignoring them; then, when he'd seen enough, he would stagger to his feet and thoughtfully select that night's companion.

Along with concupiscence, a further habit that he couldn't break was the favourite vice of old age – anticipatory meanness.

One of the few things that could still excite him was his will. On the edge of eternity, he enjoyed cheeseparing particular bequests as a final way of getting even with women he had once been fond of – even his ex-wives, Teddy and Fini, both of whose allowances he cut, as he did with that of his one-time 'honorary daughter', Robina Lund, who had somehow managed to offend him. (On the other hand, there were a number of very old mistresses he now remembered.)

But his greatest problem was the one that had been there almost all his life – the fact that part of him still had never really grown up. Even with death approaching, the financial genius was as firmly linked as ever with the emotional adolescent.

It was the childlike side of him that seems to have appealed to the women who were genuinely concerned about him. Like his secretary, Barbara Wallace, who stayed up all night holding his hand when he was terrified of dying. Or Jeanette Constable-Maxwell, who had remained a friend since he gave her that monster coming-of-age party. Or his 'dearest Pen' (as he called Penelope Kitson), who had been too wise to marry him, and was one of the few who had not allowed his money to dictate her actions or affections.

One can understand why, by the spring of 1976, when he knew he had inoperable prostate cancer and refused to see the women he could use no longer, he still wanted Penelope near him, reading those never-forgotten boys' adventure books by G. A. Henty. There was reassurance in this authoritative woman treating him as a child and reading him children's stories – just as there is something particularly pathetic in the thought of this richest of all Americans with his sad old face and his figure hunched in his arm-chair with his shawl around him, dreaming of going west with Drake or to India with Clive, and wondering about reincarnation and dreading dying.

At his death in June 1976, Getty had more than fulfilled his bargain with his mother when they set up the Sarah C. Getty Trust together, forty-two years before. He had made absolutely sure that, as ultimate heirs to nearly $2 billion in the Sarah C. Getty Trust, financially at least his children and his children's children would want for nothing.

In the first year after his death the trust produced an income not far short of $4 million each for Paul and Gordon, and the same sum was equally divided between George's daughters, Anne and Claire and Caroline. Since these five beneficiaries of the trust received all its income, the payments they received would rise steadily, as Getty Oil increased its cash dividends. These dividends rose from $1 a share in 1978 to $1.90 a share in 1980, and on to a record $2.60 in 1982. By the early eighties Paul and Gordon would be receiving $28 million each from the trust every year, while George's daughters would share the same sum between them.

But apart from money, J. Paul Getty left the members of his family remarkably little – certainly none of the things the founder of a 'dynasty' might have been expected to have left behind – no land, no appreciable heirlooms, not even a centre for the family. Apart from money, which by its nature is anonymous, there was little for members of his family to remember him by at all.

Since he had only rented Sutton Place, even the house which he had loved was sold, and its pictures and furniture dispatched to the museum. At Malibu it was as if, not trusting his descendants with his memory, he was making the museum the ultimate repository of his reputation and his sole memorial.

What he had left his family was something else – too much money, a tangle of troubles and a legacy of broken lives.

Thus one sees how important the idea of the museum must have been for him during the months before he died. It hadn't mattered that he never saw it – any more than it had mattered that he never visited the Neutral Zone until long after he had built up one of the most productive oilfields in the world from his hotel room in Paris.

He was a virtuoso of remote control, of using his money and his expertise to make extraordinary things happen far away, while seeing them in his imagination. It was a most unusual talent, and for several years before he died he had been quietly using it to build his own museum of the imagination 6,000 miles away at Malibu.

He was probably wise never to have visited it. Reality might have disappointed him – and there was always time to visit in another incarnation.

Instead, from his room in Sutton Place, he could methodically perform the tasks that he enjoyed – reading architects' reports, checking on costings, and minutely following the progress of the building. (According to Stephen Garrett, one of the old man's most exciting moments came when he watched a video he had sent him of pouring the concrete into the foundations.) Then, when his Roman villa was complete, it had been time to start to fill it with its treasures.

During the months before he died, one of his few remaining pleasures was to discuss its contents with Gillian Wilson, who as well as being the museum's official Curator of Decorative Arts was also young, intelligent and pretty. On the last occasion that she saw him he had shut his eyes and said:'I am entering my decorative arts gallery now. Tell me what I'm seeing.'

She says she talked 'as descriptively as possible' about the gallery for nearly half an hour – at the end of which he opened his eyes, smiled at her, and said, 'Well. Quite a spread, eh?'

By then the initial press reaction to the museum was forgotten. Attendance figures were already proving its popularity. In the year before he died, there were over 350,000 visitors – which, as he could not resist working out, had cost him $3.50 a head. But this had been one expense that he had not begrudged – for it was good to know that people were already appreciating what he had created.

In Rome, before the war, he had had a marble bust made of himself, and he asked that it be placed in the vestibule of the museum.

'The ideal visitor to the museum,' he once remarked, 'should fancy himself back two thousand years, calling on Roman friends who live in the villa.'

When they did, they would have found the marble bust of a middle-aged man looking not unlike a Roman emperor waiting in the vestibule to greet them.

Upon his father's death, Gordon, as co-trustee with Lansing Hays of the Sarah C. Getty Trust, became the richest – and, potentially at least, the most important – member of the family. In addition to the $3.4 million income he received in 1977 from the trust, he had an additional $1 million trustee fee, plus a $4 million fee as executor of his father's will.

But although Ann and Gordon intended to enjoy their affluence, Gordon appeared unmoved by whatever power and responsibilities accompanied it. Diffident by nature, he was no match for the lawyerly self-confidence of Hays – who, looking on himself as regent for the Getty empire after the emperor's death, treated the board of Getty Oil with scant respect – and Gordon likewise. The board of Getty Oil periodically objected to such treatment, but Gordon didn't. As Getty Oil was doing very nicely at the time, and returning steadily increasing dividends to its principal shareholder, the Sarah C. Getty Trust, Gordon had more important things to think about.

An unmalicious man, Gordon spoke well of everyone – even his father – on whom he published an amiable if enigmatic obituary:

> My father was a fathomless man, commanding and
> disarming, a philosopher and a clown. He was inscruta-
> ble, a showman, a prince of players. He was charismatic,
> even mesmeric. Many of his old employees, underpaid
> or not, would have shed blood for him. He was stoical
> in grief and at last jocular to the day he died. I think he
> meant to tell us something about courage.

Perhaps he had – although it's hard to know quite what. What *was* clear was that Gordon had no intention of learning lessons from his father over such matters as personal economy and self-denial. Money would never turn his head, but this didn't mean that he and Ann were incapable of enjoying it.

Unlike his more sophisticated brother Paul, he and Ann were not rich cosmopolitans, and their social aims were essentially confined to San Francisco, where Ann was ready to replace the memory of the Sacramento Valley by becoming undisputed queen of Pacific Heights.

So the style and quality of living at 350 Broadway rose after Jean Paul Getty's death. They glassed in the atrium, making the house ideal for full-scale parties and receptions. Getty's butler, the solemn Bullimore, was taken on from Sutton Place, together with a household staff of six. A splendid kitchen was installed, with amusing *trompe l'œil* paintings of a farmyard, and the most majestic of America's lady interior decorators, Sister Parish, was engaged to supervise the décor in the house. It was thanks to her that the pride of the house became the dining room, where electric light was banned and the Gettys and their guests would dine exclusively by genuine candlelight from elaborate candelabra (this, despite Bullimore grumbling on about the candlewax needing to be cleared up later). With its antique blue and gold Chinese wallpaper, it was a room of considerable beauty, with the lights of Oakland glittering across the bay. Guests reported *filet mignon* so tender they could cut it with a fork, *soufflés* of virtuoso lightness, and memorable wines from France and California, although they observed that Gordon generally drank water.

On a simpler level, as a family man, Gordon was anxious not to inflict upon his children the sort of insecurity he had grown up with. He and Ann read Dr Spock, and were relaxed and undemanding parents. 'We're a close-knit family but we're not big on family meals. Everyone kind of eats when they're hungry,' said Gordon. This applied to him as well – as he tended at times to disappear all day to his noiseproof workroom, not surfacing until it was almost time for bed.

No longer having any need to prove himself before his father, he was able to enjoy his freedom and do more or less exactly as he wanted. But what did Gordon want? It was none too clear, even to himself. Later he described this as a period when he was 'simply floundering around'. With little formal teaching, he was already trying to write music but was unable to complete anything to his satisfaction. He sang Schubert – *Winterreise*, which he enunciated with his eyes shut – but his voice, though powerful, was faintly but fatally off key.

According to his wife Ann, 'Gordon's favourite pastime is buying CDs at Tower Records. He practically supports the shop.' But apart from records, he spent little directly on himself. His dress sense was minimal. Lacking all taste for self-adornment, he wore a 40-dollar Casio electronic wristwatch. He preferred his Dodge convertible to a Rolls or a Bentley.

Ann, meanwhile, had started buying French Impressionists but lacked the temperament and inclinations of a serious collector. Regular contributions were made to the San Francisco Opera House and the San Francisco Philharmonic but, in general, philanthropy was done 'rather mechanically' as Ann put it, in accordance with an annual list compiled by Gordon's secretary.

As a couple, they were generous but not overgenerous, not wishing to be landed with a reputation for prodigality, and appeared somewhat less concerned about human beings than animals, prehistory, and conservation – particularly 'conservation of the world's resources before it is too late', as Gordon put it when setting up the J. Paul Getty Wildlife Conservation Prize in memory of his father, but not making it very clear what connection there had ever been between his father and conserving anything except large amounts of money.

Gordon voted Republican and Ann Democrat, 'thus cancelling each other out', as Gordon put it; and they were equally impartial in lending the house to any cause they happened to approve of.

At this stage in the marriage it appeared to be Ann who

made the running. It was Ann who bought herself a Porsche, Ann who dressed in Paris. And while Ann became the most glamorous and talked about woman in San Francisco, Gordon continued to exude the faintly baffled air of a music professor who has suddenly found himself a multi-millionaire – a multi-millionaire who sometimes happened to forget where he'd parked his car, but who, when he did find it, always insisted on driving his friends home after dinner.

During this period he seemed perfectly prepared to 'flounder' on for ever, devoted to his children, inflicting Schubert on his long-suffering friends, and ignoring what was happening in the far-off world of Getty Oil and the Sarah C. Getty Trust. At times it seemed as if he was positively inviting people not to take him seriously. Few did.

One will never know for certain why the old man didn't use the opportunity of his will to right the wrong that he had done to his eldest son Ronald. It seems inconceivable that the ancient grudge against his grandfather, Dr Helmle, still rankled. Given the somewhat bumpy history of their relationship, he may simply have felt disinclined to do Ronald any favours. But most probably he was wary of changing anything in the Sarah C. Getty Trust which could have given a point of entry to his abiding enemy – the tax-man.

Instead he offered Ronald certain consolation prizes, which made things worse rather than better. He left him the major share with Paul and Gordon in La Posta Vecchia – which none of them wanted. Still less, in the circumstances, did he want his father's diaries, which for some extraordinary reason he bequeathed to him. (The diaries were valued at a nominal value of one dollar for probate purposes.) Apart from a legacy of $320,000, the only substantial benefit Ronald derived on his father's death was his fee of $4 million as his executor, a role he shared with his brother Gordon.

After so many promises he was bitter and humiliated, so he

went to law – against the J. Paul Getty Museum and the Sarah C. Getty Trust. Fearing that his case would delay settlement of the will and threaten the tax-free status of the great bequest, the museum settled with Ronald for $10 million. But he got nowhere in his case against the trust, although he says that Paul and Gordon had been willing to include him in the trust until their lawyers dissuaded them.

So the injustice that was done to Ronald festered on, leaving him feeling doubly betrayed by his father – first at the age of six when the trust was founded, and now in this will that had continued the injustice and had set him firmly against his brothers.

Ronald, of course, was still a multi-millionaire and, sensibly invested, his money would have brought him in enough to live in comfort for the remainder of his life. But Ronald wanted more than comfort. He wanted to prove himself against his father and his brothers and before his children. So he invested his money in his business ventures, risking everything to make another Getty fortune on his own account.

Apart from Ann and Gordon, the most fortunate members of the family were George's children, Anne, Claire and Caroline. Ever since George's death, their mother, Gloria, had carefully protected them from further scandal and from press intrusion; and continuing the pattern established by their father, they kept more or less apart from other members of the family. Each received a third of the income which their father would have had from the Sarah C. Getty Trust, which in the twelve months following their grandfather's death approached $2 million each.

But although this meant that they were great heiresses, they remained wary of the world outside their sheltered circle. It was as if all three of them had learned important lessons from their father's downfall, and were determined to avoid the temptations and disasters of the very rich. They revered the memory of their grandfather. Their mother retained a strong influence on all of them, and for all their money they continued leading undramatic, very private lives.

It was as if the fault line in the Getty family continued through Paul Junior and his children; and by the time his father died, it was clear that Paul's attempt to repair it by bringing Gail and the children back to Cheyne Walk had failed.

Throughout the marriage of Paul's former mistress, Victoria Holdsworth, to Oliver Musker, her mother, Mary Holdsworth, had kept in contact with events at Cheyne Walk. Being concerned for Paul she used to bring him supper in a basket every Wednesday evening, which also gave her an opportunity to keep in touch with what was happening.

It is hard to be precise about the sequence of events that followed during the spring before Paul Getty's death. Strains had been appearing between Paul Junior and Gail and the children, as Paul was clearly finding it hard to cure himself of his addiction and continue his treatment at the clinic. Simultaneously there had been strains in Victoria's marriage, which ended in divorce some two years later – and when she decided to move back to Cheyne Walk, Gail moved out at once to a house across the river.

Gail continued visiting Cheyne Walk to look after her family, but she was increasingly upset to see that in her absence, Paul was giving up on his cure completely, and was soon as heavily addicted as before.

This was the point when Gail concluded that the cause was lost. There were angry arguments and she felt that there was nothing further she could do for him. The children were unhappy, and after one final desperate scene between her and Paul, she decided that no further purpose could be served by their remaining.

All she wanted was to remove herself and the children as far away as possible from the unhappiness of Cheyne Walk, which for her meant getting to California – first San Francisco, where they stayed with friends, then on to Los Angeles where they finally found themselves a house.

It was the most decisive move that they could take, and a total break with Europe and the past. Sometimes Gail dreamed of Italy, which appeared an insuperable distance from California.

As for Paul Junior, after his father died he made an agonized appearance at the memorial service for his father – ashen-faced, wearing dark glasses, and showing such difficulty walking that he seemed to need the support of Bianca Jagger, who came with him. This was the last time he was photographed in public for many years. He missed the children, bitterly regretted not having seen his father before he died, and his health was beginning to deteriorate as the drugs and drink started to affect his circulation.

For a man who had suddenly become a principal beneficiary of the greatest fortune in America, he could hardly have appeared more wretched.

But the greatest casualty within the family was still his son, young Paul. He was now a hopeless alcoholic, and financially his affairs were in such chaos that, since his father exercised no personal control, his grandfather, Judge Harris, filed suit in Los Angeles to be appointed his legal guardian on the grounds that Paul was 'financially improvident' and 'unable economically to handle his own affairs'.

The marriage with Martine had effectively collapsed by now. Paul was bouncing cheques, had given up on college, was drinking more heavily than ever, and was mixing with low-life characters, buying cars on the strength of the Getty name then charging them to members of the family.

In desperation, Gail invited his old friend, the journalist Craig Copetas, to Los Angeles to talk to him, 'Which', as Copetas says, 'shows how desperate she'd become.'

Copetas describes how his friendship with young Paul ended. 'I stayed with him for a few days at the place he was renting off Sunset Strip. He was drinking heavily, but he said he wasn't happy, and longed to sort life out somehow but it wasn't possible.

'While I was there his grandfather's application was due to be heard in the Supreme Court of California, and on the morning of the hearing I drove him and Martine to the court in an old red Chevrolet I'd bought. He seemed quite calm and reasonable, so I said to him, "Paul, this is your chance to show a real change of attitude. Everyone's pissed off with you, and there'll be hordes of reporters at the court. Show yourself in a new light. Just for once, be responsible."

'But suddenly he exploded and started to attack Martine. Underneath everything he had a fearful temper. I think that it was now that I realized that Paul Getty was a lost cause. I stopped the car and bawled him out. He stopped, and I got him to the court, but once again he made a scene, and that was that. I left California a few days later, and never saw Paul again.'

PART THREE

CHAPTER EIGHTEEN

DRUGS AND COMA

AFTER HIS FATHER died, it was as if Paul Junior had condemned himself to death in life in his beautiful unhappy house, and the years ticked by as he served his sentence for what had happened to Talitha. His grief alone could not explain his situation, which was also due to alcohol and drugs and money. The alcohol and drugs enabled him to insulate himself from life, and the effortless supply of money permitted him to go on living as he wanted.

The attraction of heroin is that it temporarily blanks out human misery. For the hour or so following a fix, there is absolute relief from any sense of worthlessness and guilt and from all anxiety. Reality dissolves, and in its place comes the feeling of ineffable tranquillity. The feeling does not last and in the long term the use of heroin has a cumulative effect, leading to yet more anxiety, loss of self-esteem, stifling depression, and a sense of utter isolation. When reality returns, the thought of loved ones can become a source of guilt, which helps explain why Paul saw members of his family so rarely and gave no sign of missing them. Confined within that house of many memories, there were times when he grew morbidly suspicious, and his reclusiveness increased together with his fear and his suspicion of the world outside.

For company he had his books, and books possess a sympathetic magic of their own, especially books as rare and valuable as those he was collecting – fine bindings from the history of book-making, painted manuscripts from the Middle Ages to the present day, and exquisitely printed books from private presses. These were not books to read, so much as books as talismanic objects, books as history, books as individual works of art.

His books were one of the few escape routes he possessed, for they belonged to the past, and the past is safer than the present. He could enjoy the benediction of the printed page, the smell of leather and the sensual feel of vellum. Books had become his solace, the mistresses he no longer bedded, the family he never saw. He was becoming increasingly well-read, and being clever and methodical he also studied bibliography, learning about the different styles of binding, printing, and the esoteric lore of rare editions. In his scholarly way he started to become invulnerable in a field transcending drugs and money.

For anyone in his condition it was a considerable achievement, proof that his mind was still as sharp as ever, as he started building up his library. This would be one creation he was proud of, and he was at his happiest in Rossetti's old studio, which he had made his study, the heavy curtains drawn against the light and his books around him. He was in his mid forties now but looking older – bearded, bespectacled, full-bellied, the drink and the chocolate chip cookies having made him put on weight, giving him an occasional resemblance to the bearded figure of his long-dead hero.

One of his few regular visitors was kindly Bryan Maggs, king of London rare book sellers, and virtuoso bookbinder on his own account. (His resplendent binding of John Gay's *Trivia or the Art of Walking the Streets of London* is on exhibition in the British Museum.) With Maggs to buy for him, his library increased, and all the while he went on sniffing heroin and drinking rum and hardly ever saw his children.

Being intelligent and rich, there were other interests Paul Junior was able to pursue which also passed the time and brought him no anxiety. One was the cinema. He had a huge collection of old films, and a deep knowledge of the golden age of Hollywood. He also enjoyed British movies from before the war, which became an important source of his enthusiasm for a nostalgic England he had never known but which he loved and felt at home in. Films were a window into life beyond the prison he had built so carefully around him.

There was another window, too, which opened up more unexpectedly. Living the life he did, there were long periods when sleep was impossible; killing time, he would watch interminable programmes on TV. He was doing this when Mick Jagger came to see him, and inquired why he didn't watch something more worthwhile.

'What?' he asked.

'Cricket,' said Jagger, switching to a Test Match programme and starting to explain the rules. Paul was hooked. From the days when he and Mario Lanza had attempted to establish baseball in Rome, he had always had an interest in spectator sports, and he enjoyed the subtlety of cricket, together with the drama and excitement it can offer those who take it seriously. As an increasingly Anglophile American he also found an exotic fascination in this curiously English game. Soon he was saying that cricket was to baseball as chess was to a game of draughts.

With old films, old books, and cricket on TV, he could fill the *longueurs* of his solitary life, and seemed set to continue thus until he died – which he gave every sign of doing fairly quickly, as drink and drugs and lack of exercise undermined his constitution.

From time to time he would enter the London Clinic for a cure, which never lasted; at the same time he received treatment for damage to his circulation and his liver, and for suspected diabetes, along with other symptoms of his precarious condition.

Meanwhile his children were growing up. Friends of the family often said that Aileen was the child who most resembled him, both physically and with the streak of wildness in her personality.

She was intuitively bright and very pretty, with large brown eyes and a sprite-like charm that made her mother call her her Irish leprechaun. But Aileen really liked to think herself a rebel, and after dropping out of her course at the University of Southern California she did most of the things that rebellious young women did in Los Angeles in the seventies, including painting, campaigning against the Vietnam war, and using dope and cocaine for relaxation. As part of her political protest she made artistic collages, including one of photocopied thousand-dollar bills emblazoned with the message, 'Fight Against Capitalism'. She lived for a period with a jazz pianist, followed by a film director, and attempted to ignore the fact that she would one day be a great heiress, as if the whole idea appalled her. Possibly it really did.

Less of an extrovert, her sister Ariadne was too much a traditionalist to be a rebel. But just as she had been the tomboy of the family, so she was still comparatively wild, with the mercurial personality and emotional ups-and-downs of her Irish ancestry. After studying at Bennington College in Vermont, she took up photography, specializing in landscape and architecture. She was already promising enough to have acquired her own New York dealer.

Mark was the one member of the family not to have succumbed to the lure of California. After his English education, he appeared as resolutely Anglophile as his father, but his English accent and exterior were deceptive. His Italian was as fluent as his English, and having been born in Rome he regarded Italy as home. He had been young enough not to have been as seriously affected by his parents' divorce and the ensuing dramas as Paul and Aileen – but unlike his brother Paul, the absence of his father sometimes made him seem old beyond his years, as he did his best to take his place. He was sensible and caring and responsible, qualities whose rarity among the Gettys made them particularly valuable.

Mark was not the only member of the family who was missing Italy. After the trauma of the kidnap they had all kept anxiously away, but their mother, Gail, tended to regard Los Angeles as something of a place of exile. She still owned – and longed to see – the house at Orgia, which was now closed up, while Remo the gardener kept an eye on it for her.

Finally they felt that they could keep away no longer, and early in 1980, Gail and Mark and Ariadne returned for the first time since the kidnap. Anxious to discover what had happened to the house, they did not stay in Rome but hired a car at the airport and drove at once to Tuscany. On reaching Orgia they heard that Remo had died just before Christmas. As he had been ill for some time beforehand, he'd been unable to look after the house and they found it had been badly vandalized.

It might have been a symbol for the family. But despite the mess and filth, it was still like coming home. This was where Gail and the children had been happiest, and despite the memory of the kidnap, they were determined to have the house restored. They sensed that they belonged here, and decided to return.

They felt safe in Orgia, for here in this open country, with the vines and the dark red soil, there was none of the closed-in atmosphere of Rome. Besides, they couldn't live their lives avoiding danger any longer. As Gail said, it was better to face the risk of kidnap than hide away for ever.

After Italy Gail and the children were back in Los Angeles in March for Aileen's engagement party. Tiring of her film director – or he of her – Aileen had spent some time with Elizabeth Taylor's son, Michael Wilding Junior, and through him had got to know his younger brother, Christopher. They had fallen in love, and having been together now for practically two years, they wished to marry. But although everyone liked Christopher, who was handsome, kind and charming, marrying him was not that simple.

From the start it was evident that any wedding that involved a Getty and a son of Elizabeth Taylor was a forbidding undertaking. The Hollywood protocol would be as complex as at any royal wedding; the publicity could be a nightmare; and both families had problems of their own to add to the confusion. Christopher, who was still devoted to his former stepfather, Richard Burton, insisted that he would have to be present – as well as his mother, who was now married to US Senator John Warner. The filming schedules of the two major film-stars, if nothing else, made this difficult – and on the Getty side there seemed little chance of bringing the members of the family together in tolerable harmony. There was certainly no way of persuading Paul Junior to take his daughter up the aisle.

The marital logistics seeming insuperable, Gail suggested giving an old style American engagement party for the couple – after which they could 'elope' and marry later, at their leisure. Both rather gratefully agreed, and on 17 March Gail held a formal engagement party in their honour for a hundred and fifty at her house at Brentwood

To give her blessing, Elizabeth Taylor made a regal appearance at the party 'shimmering in pearls', and Aileen, dressed as a bride with flowers in her hair, wore a Hollywood style engagement ring of imperial jade, surrounded by diamonds.

The Gettys were represented by Paul and Mark and Ariadne, and Hollywood by Sissy Spacek, Dudley Moore, and Roddy McDowell. Timothy Leary came to represent himself, and at the end of what Aileen called 'my surrogate marriage party', the bridal pair 'eloped', and married secretly soon afterwards in a chapel on Sunset Strip.

That summer further links were forged between Italy and the Getty family when Mark returned to Rome and met Domitilla Harding. Just twenty, with the face of a Sienese madonna, she was the daughter of an American businessman and an Italian mother. Her father's family came from Boston, but her mother, Lavinia Lante della Rovere, belonged to one of the oldest families in Rome. Domitilla's uncle was that same Prince Ladislao Odescalchi who had owned the Posta Vecchia and sold it to

Mark's grandfather, and the Lante della Roveres themselves had once possessed one of the loveliest houses in Italy, the famous Villa Lante at Bagnaia, near Viterbo, which had been in the family for generations until Domitilla's grandmother sold it in the 1950s.

At the end of the summer Mark had to return to England to start studying PPE (philosophy, politics and economics) at St Catherine's College, Oxford. But because of Domitilla he seemed certain to return to Rome as soon as possible.

With the children growing up, even the disordered life of Mark's unhappy brother Paul was showing signs of calming down. At the beginning of 1981, six years after the kidnap, he was still heavily dependent on drugs and alcohol; when frustrated or provoked he could be as impossible as ever. Surprisingly he was still married to Martine, but he saw her rarely and had found himself a new 'fiancée' – a smart Italian girl from a very smart Italian family, Emmanuela Stucchi-Prinetti. It was a good sign that he was beginning to work at last, in the one area he'd always dreamed of – the movie industry – working from 1978 as assistant to the film director John Schlesinger, then as an actor with an old friend of Martine's, the German avant-garde director Wim Wenders.

Wenders's early films, with their uneasy themes of alienation and male wanderlust, might have been tailor-made for Paul. He could easily identify with Wenders's characters, and after playing several minor parts was offered a major role by Wenders early in 1981 – that of a writer in his latest film, *The State of Things*.

Through his acting Paul was showing signs of coming to terms with life at last. In the past there had been his adolescent dreams of impressing his father as a figure in the counter-culture. This had never worked, despite his hippie life-style and his attempts to associate with some of the heroes of the beat generation. But now, when least expected, he found himself becoming a success in avant-garde cinema. Wenders was happy with the early scenes of the film, which they had shot in Portugal.

More filming followed in Paris, and Paul actually enjoyed his time there. He had Emmanuela with him and seemed happier with her than with any of his other women: although still heavily dependent on his daily bottle of Wild Turkey bourbon, he was almost clean of drugs.

Then in March he returned to Los Angeles with gentle, dark-haired Emmanuela to shoot the final footage for *The State of Things* in Hollywood. They stayed with friends, and Paul seemed happy to be back in familiar Los Angeles. But soon he had to face another crisis. He found working in a Hollywood studio none too easy, and once shooting started he discovered that he couldn't act and drink – so gave up drink. For an alcoholic this was a considerable shock to the system, and to help him cope with his withdrawal symptoms his doctors prescribed a formidable mixture of drugs, including methadone to help him sleep, and Placidyl, Valium and Dalmane to calm his nerves.

Despite so many pills it was still hard for him to sleep, and he tended to wake early, which was why on the morning of 5 April Emmanuela was particularly worried when she couldn't wake him from the deepest slumber. He was inert, and scarcely breathing. Thoroughly alarmed, she had the sense to call an ambulance.

Everyone suspected drink or drugs. What had actually happened was that, unable to cope with the pharmaceutical cocktail the doctors had prescribed, Paul's badly treated liver had failed to function, causing a temporary cessation of oxygen to the brain. By the time he reached the Cedars of Lebanon Hospital in Hollywood he was in the deepest coma.

Someone had telephoned Gail before the ambulance arrived, but as she was staying out at Santa Barbara it took her an hour and a half to reach the hospital. By the time she reached her son he was just alive, on a life-support machine, with symptoms of damage to the brain from lack of oxygen. When Gail asked the doctors what she could do for him, all they could say was 'Wait.' So once again Gail waited.

The doctors did everything they could to bring Paul back to consciousness, but couldn't hide their anxiety when he failed to respond. Then a few days later came a further cause of worry; X-rays revealed water on the brain, which was causing it to swell alarmingly. As something of a last resort the doctors turned to a revolutionary technique known as 'deep hibernation', which had never before been tried on human beings. Drugs were employed to send the patient into an even deeper coma, then he was gradually restored to his earlier condition.

Three days of deep hibernation cured the swelling of the brain, but Paul remained unconscious, showing only the faintest signs of breathing.

'He was alive,' says Gail, 'but only just – in the deepest of deep slumber, like the sleeping beauty. You could have pushed pins into his feet and he'd still have given no response or shown the faintest sign of waking.'

By now the doctors had nothing further to suggest – except more waiting. And it was then that Gail understood, as she had understood when Paul was kidnapped, that it was up to her to save him.

Realizing her total ignorance of coma, she visited the university bookshop and in the medical section bought everything she could discover on the subject. There was not a lot. Since 1981 the knowledge and treatment of coma has advanced substantially, but at that time there was one medical journal which gave her what she was seeking – an article on ways of maintaining brain activity in coma victims. Certain methods were suggested – continual talking to such patients, reading a book aloud to them, or playing them their favourite music. The theory was that, although unable to respond, the patient could often take in much of what he heard. Maintaining mental activity is all-important to prevent coma victims lapsing into silent inactivity.

Since then this treatment has become widely accepted, but at the time the doctors tended to dismiss it. It made sense to Gail, however. More important, it offered her and the family something positive that they could do for Paul instead of hope-lessly watching him become a vegetable.

She organized members of the family to give him round-the-clock attention. 'The aim was to make sure that there was always someone with him, either reading or talking to him or playing him his favourite music.' It was hard work, but suddenly the watchers by the bedside found they had another helper.

Mark was back at Oxford when he heard the news about his brother. He did not know that by leaving the university he would probably forfeit his chance of a degree. But as with the kidnap, he felt an obligation to be with Gail and his brother at a time of crisis. A male presence was required, and since his father was unable to provide it, it was up to him to take his place. By 8 April, three days after learning of Paul's disaster, Mark was on the twelve-hour flight to Los Angeles.

From now on he took responsibility for part of the night shift looking after Paul. Gail would stay at the hospital every evening until midnight, then Mark would take over until dawn. During the day, Aileen and Ariadne took turns to read and talk to their brother. Martine joined them. Despite the problems of their marriage, she insisted she was still Paul's wife, and that she, and not Emmanuela, was the one to be with him. As usual in a trial of wills, Martine won.

There is something quietly impressive in the idea of a family asserting its presence to avert a tragedy and willing a dormant loved one back to life. But as the days ticked by it looked as if it wouldn't work.

'With Paul just lying there,' says Gail, 'it was sometimes hard to tell that he was even breathing, but we tried ignoring this, stay-ing as positive as possible, and talking and joking with him as if nothing very much had happened.' Attempting to stay cheerful, she recounted incidents to Paul that she thought might still amuse him. Sometimes they played his favourite records, and all the time they continued talking without the faintest notion of whether he heard or understood a word they said. Sometimes it seemed a pointless exercise. But as there was nothing else to do, they continued night and day for more than five long weeks. And through it all, Paul lay still and silent as a statue.

One of the problems was that there was no way of telling how much damage had been done to his brain or how impaired he'd be if and when he did revive. All that the doctors knew, and the family suspected, was that the longer he remained unconscious, the worse his chances of recovery.

By the sixth week the doctors were no longer trying to disguise their feelings. With modern medical technology, there was no particular problem keeping Paul alive indefinitely – but everybody knew that past a certain point his hope of recovery fell dramatically – and that this point was fast approaching.

Typically, Gail was refusing to accept this. She still insisted that her son was going to recover – but for the others what they were doing was starting to appear a sad and rather hopeless exercise. Then on 14 May, nearly six weeks after Paul went into coma, came a glimmering of hope.

It was Mark who witnessed it, during one of his vigils through the small hours by his brother's bedside. Tired of talking, he had been playing Paul one of his favourite records, Wagner's 'Ride of the Valkyries', and as the loud, romantic music boomed out above the motionless figure of his brother, Mark noticed that something was happening. Tears were running down his brother's cheeks. Six weeks into coma, Paul was weeping.

Or so it seemed – except that when Mark summoned the duty doctor he was quick to damp down his excitement. He had known this before with coma victims, and it was usually a speck of dust causing minor irritation to the eye.

But Mark and Gail were convinced that Paul's tears must have come in reaction to the music. This was the only thing that gave them hope that Paul still had a future. But for several days, nothing further happened. Paul was as deep as ever in his coma, and it seemed as if the doctors had been right as usual.

To pass the endless hours at the hospital, Gail had been inviting old friends of Paul's to his bedside, and it was one of them who started reminiscing about the practical jokes he and Paul had played at school together. Some of the jokes were quite outrageous, and his friend soon had Gail laughing. When they stopped they realized that someone else was laughing too. From the direction of the bed, quietly but unmistakably, Paul was joining in.

This was proof at last that Paul really was emerging from his coma and would live. According to Gail, 'None of us quite believed it, and of course we were all in tears and highly emotional. But from that point on the coma started lifting, very slowly like a light being slowly turned up in a room.' In medical terminology this process is known as 'lightening'.

As Paul recovered consciousness, the doctors could finally assess the damage. It was as bad as the gloomiest had suspected. Although able to feel sensation in his body, he was virtually paralysed from the neck down. He was blind except for extremely limited peripheral vision. His speech, though audible, was seriously impaired. With such appalling disabilities, it seemed a final mockery that his intelligence remained completely unaffected.

The doctors were very kind to Gail when they talked about the future. But she wanted the truth, not kindness, and they gave her their honest opinion. They told her that Paul's only real hope of living out what remained of his life was flat on his back in a bed in an institution.

★

After more than six weeks struggling to keep hope alive, this was more than Gail could take. She was exhausted and the strain was telling. But just as she wouldn't give up hope when Paul was kidnapped, so she refused to give up now.

She said there could be no question of leaving her son to such a fate. But the doctors, still believing that they had to do their duty, insisted on telling her that quadriplegics as impaired as Paul were almost always better off in institutions properly equipped to look after them, and providing full-time nursing and the specialist treatment they needed. Attempts by loved ones to look after them invariably ended in disaster. However devoted relatives like Gail might be, the exhausting nature of the task ended by destroying the private life of anyone rash enough to take it on.

'Then that's a risk I'll have to take,' she said.

Had Gail had any doubts about doing this, they were banished now by Paul himself. Whenever he realized that she was in the room he'd start to weep and with an enormous effort enunciate a single word.

'Home!' he'd whisper.

Then, in case she hadn't understood, he would repeat it.

'Home! Home!'

So the work began that would occupy Gail's life for many years. Attached to the house in Brentwood was a guest house with a swimming-pool. Once it was equipped with the facilities of a private clinic it would prove ideal for Paul to live in with his helpers.

Over one thing the doctors were soon proved right – when they had warned her of the strain of looking after Paul upon her private life. Emmanuela felt this too. Her parents did not have much difficulty convincing her that there was little future as the fiancée of a quadriplegic, and she decided to return to

Italy. Martine, on the other hand, was once again a source of strength, and the two children, Anna and Balthazar, treated Paul exactly as they always had. Oblivious of his disabilities, they were soon clambering into bed with him and loving him as much as ever.

Fortunately Gail could hire nurses to provide the expert round-the-clock attention that her son required, together with the cleverest doctors and most practised physiotherapists in California. None of this would be possible without large amounts of money. But since Paul was a Getty, and money was the one thing which the Getty family possessed in such abundance, she thought this shouldn't be a problem. As so often in the past, where money and the Gettys were concerned, Gail was wrong.

CHAPTER NINETEEN

RECOVERY

WHEN HER SON Paul came out of hospital, Gail was being helped financially by her father and by Paul's uncle Gordon, who had bought the house where she and her family were living and was still providing everything his nephew needed. But for the long term this was clearly wrong. Gordon was immensely rich but so was Paul's own father, and he, not Gordon, should be paying for the treatment of his stricken son. He could obviously afford it countless times over, but when Gail began sending the bills to Cheyne Walk, they were returned – unpaid. Angry telephone calls ensued, and Paul Junior made his extraordinary position absolutely clear. Although a multi-millionaire, he was adamantly refusing to meet his son Paul's medical expenses.

To begin with nobody could quite believe it, and Gail's lawyer sent a calming letter trying to explain the situation – only to produce a fresh refusal. As she explains, 'Along with Gordon a group of us were paying for Paul's treatment and after a while it just seemed crazy and unjust to go on doing so. The very last thing any of us wanted was the publicity of suing, but with Paul refusing to listen, there was finally no alternative.'

As Gail expected, there was much unfavourable publicity for Jean Paul Getty Junior when in November 1981 he instructed his lawyers in Los Angeles to oppose Gail's court application for payment of $25,000 a month towards their son's medical expenses. The presiding judge was sufficiently shocked to rebuke

Paul in court, saying that 'Mr Getty should be ashamed of himself spending far more money on court obligations than living up to his moral duties.'

Even as close a friend as Bill Newsom described his behaviour as 'bizarre', adding that Paul had 'books in his library that cost more, much more, than it would have cost to look after his son for years'.

So what was going on?

The truth was that young Paul's coma had come at a bad time in his father's life. During a cure in Switzerland, Victoria had met Mohammed Alatas, a young Saudi businessman, and had fallen in love with him. She had once again given up hope of a satisfactory married life with Paul, so when Alatas proposed, Victoria accepted.

This had left Paul feeling more alone than ever back in Cheyne Walk. His intake of drugs and drink increased, and the more isolated and drug-dependent he became, the more his anxieties and fears grew. During the period when young Paul had been in coma, his brother Mark telephoned back to England almost every day with news for his father, who became as painfully affected by his son's ordeal as he had been in the early days of the kidnap. And once again he tried blanking out the anxiety and the pain of thinking.

What happened then provides a good example of how drink and drugs can actually distort reality, leading to emotional disruption and personal disaster. For, without making spurious excuses for Paul Junior, there was a sort of addict's logic to his behaviour over the medical bills. His refusal to pay them was generally seen as a recurrence of his father's meanness, but this was not the case at all, and his actions were really not concerned with money.

They were partly the result of the typical addict's neurosis over what he thought was happening behind his back. They were also his own strange way of attempting to play down what had happened to his son. For once he could convince himself that he was being cheated over these medical expenses, he could shift his sense of guilt for what had happened on to those he told himself had done the cheating. Stuck in his fastness in Cheyne Walk, he could even make himself believe that his son's appalling disabilities weren't as appalling as the dishonest doctors said they were. They had simply been exaggerated to extract money out of him; by challenging them, he could expose those lying doctors and prove that his son's condition was far less serious than they claimed. He wasn't the fool they took him for. And if he refused to pay a penny, he might even force them to admit that his son wasn't really sick at all.

Predictably, when it didn't work like that, Paul felt more rejected and guilt-obsessed than before – which made him more drug-dependent than ever. After the judge's remarks in the courtroom in Los Angeles, his lawyer, Vanni Treves, flew specially to Los Angeles to see young Paul on his father's behalf. He confirmed everything Gail and the doctors said, and the pathetic state that Paul was in. Paul Junior was finally convinced, and paid what he should have paid from the beginning. There were no more arguments, but the damage had been done – principally to Paul Junior himself. As a result of what had happened, his family inevitably turned against him.

'Gordon is light, and my father is the dark side,' Aileen told a journalist. And locked away in the house on Cheyne Walk, Paul Junior became more wretched than ever and determined to have done with his family.

Even Mark, loyallest of sons, was firmly on the side of Paul and Gail after so many bitter angry things had been muttered down the telephone from London.

This abrasive contact with his family and its sufferings brought further threats to Paul Junior's precarious stability, and he reacted as he always did: by relying more heavily on his trusted sources of relief, which produced the inevitable relapse, followed by a further lengthy stay in the London Clinic, which was becoming a home from home for him.

While what was left of his health and self-esteem were undergoing yet another battering, Gail and the children in America were doubly grateful for level-headed Uncle Gordon, who, in contrast with his brother, was happier than he'd ever been.

In a Paris bookshop just the year before, Gordon had found a copy of the poems of the nineteenth-century American mystical recluse Emily Dickinson, some of which struck him as ideal to put to music. Inspired by the poems, he overcame whatever had been holding him back as a composer and, in a fevered period of work, produced settings for thirty-two of them – from which he finally created the song cycle he entitled *The White Election*.

The White Election marked the beginning of a whole new life for Gordon and the beginning of his true ambition – to become a serious composer. All his enthusiastic energies went into it, and this was the point from which he always claimed his life had really started.

As a composer he had great ambitions. As he put it, 'composers are remembered by posterity when businessmen are forgotten', and he staked his claim in no uncertain fashion. 'I should like to be a composer who is remembered alongside the masters of the past, like Bach, Beethoven, Schubert, Wagner, Mahler and Brahms. Maybe it's hubris to put my name in that group. And maybe hubris is a damned good thing.'

Gordon's confidence and newly found creative happiness formed the greatest contrast to his brother Paul's addictive misery. Gordon was a genuinely happy man, with everything he wanted now as well as money. For Gail and the children, he was what they would have loved his brother to have been – supportive, kind, and quietly concerned about them all.

But Paul Junior had started to suspect his brother of usurping him in his family's affections, and grew jealous of everything he represented.

It was typical of Gordon to be the only one who didn't seem to notice his brother's change of attitude or to take offence, and he continued treating him as if nothing very serious had happened. It was here that the brothers' shared passion for the opera took on a particular importance as a slender bridge between them. Gordon would send Paul information about the great singers that they both enjoyed.

'Domingo greater than ever at la Scala.'

'Pavarotti greater still,' Paul would answer.

After the dramas of the year before, 1982 started with a period of calm throughout the family – and witnessed the beginning of a partial recovery for paralysed young Jean Paul Getty III.

At first he had seemed so terribly afflicted that his grand-mother Ann's first words on seeing him had been, 'They should have put him down to end his misery.'

Muscular cramps were causing him excruciating pain, and his body was so stiff and rigid that even the touch of bedclothes on his limbs was intolerable. Agony, tears, periods of deep depression followed, but after a while something miraculous began. To almost everyone's surprise, Paul started showing extraordinary willpower as he struggled to make something of the little that was left him.

It was now that the Getty money really helped. Just as it had been the origin of so many of his problems, so now it helped relieve his ghastly situation; for without it the specialist nursing and equipment he relied on would have been impossible. But Gail insists that there was more to Paul's treatment and recovery than money. 'It included not being afraid and negative. It called for courage and perseverance. It was about never giving up.'

And beyond this lay the most important fact of all – that the lost boy had found himself at last; that thanks to the disaster which had struck him, the suicidal, self-destructive urges which had practically destroyed him had been replaced by their opposite, a clinging on to life, which in turn was followed by a resolute will to live.

Finding himself with nothing, he was being forced to fight to be a human being – which he did with increasing power as his stamina improved. Everything in life that had previously been boring, gratuitous, taken for granted, had to be struggled for now. Since the kidnap there had been few challenges in his life. Now everything became a challenge.

Although he couldn't see, he asked to be taken to his grandfather's museum at Malibu on the day when it was closed to visitors, and while he was pushed around the empty galleries on a stretcher he had the paintings described to him, and the paintings became precious to him as paintings never had been when he could see them.

Every morning he exercised with his physiotherapists in the pool beside the house – boring, repetitive exercises, but he endured them and gradually his strength improved. His speech remained a problem, as there was motor damage to the brain causing a condition known as aphonia – making it hard to pronounce consonants correctly. So the following year Gail would take him to work with the speech therapists at New York's Rusk Institute of Speech and Hearing, which brought a slow but definite improvement.

He became hungry for books and his friends took turns reading to him. Martine was a lifeline for him, as were the children, giving him yet further strength to carry on. Gail's devotion was unstinted.

One of his heroes from the past, Dr Timothy Leary, came to visit him.

'His willpower is like Niagara. He is a miracle,' he said.

Nineteen-eighty-two saw another marriage in the family.

When, just before Christmas, Mark married Domitilla Harding in Rome's ancient basilica of the Santissimi Apostoli, he was the third generation of the Getty family to marry in the Holy City. But unlike the other weddings, his was a very grand affair which not only guaranteed that the Italian connections of the Getty family would continue, but also linked the family with Italian history. Along with its famous relics of St Peter and St Paul, the church of Santissimi Apostoli contains the tombs of numerous Riario and della Rovere cardinals, all of them antecedents of the bride; and part of the church itself had been built by the most famous member of her family, the warlike della Rovere Pope Julius II (patron of Michelangelo, painted by Raphael, and played in the film *The Agony and the Ecstasy* by the late Rex Harrison).

Although the bridegroom had now made peace with his father, Paul Junior was unable to attend, as he could barely walk and was still unwilling to return to Italy. And on the day of the wedding, in spite of all the detailed preparations, things soon started going wrong. First the bride failed to arrive at the church. Her grandfather, John Harding, had flown all the way from Boston to give her away but, owing to a typically Roman muddle, he was driven to collect her not from her flat in Parioli where she was staying, but from the family's summer house along the coast at Fregene. By the time John Harding found the right address, and had got his granddaughter safely to the church, the bridegroom and the congregation had endured two anxious hours wondering what had happened to the bride.

She arrived looking beautiful and quite unflustered, but this did little to resolve an even more disturbing mystery – where was the bridegroom's aunt, Gordon's wife Ann Getty? Since she wasn't there, the service had to start without her.

When Mark and Domitilla had announced their intention of marrying in Rome, Uncle Gordon had put his foot down rather firmly. Still worried by the memory of his nephew's Roman kidnap, he had reluctantly decided that it was still too big a risk for him or his family to attend. But Ann, by nature less anxious than her husband, thought otherwise. She was on a trip to

Europe at the time, and without informing Gordon had flown to Rome to be present at her nephew's wedding.

She was staying at the Excelsior Hotel on the Via Veneto, and Bill Newsom had arranged to meet her and bring her to the church. But once again something had gone wrong. Somehow they missed each other, so Ann took a taxi to the church alone, only to discover that while she spoke no Italian, and the driver spoke no English, she had forgotten what the church was called. For the next three hours she and her taxi-driver toured Rome, visiting every church where a wedding might be taking place.

With the memory of young Paul's kidnap never far away, Bill Newsom, Gail and several members of the family were alarmed that the worst might well have happened. Gordon could have been right. Ann should never have come to Rome alone.

She and her taxi-driver never found the church, and eventually returned to the hotel where she was reunited with the family when the service was over. Only then, with the nightmare of a second potential Getty kidnap behind them, could all the guests enjoy the party.

Next day, while Ann was flying safely back to San Francisco, Mark and Domitilla were *en route* for their honeymoon in Switzerland. Elizabeth Taylor had invited Gail and the family to spend Christmas with her at her chalet in Gstaad, and the newlyweds joined them. The snow was thick, the threat of kidnap was forgotten, and even with Elizabeth Taylor as their host, Christmas in Switzerland proved a more peaceful proposition than a Roman wedding.

CHAPTER TWENTY

GORDON THE PEACEMAKER

GORDON GETTY WAS a late developer – and rather proud of it. 'You know, for me it's true,' he used to say, beaming at the world around him. 'Life really did begin at forty' – for it was then that he had begun to realize his true potential, as a composer, an intellectual and a businessman.

Unlike most other members of the family, Gordon had always seemed to keep his fortune from obsessing or distracting him by the simple expedient of ignoring it. He still loved his enormous house at the top of Pacific Heights, he was as devoted to his family as ever, and he obviously enjoyed the freedom from the daily grind that his money gave him.

But he also insisted that he'd 'scarcely notice the difference in my lifestyle if I didn't have my fortune. I think I'd drive the same car I'm driving now, watch the same TV shows, the same movies. I might not have had the luxury of being a composer, but I'd probably have taught literature in a college somewhere and been just as happy.'

Perhaps he would, for currently his greatest problem was that of being taken seriously for anything except his money. Reactions to *The White Election* had been mixed, but he showed a commendable unconcern about the words of critics. 'My philosophy has always been that the next guy's taste is just as good as mine, but I won't defer to his.' What was difficult was to know how much the critical reactions either way were influenced by the fact that he was a multi-millionaire.

'I'd describe Gordon Getty as the best millionaire poet in the language,' the Irish poet Seamus Heaney told Bill Newsom after reading some of his extraordinarily fluent, highly polished and romantic poetry. Much the same applied to Gordon's music and his economic theories, which tended to be placed in a special category just because he was a Getty.

This was not entirely fair, for Gordon, far from being a wealthy dilettante, worked immensely hard at anything he did. Unlike his brother Paul he had always been a workaholic, a tendency inherited, like his money, from his father. And like his father, when the mood possessed him, Gordon would work in massive swathes of energy, rising at 6.30, confining himself to his workroom, and labouring throughout the day without pause for food or exercise or conversation, until, as he put it in typical Gordonese, 'I'm bushed.'

Apart from his record collection – by now probably the largest in private ownership in America – he remained entirely unacquisitive. It was Ann who had recently bought the three paintings of the Degas ballet dancers in the bedroom, and chosen the furniture in the spectacular drawing-room. Ann loved jewellery and grand furniture and Impressionist paintings. Gordon preferred ideas.

At around this time a friend, calling at the house, saw a painting of a dog propped against a sofa and, remembering that Ann had recently bought a painting of a dog by Manet, asked if this was it.

'Gee, I wouldn't know,' said Gordon. 'Ask anyone but me.'

Someone once described him as 'opaque', which was due partly to his apparent vagueness and also to his size, which gave him a sort of massive impenetrability.

But as the next few months would show, Gordon could be made to care as deeply about money as the next multi-millionaire. And anyone who challenged Gordon would be ill-advised to place excessive store on his naïvety and absent-mindedness. Opaque he might be – but in a financial battle, for all his talk about ignoring money, Gordon was someone to be taken seriously.

By the time of Mark's wedding, trouble was already brewing between Gordon and the board of Getty Oil, after the death a few months earlier of Gordon's solitary fellow trustee of the Sarah C. Getty Trust, the powerful lawyer Lansing Hays.

Since the trust owned 40 per cent of the capital of Getty Oil, Hays had been dominating the company management on the trust's behalf ever since Jean Paul Getty had died in 1976. Hays had made no secret of his contempt for the head of Getty Oil, the ex-accountant Sid Petersen. Now, with Hays departed, Petersen felt freer to assert himself.

But it was unwise of Petersen to have been so tactless in his dealings with Gordon Getty. For now that he was sole trustee of the Sarah C. Getty Trust, Gordon felt a need to know more about the state of Getty Oil, where all its money was invested. Petersen, however, like others in their time, regarded Gordon as something of a simpleton – and treated him accordingly.

By that autumn, Petersen's behaviour was seriously annoying Gordon, less on grounds of affronted dignity than because he felt that Petersen and the board of Getty Oil were insulting his intelligence. Since he effectively controlled the great family trust, Gordon felt he had a duty and a right to know why the shares of Getty Oil had reached an all-time low of under $50 a share. But as he complained to Bill Newsom, 'Whenever I ask about it, Petersen treats me as a nonentity.'

Unable to get the information he required from Petersen, Gordon turned to others who might help, and flew to New York to consult a firm of Wall St investment bankers. Were shares in Getty Oil, he asked them, seriously undervalued – and if so, what could be done about it?

He was being just a touch naïve to act in such a manner. With takeover warriors like Ivan Boesky and T. Boone Pickens on the prowl, such inquiries by anyone as unmistakable as Gordon

Getty would inevitably suggest that Getty Oil was ripe for their attention. So when Petersen caught wind of what was happening, battle between him and Gordon was inevitable.

It was a curious fight, for while Gordon continued to pursue what he felt to be the interests of the Sarah C. Getty Trust with a sort of rugged innocence, his opponents went to extraordinary lengths of cunning to thwart him. Their action took the form of a secret plot to persuade some member of the Getty family to petition the court in Los Angeles that the Bank of America should be appointed as an additional trustee to the Sarah C. Getty Trust on the grounds of Gordon's incompetence.

The plotters were not over-clever when they did this, for apart from underestimating Gordon they also made a bad misjudgement in their first choice for a family petitioner. In October 1983, Mark Getty was so surprised to be asked to present the petition against his favourite uncle that he flew to San Francisco especially to ask him what was happening. Gordon himself was baffled – at least to start with. But Mark's query served to warn him that something was afoot, so that when a petition did arrive, Gordon was prepared to meet it.

By now the lawyers representing Getty Oil had persuaded Gordon's brother Paul Junior to petition the court on behalf of his fifteen-year-old son Tara.

The fact that Paul Junior hardly ever saw his child by Talitha made this appear a fairly cynical manoeuvre. But from the point of view of Getty Oil, it was also singularly inept. For as Gordon's opponents might have foreseen, he possessed one weapon which they couldn't beat. Aware of what was going on by now, the bumbling Gordon used it – and the fate of Getty Oil was sealed.

Gordon's strength lay in the fact that most of the money which his father had left to his museum at Malibu was in the form of a 12 per cent holding in the shares of Getty Oil. Until this point, the museum chairman, Harold Williams, had purposely remained aloof from what was happening. But now, thanks to the behaviour of the board of Getty Oil, Gordon had little difficulty persuading him that the museum's best interests – especially their financial ones – lay in helping him defeat them.

Together, the shareholders of the Sarah C. Getty Trust and the J. Paul Getty Museum formed a majority able to dismiss the board of Getty Oil – and duly did so.

This was the point at which a takeover of Getty Oil became inevitable – and promptly arrived in the form of a cash bid of $110 a share from the medium-sized Pennzoil Company. This offer suited Gordon, who reached an understanding with Pennzoil's chief executive to become chairman of the reconstituted company.

But completion of the Pennzoil deal was delayed by a lawsuit from one of 'the Georgettes' (as someone had christened George's daughters), his second child, Claire, who was sentimentally opposed to this impious attempt to break up Grandpa Getty's precious company and petitioned the courts accordingly.

'Why, Uncle Gordon, does a trust already worth $1.8 billion need to be increased in value?' she had asked him.

'A very interesting philosophical question, Claire,' said Uncle Gordon, scratching his curly head and searching for an answer. 'It is my fiduciary duty,' he said at last, 'to maximize the wealth and income of the Trust.'

Maximize he did, and largely thanks to Claire. For while her lawyers were arguing the legality of the Pennzoil deal, the oil giant Texaco slipped in a higher deal of $125 a share for Getty Oil. And in January 1984, when Gordon accepted the Texaco offer on behalf of the Sarah C. Getty Trust, the value of the trust was doubled overnight, from $1.8 billion to nearly $4 billion.

Even this was not the end of it. To forestall yet another legal intervention from yet another quarter of the family – this time from Ronald's children, claiming that the price was still not high enough – Texaco actually increased their price to $128 a share, and that was that.

If the word awesome can be properly applied to a financial deal, then the sale of Getty Oil was awesome. By paying a total of $10 billion for the whole of Getty Oil, Texaco had just made what was then the largest corporate acquisition in American history.

Some of the results were less than beneficial. With Getty Oil now swallowed up by Texaco, the family company lost its identity – and 20,000 Getty Oil employees their jobs. For Texaco too the monster deal proved ultimately disastrous – with Pennzoil successfully suing them for $10 billion over the affair, and making the company bankrupt in the process.

Within the family few seemed happy at the outcome and the legal battles rumbled on. Ronald used the sale as the occasion for one more attempt to right the injustice which had dogged his life – and petitioned the court to 'equalize' his share of the Sarah C. Getty Trust with those of his three siblings. (Two years later, Los Angeles Superior Court Judge Julius M. Title would finally express his sympathy for Ronald's situation, but reluctantly rule that 'in law there was no proof that his father ever promised to correct the inequity'.)

'The Georgettes' also went to law – in an attempt to punish Uncle Gordon for what he'd done to Getty Oil, by trying to make him pay all taxes due on the sale. And the earlier attempt in Tara's name to have a co-trustee appointed to the Trust continued. But despite the anger and upheavals which still echoed from this earthquake of a sale, one thing was undeniable. While the Sarah C. Getty Trust had been under the solitary control of an absent-minded, would-be poet, composer and economic theorist, its capital had more than doubled and now stood at something over $4 billion.

Whether by extraordinary cleverness or the luck that protects the innocent, Gordon in this one traumatic deal had made almost as many billion dollars for the Sarah C. Getty Trust as his father had within his lifetime. This time, *Forbes* magazine was proclaiming a Getty the richest human being in America.

★

This wasn't strictly true, as Gordon didn't own the Trust money he controlled, and he was limited to an annual income as its principal trustee of a mere $200 million. But this did not prevent him and Ann attempting to enjoy a little of their new-found increment.

Left to himself, Gordon would almost certainly have stayed exactly where he was and carried on composing his opera based on the character of Shakespeare's Falstaff, which the Globe Theatre Trust in London had recently commissioned. Apart from finding fame as a composer, there was little new in life that Gordon truly craved, and San Francisco suited him to perfection. 'I can go down into the street and get into my own car and don't have to call the chauffeur as I have to in New York,' he said. Besides, his friends were there, along with his precious workroom with his two computers, his Macintosh loudspeakers and his Yamaha piano.

But Ann felt differently. Under California law, she is theoretically entitled to half of Gordon's income, and within the family it was Ann who had the role of mover and spender. Even so, she had a problem over what to do with such a massive sum of money. For like Gordon she appeared to have more than enough of almost everything.

They already had their private Boeing 727, with Ann's initials painted on the tail, and its own bathroom with a real shower, which for some reason seemed to fascinate her husband. She had been known to redirect the plane to Paris on a sudden whim to do some shopping, but by now she had sufficient scarves from Hermès, bags from Gucci, shoes from Ferragamo, to last a lifetime.

She and Gordon made donations to causes they believed in – still principally concerned with conservation. The Leakey Anthropological Trust was supported in its work on the origins of man – as was Jane Goodall for her work on the behaviour of chimpanzees. When Gordon gave $5 million to the Leakey Trust, he said, 'There is a now-or-never quality to anthropological research, as human encroachment and deforestation threaten sources of fossil data-base.'

Simultaneously Ann decided to rebuild her family home in the Sacramento Valley. Although inclined to refer to her mother as a 'tough old bat', Ann was a good daughter, and hoped she'd please her with this brand new home in the shape of a Tuscan villa, complete with courtyards, flower-beds and tower. But the 'tough old bat' stayed fairly cool about it all – and the building used up only $2 million out of all that money.

It was around this time that a glamorous-looking Ann, when interviewed on television by Barbara Walters, tempted fate by setting out her current credo. 'Not at all,' she replied to a suggestion that too much money was an instant recipe for misery. 'I think it's possible to be very rich and happy, and I suppose, very poor and happy. But it's easier to be very rich and happy.'

Determined woman that she was, she now set out to prove this to her private satisfaction.

Ann is the sort of woman who likes challenges as well as money, and, since there was little left to challenge her in San Francisco, she decided it was time to focus her attention on New York. Having made herself the undisputed social queen of Pacific Heights, she now planned to do the same from the large apartment she and Gordon had acquired on New York's Fifth Avenue.

It was a spectacular, expensive operation, an adventure into what is sometimes called 'the regality of wealth', with Ann, if not exactly Gordon, apparently set to become the nearest thing to royalty for America. She entertained lavishly, dressed superbly, and soon acquired courtiers – like Jerry Zipkin, famous for his friendship with the Reagans, and the Greek financier and socialite Alexander Papamarkou. It was Papamarkou who introduced her to a real king, or rather ex-king, Constantine of Greece, and when she decided to convert to Greek Orthodox Christianity, King Constantine stood beside her as her godfather.

But despite this royal connection, Ann remained at heart the

girl from Wheatland, California; and, to satisfy her puritan conscience, she attempted to become what is known as 'working
rich' – by joining the boards of Sotheby's and Revlon, and
becoming a trustee of the Metropolitan Museum and the New
York Public Library.

It was not enough. For what she craved secretly was not so
much work as self-improving culture – the subtle conversation
of philosophers, evenings with distinguished authors, enriching
contact with gigantic minds. All of which were suddenly on
offer, thanks to an unlikely friendship with a portly, polyglot,
cigar-loving publisher of Austrian Jewish origin, who happened
to be a member of the British House of Lords.

Since the early seventies Ann and Gordon had been flying regularly to Europe in their Boeing 727, doing the rounds of the
music festivals, such as Salzburg, Spoleto and Bayreuth, which
they thoroughly enjoyed. It was at Salzburg back in 1972 that
they had first met Baron Weidenfeld of Chelsea, and the friendship subsequently flourished.

Although a publisher by profession, George Weidenfeld was
essentially an old style central European cultural magician.
Everything about him had a touch of magic, including his bar-
ony, conferred upon him by the socialist premier Harold Wilson, and the equally magical survival of his London publishing
house, Weidenfeld & Nicolson. Meeting Ann now to discuss her
aspirations, he suggested that the answer to her problems was to
become a publisher like him.

It was an original suggestion, but not impossible for the
wife of the richest man in America, particularly as Weidenfeld
knew that Barney Rosset of Grove Press, famous publisher of
Henry Miller, Jean Genet and the Marquis de Sade, was keen to
sell the business and finally retire with 2 million dollars.

Ann had always been an eager reader – though whether of
books from Grove Press is another matter – and the idea captured her imagination.

'I love to read all day,' she said. 'But as I'm of puritan stock and grew up believing that you have to work all day, I decided to make reading my work.'

Buying Grove Press suited her, for as well as reading for her living she could now begin to meet those strange Houyhnhnm-like characters, famous living authors. She even went on a promotion tour with one of them, Nien Cheng, author of the best-selling *Life and Death in Shanghai*.

The purchase also suited George Weidenfeld, who had persuaded Ann to become a partner in Weidenfeld & Nicolson in London, and simultaneously help finance a new and independent branch of Weidenfeld & Nicolson to operate from New York, in close cooperation with the Grove Press.

For Ann and for Weidenfeld, publishing became a game that two could play. He would fly Concorde to New York, where they would get together to discuss the publishing conundrums of the 1980s – could they encourage Joseph Heller to create a proper sequel to *Catch-22*, or J. D. Salinger to do likewise with *Catcher in the Rye?* Could Ann entice the susceptible Norman Mailer or the saturnine Philip Roth to their imprint – or should they go for less expensive, lesser-known authors? They also planned to enter films, preparing to bring Weidenfeld's old home town, Vienna, to the screen 'in all its intellectual and cultural splendour', as the publicity put it. There was talk of an impressive cultural magazine. A TV series on 2,000 years of archaeology was commissioned.

'Everything I do is related to everything else I do,' said Ann, as she set up the Wheatland Foundation to further her different interests in the arts. The Foundation went to Venice to discuss the future of opera, and to Jerusalem to discuss the symphony. Writers were taken up the Nile to discuss literature, and others brought to talk about their books beside the Tagus.

And through it all Ann paid large advances to her authors, which is the best and noblest way for anyone to offload fairly large amounts of money.

There were also dinner parties for authors and their agents at the Getty apartment on 5th Avenue, the like of which have not been seen before or since in the world of publishing – exquisite food, exotic flowers, twenty-four sitting down to table, all this together with the aroma of George Weidenfeld's Corona Corona and his fluent conversation in five European languages.

Throughout these dinner parties Gordon, being Gordon, sat in the background, smiled his Gordonesque smile, said 'Heck', and 'Gee', and tried working out the latest puzzle that had started to obsess him, an odd one for a billionaire. How can modern capitalist society operate without money? Money causes such a lot of problems. Surely, he told himself, there had to be a better way.

Gordon couldn't meditate for long, since the fall-out from the sale of Getty Oil continued. In all, Gordon found himself facing fifteen separate lawsuits, most of them from members of the family. This genuinely disturbed him. 'There's nothing more rancorous and upsetting than a family lawsuit,' he said sadly. Besides, he was longing to return to his composing.

As a close witness to the effects of past family dissension, Gordon wanted peace. According to Bill Newsom, he was 'astonished at the way the sale of Getty Oil had gone', and confessed to him, 'Bill, I just don't *want* 4 billion dollars.' Nor did he want the trouble that accompanied the position of sole trustee of the Sarah C. Getty Trust. Nor, for that matter, did he see much mileage in prolonging the existence of the trust out of loyalty to his father. It had done its work. It had played a major part in creating and preserving the family's amazing fortune. Its usefulness was over.

So acting like the philosopher billionaire he was, Gordon Getty bowed to the inevitable, and killed the Sarah C. Getty Trust stone dead. First he paid practically a billion dollars to the taxman – then, Solomon-like, divided up what remained of the corpse four ways. Each part was roughly 750 million dollars. One part went to his brother Paul, another to 'the Georgettes', the three daughters of his half-brother George, yet another to the heirs of his half-brother Ronald – and the fourth part he kept for himself and his family.

As Ronald's exclusion from the fruits of the trust continued, this brought a certain complication to the situation. Apart from the Georgettes, none of the grandchildren of J. Paul Getty would inherit until the death of the last of his three remaining sons – which by actuarial computation could be expected around twenty-seven years hence. In the meantime the money which would go to Ronald's children was in turn divided into three separate trusts, the profits from which would go to Paul, to Gordon and to the Georgettes until the next generation was in a position to inherit.

The dismembering of the Sarah C. Getty Trust was an important moment in the history of the Gettys, for it offered the family the possibility of peace at last, by giving each section of the 'dynasty' control of its own finances. The immensely profitable sale of Getty Oil had already freed the family from its dependence on the uncertain future of the oil business. Now the family possessed this vast new acreage of wealth, which with appropriate investment could last for ever, with the capital within the trust steadily increasing and the income beneficiaries living immensely well off the interest.

At the same time, Gordon made one further contribution to the future well-being of the family. Appreciating the danger of having vast amounts of money locked away within the separate trusts for years, to gush forth only on the death of the last of the older generation, he devised a way of ensuring what by Getty standards was a relatively modest income for younger members of the family in return for their participation in the workings of the different trusts.

He personally gave up the 5 per cent trustee fee to which he was entitled in order to provide annual fees for younger members of the family, who were to be appointed co-trustees of the family trusts at the age of twenty-five. In this way he hoped that his children and their cousins would gain experience in the financial affairs of the family, and have an early stake in its prosperity.

Already he was looking forward to a future for his children free from the disasters that had dogged the Gettys in the past. He put his hopes for them into a poem which he wrote around this time entitled 'My Uncle's House'. It ended thus:

> *I wish my sons no finer birth;*
> *I wish them this, to find*
> *How patience and the generous earth*
> *Make life, how work makes wealth and worth,*
> *And song the graced mind.*

CHAPTER TWENTY-ONE

KNIGHTHOOD

THE $750 MILLION Paul Junior received from the division of the Sarah C. Getty Trust made him overnight the sixth richest man in Britain. The capital was credited to his Cheyne Walk Trust, where it was expertly invested by fund managers across a whole range of investments to guarantee security and growth – which with interest rates at an all-time high in the early eighties meant that while the core capital would steadily increase for the benefit of future generations, Paul would immediately receive more than a million dollars every week in interest.

In terms of disposable income he was even richer than most of Britain's other hyper-rich. With his children and grand-children's inheritances taken care of by the capital in the trust, and with no extraneous demands upon his income, he was free to spend entirely as he wanted.

But it would have been hard to find a neater parable on the futility of excessive wealth. What use a million dollars every week to someone who despised himself, who barely left his home except to enter a clinic, who derived no pleasure from family or food or travel, and who was suffering acute phlebitis, impending diabetes, suspected cirrhosis of the liver, impaired lung functioning, brittle bones and dreadful teeth?

The poverty of his desires made the richness of his inheritance distinctly pointless. Yet by an unexpected twist of fate, it was the arrival of this vast inheritance that marked the beginning of Paul's personal salvation.

The arrival of the money coincided with a personal crisis. Paul was very ill indeed, and with Victoria still married to Moham-med Alatas – and now the mother of two sons, Tariq and Zain – it was particularly hard for him to remain at Cheyne Walk without her. With his health in ruins, he re-entered the London Clinic for what would clearly be a lengthy stay.

It was around this time that his thoughts returned to the Catholicism to which he had been converted at sixteen by the Jesuits of St Ignatius. He had subsequently lapsed, but during this period in the clinic he was influenced by the Jesuit chaplain, Father Miles, from nearby St James's, Spanish Place. Under his guidance Paul returned to the Church.

Restored to the Faith, and having severed most connections with possessions and the world outside, he was living rather like a monk within the London Clinic. Here he had no responsibil-ities and was blessedly free from fear and worry.

So his first reaction to his money was a Christian one. He remembered Christ's remarks comparing rich men's chances of heaven to a camel's odds of getting through the eye of a needle. He was prepared to follow Christ's advice. Having no need of so much money, he was perfectly prepared to give the greater part of it away. But this wasn't easy. As a one-time hippie, he was uncomfortable with very large amounts of money anyhow, and had few clear plans of what to do with it – apart from wanting to see it used to good effect.

His first large donation went to a cause he personally believed in. As a lover of the cinema, he had discovered that the whole legacy of early British movies was in danger. The only copies of countless British films in the archives of the British Film Institute were on perishable nitrate stock, and the Institute lacked the funds for the expensive process of transferring them to modern media. Paul financed this – very quietly, as he wanted no publicity – finally contributing to the tune of nearly £20 million. It is largely thanks to him that the early history of the British cinema has not been lost for ever.

Shortly afterwards he offered £500,000 to Manchester City Art Gallery to prevent a small painting of the Crucifixion by the Sienese master Duccio being purchased by the J. Paul Getty Museum at Malibu. This aroused speculation in the press that he was getting even with his father's memory – or alternatively with his brother Gordon, who was a trustee of the museum. But his own explanation for his gift was simpler. He remarked: 'I'm fed up with everything streaming to Malibu. It's time that someone stopped it.'

Influenced by Father Miles, Paul now made a firm commitment to give up drugs for ever. But he had made the same decision many times before, and was painfully aware of the difficulty of sticking to it. Because of this, he intended continuing his treatment, supervised by his doctors, in the safety and obscurity of the London Clinic for as long as possible.

He would in fact stay fifteen months – but his desire for obscurity was not to be respected.

By the beginning of 1985 the government of Mrs Margaret Thatcher was facing problems over its policy towards the funding of the arts, a minor but potentially embarrassing area where supply-side economics, as practised by her monetarist administration, patently failed to function. In theory, as the state cut taxes and the rich grew richer, the so-called 'trickle down effect' would start, with grateful multi-millionaires offering up their surplus capital to fund the arts rather as wealthy donors had been doing in America for years.

But England's greed decade was so extremely greedy that it hadn't worked like that. (More to the point, perhaps, contributions to the arts were still not tax-deductible as they had long been in the United States.) And the fact was that by the mid eighties many of the country's great museums and galleries, endowed in more civilized eras, were strapped for cash in a world of monetarist plenty.

Ironically, the Getty Museum at Malibu – itself the product of private benefaction and with its wealth increased, like Paul and Gordon's, from the recent sale of its stock in Getty Oil – was making the situation worse by pushing up the prices of major works of art and being able to outbid any major gallery in the world. Without serious funding by the government – which would upset the Prime Minister and her spending limits – the National Gallery would be pauperized and left unable to bid for further acquisitions in the market-place of international art.

There was one bright spot in the gloomy scene of artistic patronage – the gift of money to the National Gallery in London by the Sainsbury family to construct a brand new wing on a neighbouring site which would ultimately bear their name. The prime mover had been the artistically enlightened scion of the Sainsbury family, Simon Sainsbury, who coincidentally happened to be the business partner of Christopher Gibbs. While the Sainsbury gift was being finalized, one of the gallery trustees, the Marquis of Dufferin and Ava, had talked to Gibbs about the gallery's need for 'an equivalent great endowment' which it could invest to provide an annual income for its major purchases.

Gibbs pondered – but he can't have pondered very long. For it was shortly after this that some influential members of the government and the world of art became extremely interested in a previously neglected hermit billionaire currently residing in the London Clinic.

It had been nearly twenty years since Christopher Gibbs had first met Paul, and he was one of the few who had continued seeing him regularly through the bleak years following Talitha's death.

During this period, Gibbs himself had prospered. With Simon Sainsbury as his partner, he had become a successful West End art dealer, with a rich clientele and a fascinating shop in Mayfair.

At the same time he had transformed himself from the wunderkind of 1960s Chelsea into a serious social figure, with a house beside the Thames at Abingdon, an apartment in Albany and a wide range of influential friends.

During his own ascent, there had been little he could do to halt his friend's decline, but now he detected in the current situation a chance for Paul to help himself while helping the National Gallery solve its problems. If he could be persuaded to make the gallery the sort of grand donation it required, the result might well work wonders for his public image – and thereby for his private self-esteem and precarious morale.

Despite his gifts to Manchester City Art Gallery and the BFI, Paul still had far more money than he knew what to do with. So when Gibbs described the plight of the National Gallery, Paul agreed in principle to a £50 million gift without demur.

But Gibbs wanted to ensure that Paul received full credit for his generosity, With so much money – and such dubious publicity from the past – the gift could easily backfire if handled badly. To prevent this, Gibbs relied upon a number of strategically placed allies who understood the situation, and who would be able to ensure that the gift became a coup for the gallery – and something more than this for Jean Paul Getty Junior.

The most important of these allies was the newly appointed chairman of the Gallery trustees, the financier and art collector Lord Rothschild. A perceptive human being as well as a successful banker, Jacob Rothschild was swift to appreciate the irresistible nature of the gift – and what it would entail.

'It just never happens that you get an offer of £50 million even for the National Gallery,' he says. 'So when it *does* occur, you go for it with everything you've got, and throw in the whole boiling – support from politicians, from royalty, from anybody who can help. It's your job to be an opportunist, and do everything you can to make it happen. I knew that Christopher was seeing this as part of Paul's return to life, and hoping it would change the perception people had of him. That was something I was obviously prepared to go along with.'

Another of Gibbs's influential friends, Mrs Thatcher's Minister for the Arts, Lord Gowrie, felt much the same once he
heard what was on offer. As a member of the government he
had a stake in ensuring that the donation went ahead, and he
was fully aware of the political significance of so much private
money for the arts. So, like Lord Rothschild, he visited Paul
Getty Junior in the London Clinic to express his gratitude and
finalize the details of the gift.

He was quick to tell 'the Boss', as he referred to Mrs
Thatcher, who was equally delighted at the news. High art was
fairly low on the Thatcherite scale of values, but an unsolicited
gift of £50 million to the nation brought out the gentle side of
the Iron Lady, and her immediate reaction was that she should
thank Paul Getty Junior in person.

In the USA it would have been unthinkable for the head of
government to associate with a well-known addict with a history such as Paul's, but for Mrs Thatcher it would have been
unthinkable not to.

She liked rich people, and was particularly moved that one
of them was showing such patriotism to his adopted country.
Since he was in the London Clinic, what else could a caring
premier do but don the mantle of Miss Nightingale, come to
the bedside of the invalid billionaire, and thank him warmly for
his generosity.

Before this happened, Gowrie felt it prudent to inquire of
Paul how he felt about meeting Margaret Thatcher. He relates
that he found him 'rather excited by the idea, but being a very
shy man he was also wary and asked me to brief him over what
would happen. I told Paul, "Just don't worry. You'll find that
she'll be very charming and very easy to talk to and as soon as
she sees you, she'll say, 'Now my dear Mr Getty. What on earth's
the matter?' Then before you know where you are she'll have
taken over your case medically." '

When Lord Gowrie brought Mrs Thatcher to the London
Clinic a few days later, he was understandably relieved to see
that 'Paul had spruced himself up and was sitting on the edge of

his bed like a schoolboy waiting for matron'. Once introduced, the Prime Minister treated Paul almost word for word as Gowrie had predicted.

'My dear Mr Getty,' she began. 'Now what's the matter? We mustn't let things get us down now, must we? We must have you out of here as soon as possible.'

Gowrie saw Paul looking worried, for, as he says, 'He was obviously as happy as a clam in the London Clinic, where he was taken care of and had no intrusions on his privacy, and had everything he needed – his records, and his books and television.'

The thought of being forced to leave this haven must have shocked him deeply. But this apart, the visit went off admirably. Everyone was very charming, and Paul himself was genuinely touched by the Prime Minister's concern. When a signed photograph arrived from Downing Street it was given pride of place beside his bed; and during the months ahead Paul and Mrs Thatcher met several times and got on splendidly together. Meeting Paul's half-sister Donna (neé Wilson) later in America, Margaret Thatcher told her that her brother had one of the most remarkable minds in Europe.

Despite the Prime Minister's concern to get him out of the London Clinic as soon as possible, Paul had nearly nine more months of clam-like bliss within its pricey portals. According to his lawyer, Vanni Treves, he was treating it 'more like a hotel than a hospital' – but this did not belie the fact that he had been extremely ill, and that the process of recovering from such long and deep addiction required time.

Fortunately there was no pressure to economize on the £250 a day, plus treatment costs and incidental extras, which his room was costing. Methadone could take the place of heroin, lager in the icebox could become an acceptable substitute for rum – but there were no short cuts to help his wounded spirit to recover.

In the meantime, since he was still determined not to spend

his enormous income on himself, it was announced that he was placing much of it in a charitable trust and keeping 'only what is necessary to maintain a relatively modest lifestyle'.

It was now that he contributed £20 million to establish the J. Paul Getty Jr Charitable Trust. The trustees were Christopher Gibbs, Vanni Treves, and James Ramsden, former Conservative minister and chairman of the London Clinic – and Paul was careful to designate the sort of groups on whom the annual income should be spent.

Two key categories were to be conservation and environment, but the rest of the money was to go to what he termed 'unpopular causes', generally involving 'poverty and misery'. Most of the grants would be of the order of £5,000 and £10,000 for small community and local projects – such as work with the mentally ill, drug addicts, ethnic minorities, and the homeless. The trust should also 'offer support for people under stress', such as battered wives, victims of sexual abuse, and families in difficulty. Most of the suffering Paul was hoping to relieve had definite connections with his own experience. He had never known poverty – but otherwise was fairly well acquainted with most forms of human misery.

The Trust established, he continued giving on the widest scale, often on the spur of the moment to something he had seen on television. Hearing that the virtuoso pianist John Ogdon was so short of money that he had been forced to sell his piano, he told him to choose himself a new one and send him the bill. (Ogdon did and it cost £18,000.) Touched by the plight of a group of breakaway striking miners, he sent them £50,000. £250,000 went to preserve the environment of Ely Cathedral from the threat of building, and £10,000 to conserve a medieval field in Somerset.

(Since then he has made large donations for famine relief in Eritrea, medical supplies for Poland, the Special Air Service and the Imperial War Museum. He also paid $1 million for Claus von Bülow's legal fees for his successful defence against charges of attempting to murder his wife Sunny – 'because my father would have done so'.)

By giving he was generating great goodwill. Britain is not a generous country, and gratitude was palpable around him. Meanwhile from his room within the London Clinic, he continued to adhere to that 'fairly modest lifestyle' he apparently enjoyed. His only personal extravagance that year was the purchase of Wormsley Park, a run-down country house with a more or less derelict estate 38 miles from London, for £3.4 million.

Built in 1720, Wormsley had been home to the Fane family for two centuries until they found it too expensive to maintain. The house needed more or less rebuilding – or demolishing – and its greatest asset was its romantic position in an upland valley on the edge of the Chilterns, surrounded by 3,000 acres of meadowland and seriously neglected beechwood.

Why Paul had bought the place was anybody's guess. Had he needed a country house (which currently he didn't), why a derelict edifice like Wormsley when he could have purchased almost any stately home in Britain? To make his attitude towards the purchase clear, a spokesman told the press that the house and the estate would be restored 'regardless of cost – and then given to a charitable trust for deprived children'.

Perhaps it would. But as with his gift to the National Gallery, the initiative behind the Wormsley purchase came from Christopher Gibbs, who cheerfully admits to having 'bullied' Paul into it. Gibbs was a man of many interests, but creating homes at great expense for deprived children was not among them.

When Paul's gift to the National Gallery was announced, the Establishment united to express its gratitude.

'Maecenas has come among us,' hymned Gowrie's deputy, William Waldegrave, as he brought the news to an awed and grateful House of Commons. Simultaneously a missive of considerable distinction arrived for Paul at the London Clinic. It was from the Secretary to the Cabinet, and conveyed the news that 'the Cabinet agreed that the standing of the Institution and the munificence of the gift combine to render this an occurrence of national significance, and express their warm appreciation of, and profound gratitude for, your magnificent generosity'.

Meanwhile from America came congratulations couched in less tortuous vernacular. 'Three cheers for your magnificent support,' cabled Gordon. 'If that means Britain can keep art works that might have gone to the J. Paul Getty Museum, that's fine. And if you personally were to target Getty Museum acquisitions for retention funds, picking on us and not on other purchasers, I don't see how I could find much fault with that either.'

Since Gordon was a trustee of the museum in Malibu, it was generous of him to write like this. And against the background of the treatment he had been receiving from Paul until quite recently, his note seems positively saint-like in its attitude. But Gordon was wanting bygones to be bygones. So was Paul. A new and unaccustomed mood of reconciliation had started in the family.

At the same time, public approval was beginning to have the effect on Paul's morale that his friends had hoped for, encouraging him to stay off drugs and be worthy of the glowing reputation he was gaining. He had tried to break the habit many times before, but failed to sustain the resolution. This time, however, he was revealing unsuspected strength of will.

Even so, it wasn't easy – and his 'cure' was by no means completed. He had been addicted now for nearly twenty years, and the psychological dependence over such a period is often more difficult to break than the purely physical. Prolonged addiction can inhibit emotional development so that former addicts find themselves subject to relapses, to panic attacks, and are painfully at risk.

Strong-willed though he was, Paul remained vulnerable, and

his damaged psyche needed reconstructing rather like an injured body. In the process much of his former self was being quietly replaced by something very different.

This explains why Jean Paul Getty Junior, one-time hippie, heroin addict, unemployed billionaire, was getting on so well with Mrs Thatcher, who as a person and a politician stood for much that he would once have almost certainly derided – middle-class morality, hard work, and family values.

Paul was changing. He was now fifty-two, and, in place of the Pre-Raphaelite hippie of the early days in Cheyne Walk, an increasingly conservative middle-aged Englishman was emerging.

That autumn came his biggest test of all – reunion with his son, Paul. This was young Paul's first flight to Europe since his coma. He flew from Los Angeles with his two male nurses, and once in London the first thing he wanted was to see his long-lost father; or rather, since young Paul was all but blind, to hear his father's voice, be with him again, forget the past, and start a new life with his blessing.

It would have been hard for any father to have coped with such a situation. Inevitably there were tears, especially from Paul Junior, whose sense of horror and regret when faced with what had happened to his broken son can be imagined. It was a harrowing ordeal for him, particularly as he could no longer dull his sense of guilt with drugs or alcohol. But there was also joy, and the chance of making restitution in the future. He was learning his first lessons in coping with his guilt unaided, and with every day that passed, the future seemed more hopeful.

By the second week of March 1986, Paul was sufficiently recovered to take Mrs Thatcher's advice and leave the London Clinic. He had stayed hidden away for so long that, despite the fame his generosity had brought him, he was regarded as something of a mystery by the general public, and bizarre rumours of his physical condition prompted Vanni Treves to assure reporters that 'his health is now actually very good'.

Like most lawyers' assurances, this was true to a point. Paul was off heroin and booze, his circulation had improved, as had the condition of his liver, and his general health was certainly better than eighteen months earlier. But his physique remained impaired. He tired easily, and was liable to fall and break bones if he wasn't careful. To Lord Gowrie he appeared 'as if he had received a bad wound some time in his past, and had never quite got over it'.

Wise for once, Paul decided against returning to Cheyne Walk to live, the excuse being that the house had been so seriously neglected that it needed renovating. But the truth was that Cheyne Walk contained the dead weight of his past – regret for his children, guilt for Talitha, drugs, drink, the influence of Dante Gabriel Rossetti – and to leave now was to make a break with all that it had represented.

His new abode could not have been more different – a flat in a modern block created for the very rich just behind the Ritz. There were no ghosts here. It was quiet and discreet and somewhat clinical, its principal features being the views from its plate-glass windows of trees *ad infinitum* in Green Park, and the occasional elusive presence of Rupert Murdoch as a neighbour. Paul had actually purchased the flat some months earlier for his mother, but as she was now dying of cancer and her doctors were in America, she had little use for it.

The final accolade for Paul arrived in early June in the Queen's Birthday Honours List, when, not entirely unexpectedly, he was appointed Knight of the British Empire, 'for services to the arts'.

For a man suffering low personal esteem there is nothing like a knighthood, and it was touching to observe his obvious delight at what was happening. This was the final seal of acceptance by the British establishment, proof that as far as Britain was concerned the past was over and the slate wiped clean. However, as a foreigner he could not style himself 'Sir Paul' – which would have rather suited him – because foreigners are given only honorary knighthoods. To enjoy the curious pleasures of a title, he would have had to change his nationality, something he had already contemplated doing, having come to the conclusion years ago that 'Britain is Utopia'.

But he reluctantly explained that 'my advisers have asked me not to, because of the enormous tax consequences. [It would have involved him in double taxation, by the USA and Britain.] If I became a British citizen it would prevent me putting my money where it is needed.'

One sees his point. His knighthood had already cost him £50 million. To pay yet more money to the British Treasury for the right to use it would have been excessive. So he remained plain Mr Getty, KBE – joining a distinguished group of his fellow Americans, including Ronald Reagan, Gerald Ford, Henry Kissinger and Douglas Fairbanks Junior.

Receiving the KBE insignia from the Queen at the official investiture at Buckingham Palace was Paul's first appearance at a public event since his fraught arrival with Bianca Jagger at his father's memorial service ten years earlier. In its way this was even more of an ordeal, given the forbidding nature of the Palace and the fact that he was still far from well and had grown even shyer and more reclusive with the years.

But he had to go, not only because the Queen had summoned him but because his mother and his half-sister Donna had flown in from America to be present at the great occasion.

In place of the bustling Aunt Mame figure, Ann was now skin and bone, and so ill that her daughter Donna had had to accompany her. Ann had borne witness to the troubles that had hit the Gettys, and to the pain and disappointment Paul had caused her. But now, for the first time in many years, she could be proud of him, and could die having seen the Queen of England honouring her 'dearest Pabby'.

★

By now Paul was following several paths towards salvation. His Catholicism was one, his philanthropy another – and the third, and most pleasurable, was cricket.

Ever since Mick Jagger had introduced him to the game, he had continued watching it on television; given his addictive nature, he was soon a dedicated fan. Cricket can have extreme effects on grown men. Harold Pinter once seriously insisted that 'Cricket is the greatest thing that God ever created on earth, certainly greater than sex, although sex isn't too bad either.'

Paul would have agreed, and, scholar that he was, he began studying the history of the game from the days in the 1790s when the members of the Marylebone Cricket Club adjourned to the room at Lord's Tavern to codify the 'laws' of the game. In love with England, he loved the Englishness of cricket, and the way it had been patronized by the aristocracy when they played it with any labourer from the estate who could hit a ball for six. He learned all he could about cricket's famous players, past and present, rather as he had once learned everything he could about the greatest opera singers.

So it was that when James Ramsden, chairman of the London Clinic, introduced him to the distinguished-looking fellow-patient who was recovering from an operation, he knew exactly who he was and felt honoured to be meeting him.

Sir George 'Gubby' Allen was one of the grandest of the grand old men of English cricket. The son of a former Police Commissioner, educated at Eton and Trinity College, Cambridge, he was one of the last of the great amateur all-rounders. He captained England against Australia in 1936, and is remembered for refusing to indulge in Douglas Jardine's ruthless 'bodyline bowling' against the Australians in 1932, on the grounds that it 'wasn't cricket'.

Gubby came to be Paul's ideal Englishman, and after his death in 1989 someone suggested he had been like an elder brother to him.

'More like a father,' he answered.

It was a telling remark from someone who had missed out

badly over fathers, and Gubby became something Paul had always wanted – the sort of father figure who exemplified the virtues he was needing, self-discipline and courage in particular.

For any cricket lover, election to the Marylebone Cricket Club is one of life's golden pinnacles, taking much time and influence to reach. If one is very lucky one is put down for the MCC at birth, and might just get elected in one's thirties. But with Gubby President of the MCC, and Gibbs's brother, Roger, a committee member, Paul's election proved what everybody knows – that in England most doors open in the presence of extremely large amounts of money and the right connections.

But for Paul, election to the MCC was like acceptance into Paradise. Outcast no longer, he was entitled to wear one of the marks of English upper-class acceptance, the maroon and gold MCC tie (known among cricketers as 'rhubarb and custard'). He also had the entrée to one of the last male bastions of England, the historic Long Room in the MCC Pavilion.

Sitting beside his friend, the great Gubby Allen, in this cricketing Valhalla, Paul could participate in the ritual of the national game, watching the batsmen pass through the Long Room as they strode out to bat, following their innings from the vantage point of the pavilion, and then applauding – or sitting in commiserating silence – on their return.

The Long Room experience did more than anything to draw Paul out from the isolated world he'd lived in for so long. Old cricketers will always talk about two things – cricket and themselves – and for Paul the idea of a cricket bore was inconceivable. Before long he was numbering some of the greatest names of cricket among his friends – the fine Australian all-rounder Keith Miller, Denis Compton, and the oldest surviving English Test Match captain, R. E. S. 'Bob' Wyatt. These great men treated Paul with the easy camaraderie experts tend to show to wealthy seekers after truth, and his natural shyness didn't seem to matter.

Gubby continued to be very kind to Paul, but it would be pointless to pretend there wasn't method to his kindness. He had been a crafty bowler in his time, and as a successful stock-broker and former treasurer of the MCC he was not financially naïve. Cricket was seriously underfunded, and Gubby had long had plans to improve the standards of the game and the amenities at Lord's cricket ground.

Paul soon agreed with him, and with Gubby to advise him he felt honoured to become the self-appointed godfather of English cricket. Soon he was dispatching anonymous donations to hard-pressed county sides, paying for schools for youthful cricketers, and helping a group of Britain's worthiest recipients – old and needy cricketers – with pensions. Then in 1986 Paul crowned his benevolence to cricket by donating £3 million for a badly needed new spectator stand at Lord's.

His £50 million donation to the National Gallery had earned Paul his knighthood and acceptance from the British establishment, but his support of cricket brought him something different – genuine and lasting popularity. And, paradoxically, while establishing his popular appeal, cricket also endeared him to the English upper classes.

He understood the game and genuinely loved it, and, from his private box in the new stand he had paid for, he could watch its arcane rituals as he sat in splendour, offering excellent champagne to his friends among the cricketing fraternity, and alleviating the boredom of the English summer. But as far as Paul's private future was concerned, something more important still was taking place beneath the beechwoods in a long-forgotten valley in the Chilterns.

CHAPTER TWENTY-TWO

WORMSLEY

EVEN IN THE lost years of Paul's addiction, when Christopher Gibbs was making weekly visits to Cheyne Walk, he had always found his friend 'a very clever, funny, erudite man'; and, despite the anguish and the heroin, Gibbs insists that it was during these years that Paul taught him 'most of what I know about books and the book arts, and everything I know about the movies, and much, much else besides'.

Having known each other so extremely well for many years, they had developed much in common – interests, tastes, a shared sense of humour – so that once his friend received his monster fortune after the sale of Getty Oil, Gibbs could see, better than anyone, how this vast amount of money could be used to rescue Paul and steadily enrich his life.

One of Gibbs's many passions is his love for the English countryside, and even when Paul had seemed stuck for ever in the London Clinic he was already planning how to introduce him to the serious pleasures of country living.

When Paul left the clinic, it was obvious that, for all the talk about that 'fairly modest lifestyle' he intended leading, he would not reside exclusively in his flat beside the park for ever. But Gibbs knew Paul well enough to understand that in his present mood he had no interest in buying a stately home like Sutton Place, which would have worried and constricted him. It was because of this that he had pushed him into buying Wormsley.

At the time of the purchase, Gibbs saw Wormsley as little

more than 'a dullish house in a romantic setting', but he could also see how something extraordinary could be made of it. The 'romantic setting' could become the ideal background for what he was envisaging for Paul, a place so perfect that it would satisfy his every need and whim and speed his recovery.

In fact the whole idea of creating such a house had been haunting Gibbs for years. He had always been deeply interested in architecture, and had become fascinated by a recurrent architectural fantasy – of an earthly paradise where its occupants could effortlessly find true happiness. In the past, the would-be paradises of the very rich have had many names – Xanadu, Shangri-La, Schifanoia, Sans Souci – but Gibbs had become particularly intrigued by an English version of this dream, that of re-creating Adam's House in Paradise in the English countryside.

It was an idea associated with an unlikely figure who had come to fascinate both Paul and Gibbs because of his close connections with Rossetti and the Pre-Raphaelites – William Morris, the artist, typographer and early socialist, whose wife Rossetti was in love with.

Gibbs says that he has 'always had a vision (which comes and goes like all things mystical) of an English paradise like the one in William Morris's novel, *News from Nowhere*'. Paul was acquainted with this vision too. And here in this upland valley of the Chilterns, an area he had known since childhood, Gibbs saw how Wormsley could become a sort of rural paradise on earth. It could bring back Paul's appetite for life, reunite him with his family, and make him happy.

Once the house was bought, a few visits were enough to make Paul equally enthusiastic, thus putting paid to his hermit life for ever.

Once started, work on Wormsley soon built up its own momentum, which would last for more than seven years, keep over a hundred men permanently employed and cost around

£60 million. It would be such an extraordinary creation that, having seen it, one recent writer claimed that, 'as the expression of one man's taste on a grand scale, Wormsley has no equal in modern Britain'.

Even from the start it was obvious that more would be involved than just transforming 'dullish' Wormsley into the 'fine country house' Gibbs wanted for his friend. The house would virtually need rebuilding – but, above all, Paul was concerned about housing his precious book collection. He had bought so many books by now that the bulk of them were in store in London warehouses, and he couldn't wait to bring them all together in one building which would make a perfect library. But what was the perfect library?

The simplest solution would have been to have built an extension to the house in a style to match its eighteenth-century architecture, but as Gibbs put it, 'It would have ended up looking like a nursing home.' Instead he remembered seeing eighteenth-century houses in Ireland and the Scottish borders built close beside much older castles. A castle would also offer just the touch of fantasy that Wormsley needed, and someone suggested building it from local flint. No one had built a flint castle in England since the Normans, but Paul agreed to it.

He also wanted the most up-to-date modern cinema, along with unobtrusive garages, a nuclear-bombproof shelter, an indoor swimming-pool, a deer park and a four-acre lake. Wormsley had no lake, but Gibbs believed that any proper country house just had to have one. So an artificial lake would have to be created. And since there was no water for it, bore-holes would have to be sunk and water pumped from depths of over 400 feet through the chalk to fill it.

The 1,500 acres of beechwood also needed careful refor-estation. The fields required hedging, as the estate had been ter-ribly neglected and Paul had set his heart on having a herd of his favourite long-horned old English cattle at Wormsley. But the first priority was to put the house and cottages in order. Paul desired a centre for his family, for now that relations with them were improving, he was already picturing himself with his children staying on the estate. The picturesque New Gardens Cottage was needed urgently for young Paul's visit in December, which meant a rush to build a heated swimming-pool where he could continue his exercises.

For the future there still remained one all-important matter to consider – the creation of a cricket pitch, which Paul had also set his heart on. He was excited by what he'd read of the great days of English country house cricket – hot summer afternoons, white flannelled figures at the crease, and the effortless pursuit of the best game in the world. Before Wormsley was complete, it would need a perfect cricket pitch to match.

The creation of a billionaire's Shangri-La in the Chilterns might all too easily have ended as a nightmare or a joke; for Paul, either would have been a personal disaster. It was really Gibbs who stopped this happening, thanks to the guidance he exerted and the experts he produced to work upon the project. For just as it was largely through his friends that he had helped Paul get his knighthood, so now he turned to other friends to bring his hopes for Wormsley to fruition.

With the wrong architect, the library castle could all too easily have become something from Disneyland – but Gibbs had in mind an architect he knew and trusted, Nicholas Johnston, a man with a talent for interpreting the whims of wealthy clients. Gibbs had known him even before he had made his name by designing a mock-Georgian extension to the Ian Flemings' house near Swindon, and had grown to admire his taste and ingenuity. As Gibbs expected, Johnston got on well with Paul, and the Wormsley library is one of his most successful creations. From outside it is essentially a happy castle, living benignly with its next door neighbour, but, once inside, one sees what a sophisticated building Johnston, with his collaborator, Chester Jones, has created for its owner's fabled book collection.

For ever since the sale of Getty Oil, Paul had been stepping up his spending on priceless books and manuscripts. Apart from buying Wormsley, this remained his one authentic self-indulgence, but even with virtually unlimited resources and an expert like Bryan Maggs to advise and buy for him, the days were over when one individual, however rich, could build a comprehensive major library. The books are simply unavailable today.

But there remain individual treasures to be bought – and Paul had been assembling a collection of what he calls 'milestone books' in the history of book production to enrich his library; among them a priceless twelfth-century gospel from the monastery of Ottobeuren in Germany, Flemish illuminated Books of Hours, and elaborate nineteenth-century French *livres d'artiste*, luxuriously printed and produced editions illustrated with original paintings by contemporary artists. The strength of the library consists in great bindings (a passion of Paul's), English aquatint books, and wonderful examples of the private press movement.

Such books are a most recherché way of spending large amounts of money, and must have formed a very private source of pleasure to their owner. When converted into books, capital acquires a semi-sacred aura, and Johnston's library, with its scholarly interior and carefully controlled humidity and temperature, has something of the atmosphere of a secular chapel built to serve the house beside it. On the ceiling are painted the stars in their courses as they were on the night of 7 September 1939 above the Ligurian Sea when Paul was born. When some of the treasures of the library have been brought up from the vaults and placed on display they make a splendid sight.

Once it was completed and the precious books had been reverently set in place on their barathea-covered bookshelves, Paul was soon pottering between the book-strewn sitting-room, where he habitually watched television, through the conservatory and into the leather-scented silence of his library – which soon became his favoured place for reading.

But as well as designing the library, Johnston also supervised the transformation of the run-down country mansion into an up-to-date vision of a perfect eighteenth-century country house.

Once again there was a danger of Wormsley exhibiting what Gibbs himself once called that 'frightful uniformity of richness where everything shrieks that Mammon's worshipped'. To avoid this happening at Wormsley, he introduced another friend whose work he trusted, the interior decorator David Mlinaric. An amiable charmer, Mlinaric is essentially a scholar who has made himself the Pope of the English classical interior – and like the Pope he tends to be infallible, as he has shown in his work for the Rothschilds at Warwick House, at the National Gallery in London, and for the British embassy in Paris.

At Wormsley the result of his extensive operations has been a very gendemanly blend of comfort and understated opulence, together with a touch of the atmosphere you sometimes sense in great historic houses. The priceless carpets underfoot are very slightly worn. The new oak floors have been distressed artificially but as if by generations of the feet of gentry. And the furniture, mostly found by Gibbs, manages to look as if it had arrived at Wormsley over the last 250 years.

Perhaps the most interesting thing about this curious period, when Wormsley and Paul Junior were being reinvented, was how effortlessly he became accepted by the English upper classes. This was something that his father had desperately wanted, having been infatuated with the English aristocracy, who were perfectly prepared to visit Sutton Place and eat his food and take his hospitality. But although intrigued by the old man and deeply fascinated by his money, the English upper classes never saw him as remotely belonging to their own sub-species of humanity.

But with Paul Junior it was different. Times had changed and his previous vices could be easily forgotten. In a way this seemed unfair, since until quite recently he had been exhibiting a much wider range of human failings than his father. But it is important to remember that while his father had become notorious for a particularly *déclassé* brand of meanness, none of

Paul's vices was particularly shocking to the British upper classes. Drink, drugs, marital carelessness and being beastly to one's children are largely endemic to the English aristocracy, where they tend to be accepted on the grounds of eccentricity.

Paul had also made himself accepted through his love of cricket, which is widely taken as the purest proof of love for England. Indeed, at a time of faltering national self-confidence, there was something reassuring in the thought of this wealthy Californian taking England quite so seriously. His philanthropy also showed how genuinely he cared for his country of adoption, and there was a certain grandeur to his generosity. At a time when the native aristocracy had, by and large, abandoned the remotest interest in philanthropy, he was giving on a scale traditionally reserved for princes.

But another element in Paul's acceptance lay in Wormsley. Had the house revealed that fatal touch of Mammon as Sutton Place had done, he'd not have stood a chance. But because Wormsley was so understated and romantic, with the correct class connotations in the décor and the furniture, it could not be faulted. Nor, by association, could its owner.

One must remember too that at Wormsley he was indulging in a massive exercise in pure nostalgia, and attempting what the English aristocracy had been doing since the Reformation but because of the expense can do no longer – creating a classic nobleman's establishment in its entirety, complete with its castle, its mansion with its pillared portico, its home farm, deer park, lake and cricket pitch, together with one of the richest libraries in the country, crammed with treasures held in trust for future generations.

But the final element in Paul's acceptance was the way that members of the royal family gave him their seal of personal approval. This had started when the Queen awarded him his KBE, but in 1987 there came a setback in his royal progress, making one realize just how delicate was his recovery.

Early that May he was due to be presented with the prestigious National Arts Collection Fund's 'Art Benefactor of the Year Award' by Prince Charles at a dinner at the Dorchester. Paul had already shown that he was not averse to honours, but receiving them in public was a form of torture. On this occasion he was unable to go through with it and cried off, pleading toothache, shortly before he was due to arrive. Luckily, seventeen-year-old Tara was staying with him and, being commendably relaxed about such matters, collected the award for his father.

Three weeks later one more chance to meet another member of the royal family nearly failed as well. One of Gibbs's friends and neighbours, Lady Katherine Farrell, had invited him and Paul and Victoria to a small luncheon party she was giving for her friend, Queen Elizabeth the Queen Mother, whose curiosity had been aroused by what she'd heard about this strange American philanthropist. But while Paul was waiting for the Queen Mother's arrival, panic overcame him, making him feel so unwell that he had to lie down in a room upstairs.

'Such a pity,' said the Queen Mother when informed of Mr Getty's indisposition, but, practical as ever, she added, 'I suppose we'd better have a little something and begin without him.'

Luckily Paul recovered by the time the meal was over, and he was able to accompany the Queen Mother and show her Wormsley. Her Majesty was fascinated – by Paul as much as by his house – and they met later on a number of occasions.

Like almost everyone, Victoria fell in love with Wormsley, as did Tariq and Zain, her two children. Hardly surprisingly, her marriage with Mohammed Alatas wasn't working now that she was seeing Paul again. His health was improving, and the stronger and more confident he became, the happier he seemed when with Victoria.

Now in her mid forties, she was still an elegant, rather nervous English beauty. As he was haunted by Talitha's memory, her role with Paul had never been particularly easy and had been complicated by her diversionary marriages and romances. But by now she knew and understood him better than anyone, and he was particularly relaxed in her company. He bought her a comfortable house in Chelsea, but for Victoria, Wormsley was the house that really mattered, and inevitably she became the châtelaine of the establishment.

Rossetti had gone – except for his famous painting *Proserpine*, which hung in Paul's London flat like a souvenir from Cheyne Walk. Talitha's portrait by Willem Pol still hung in his dressing-room. Queen's House itself would soon be sold – to Gibbs's partner Simon Sainsbury and his friend Stewart Grimshaw.

Occasionally Paul would venture forth incognito to the world outside, sometimes bearded, sometimes not, and apparently enjoying the new-found freedom of his anonymity.

That autumn he spent £4 million buying the *Jezebel* – a wonderfully elegant motor yacht built in Germany before the war for the head of the Chrysler car company. He would spend more than twice as much again restoring her, and although she would lie for several years in lonely luxury on the River Dart, her presence was a promise of foreign lands and travel and a more exciting life around the corner.

It was as if his life was slowly starting up again after a massive interruption. Paul was building up an inner circle of extremely faithful friends. He was also rediscovering his past by bringing over some of the old members of the 'Getty Gang' from San Francisco like James Halligan and John Mallen, and having them to stay at Wormsley.

There seemed surprisingly little bitterness about the past among his children. Tara was particularly relaxed and seemed to have inherited his mother's happy nature. Although devoted to the Pols, and spending much of his time with them in France, he was also seeing more of his father now, and got on well with him and with Victoria, just as he got on well with almost everyone. The two girls had remained in California (Ariadne would marry the actor Justin Williams in 1992). Paul was hoping to see both his daughters at Wormsley in the near future.

But as far as the family's future was concerned, the most important of his children was turning out to be his second son, Mark. Realizing how important the control and direction of the family finances would inevitably become, Mark had decided on a career in high finance. Because of this he had taken Domitilla to New York and had landed a job with the banking house of Kidder Peabody and Co. He admits that 'the fact that they'd recently made $15 million out of the sale of Getty Oil might have helped'.

In 1982 Mark and Domitilla had a son and, wanting a name that sounded equally good in English or Italian – and thinking there had possibly been sufficient Pauls in the family – they called him Alexander. But they disliked the idea of bringing up a family in New York, and, wanting to be nearer Italy, moved to London, where once again Mark didn't find it difficult to get a job – this time with the influential merchant bank of Hambros.

The only person who was none too pleased by this was his father, who wanted him to return to Oxford to finish his degree (something he had never done himself). 'For someone who has been so unconventional himself, he was getting very conventional about it all,' says Mark, who as a married man was not particularly keen to become an undergraduate again. Largely to please his father, he did return, took a degree in philosophy – and then returned to Hambros.

But the more he learned of banking and finance, the more concerned he was becoming for the future of the family. It was clearly going to be of great importance how its resources were managed as the rest of his generation grew to manhood; and what particularly concerned him was the human problem of avoiding the misery and wastage he had witnessed in its past.

Already he was becoming something of a bridge between the different sides and generations of the family. He had remained extremely close to his Uncle Gordon and his cousins in San Francisco, and also to Uncle Ronald's eldest son,

Christopher. He remained as devoted as ever to his mother. Two more sons were born – Joseph in 1986 and Julius two years later – and Mark was happiest when staying with his own small family at his childhood home in Orgia.

After the bitterness and battles of the past, what he wanted most was peace among the Gettys so that his children could grow up unscarred and unaffected by the past – and free to make the most of what they would finally inherit.

For him the Christmas of 1987 was a very special one. At Wormsley the covered pool had now been built beside New Gardens Cottage, so that everything was ready when his brother Paul and his nurses flew in from California to join the family for Christmas. Paul was still paralysed, and his speech and sight remained impaired, but he had now transformed himself from the hopeless, totally dependent invalid he had been in the aftermath of his coma. Mark had not seen him so optimistic or so full of life for many years.

Paul had made up his mind to live as if his disabilities didn't matter – and to an extraordinary degree he had succeeded. He had recently been to university level classes in English literature and history at Pepperdine University, the school he had flunked out of before his coma. Once a week he attended classes at the university, and one of his nurses made tapes of texts for him, and interpreted his answers for his tutor.

He loved concerts and the cinema, and had made himself something of an expert on San Francisco restaurants. He had even started skiing once again – strapped to a metal frame on skis, with a ski instructor fore and aft. He dreamed of some day returning to Orgia.

In the meantime, in preparation for the Wormsley Christmas, Gail had arrived, and was delighted to be with her sons and her grandson, Alexander. Remembering how hopeless her son Paul had seemed after the coma, there were still times when she found it hard to believe all that he'd accomplished. The recovery of her ex-husband, Paul Junior, was almost as miraculous in its way, and she was glad to see him happy and relaxed at last – and able to enjoy a traditional English Christmas in his own home. He was now fifty-five, and it seemed as if the family's troubles could be over. But even then the past could not be so easily evaded.

CHAPTER TWENTY-THREE

AILEEN

TOWARDS THE END of 1985, Elizabeth Taylor, as President of the American Foundation for Aids Research, had gone to Paris on a short fund-raising trip. Earlier that year her daughter-in-law, Aileen, had finally given birth to a son called Andrew. Afterwards she had been seriously depressed and, thinking that a holiday in France would do her good, Elizabeth decided to take her along.

But for Aileen the holiday became more of a nightmare than a treat. The constant discussion of Aids made her suddenly aware of risks that she had taken in the past. There were things that she would rather have forgotten – and after a sleepless night in her hotel, she told Elizabeth that she might well be HIV positive herself.

As something of an expert on the dread disease, Elizabeth did her best to reassure her, but the blood tests Aileen took on returning to America proved positive. It was like a sick joke. Apparently the daughter-in-law of the President of the American Foundation for Aids Research was in danger of developing Aids herself.

After the first shock of the discovery, Elizabeth was the only person able to comfort the terrified Aileen, who seemed to dread other people knowing as much as she dreaded dying. She clung to Elizabeth pathetically, and to help her start the painful process of adjusting to the situation, Elizabeth let her stay in the privacy of her Bel Air mansion. Aileen's fears were worst at night, and the star would calm her terror by letting her share her bed.

For Elizabeth the situation was complicated by the fact that Aileen was mother to her two grandchildren (Aileen and Christopher had already adopted a son called Caleb before Andrew was born), and that her problems didn't end with being HIV positive. The illness was in fact the culmination of a series of dramas and disasters in her private life. For quite some time, Aileen had been as just as much at risk as her brother Paul before his coma.

Aileen had become the last of the sacrificial children, the latest victim of the great fortune. She was extremely pretty – with her heart-shaped face, her nervous manner, and enormous dark brown eyes – but she was also flighty, and the combination gave the impression of a nervous animal about to bolt, like a faun on speed. For several years she had been increasingly desperate and depressed, and had seemed heading for disaster.

Her fate still mystifies her brother Mark, for, as he says, 'One could have expected my brother Paul to have broken up, but not Aileen, who always seemed the liveliest and best adjusted of the children. She seemed so full of life, and had so much going for her. Perhaps she just wanted everything too quickly and grew up much too fast as a result.'

As usual in such situations, it is difficult to know exactly where her troubles started. Aileen has claimed that her insecurities began when her parents parted. She has also said that her rebelliousness started after her brother's kidnap, when she learned to distrust the Getty family, fearing that it would destroy her and isolate her from reality.

'I see money as a toxic element,' she said. 'I think it separates those with it from knowing what it's like to be without it. This takes much that is important out of life.' More to the point perhaps, she could see the trouble which the Getty money had brought to those she loved – the difficulties of her parents, the horror of her brother's kidnap, and the suspicion and unease which she, like many of the children of the very rich, had learned to adopt against the world around them.

Even in England, during her time at Hatchlands, she was already starting to reject what she saw as the obligations of 'being a Getty'. But it was not until she returned to California that she became a full-time rebel. As a rebel, she could go with unsuitable companions if she felt like it, sleep with them, drink with them and take drugs with them. Above all she could assert the one thing Gettydom denied her – freedom.

There was no shortage of drugs – or sex – in California in the mid to late seventies, and Aileen used them as weapons in her battle to be free. The drug she turned to was the favourite standby of the famous and the rich, which can become the most insidious of all – cocaine.

She had clearly inherited a strongly addictive nature, sniffing cocaine in such quantities that by the time she was in her early twenties her nose required medical treatment. By then drugs were giving her what she called 'emotional overload' – principally horrendous panic attacks and sleeplessness. By the time she 'eloped' with Christopher, she had already had the first of several nervous breakdowns.

Marriage to Christopher, far from sorting out her problems, helped to make them worse. Part of the trouble was her husband's kindness. He was a gentle man who happened to be in love with her. Cocaine addicts can react cruelly to those who love them, and her mood swings made their existence a misery – and normal married life impossible.

Overshadowed since childhood by a mother who was one of the most famous women in America, Christopher was hardly likely to stand up to a character as strong as Aileen. With nothing particular to do with their lives, they first tried gold-prospecting, then photography, neither of which succeeded.

Aileen had several miscarriages, followed by further periods of deep depression, during one of which she vanished to New York for several weeks. On her return she had a full-scale nervous breakdown requiring electric shock therapy.

Soon, as a friend remembers, 'Christopher was getting sick of acting as a nurse to Aileen' – as well as overlooking her absences and infidelities. It was in a last attempt to save the marriage that they adopted Caleb; and as often happens, no sooner had they done so than Aileen discovered she was having a baby of her own. Their son Andrew was born early in 1985. Eight months later Aileen was sobbing out her fears to Elizabeth Taylor in Paris.

Aileen has a strong touch of drama in her make-up, and after the initial shock of discovering she was HIV positive, and knowing she could not remain with Elizabeth indefinitely, she fled once more to New York – where she tried to lose herself in drink and drugs on the Manhattan nightclub circuit. Dangerously self-destructive, she was taking what she calls 'extreme measures to deal with an extreme situation', and adds that 'Funnily enough, I thought it would be more acceptable – this shows how unacceptable the virus was – if I died now of an overdose.'

But Aileen didn't die. Instead, she returned to Los Angeles where the two children were waiting for her. Christopher was talking of divorce. And there was, of course, one further problem. Her greatest fear was for her baby, Andrew, but thankfully blood tests showed that he was unaffected by the virus.

For a time she tried confining the truth about her illness to Christopher, Elizabeth and herself, and said nothing about it to the rest of her family. They were finding it increasingly difficult to help her while she was on cocaine, and were hoping she would reach a crisis point from which she could finally be cured of her addiction.

She underwent several cures – without success. And when

her family were starting to despair of her, she broke the news to them that she might well be getting Aids as well.

What particularly upset her was the contrast between Elizabeth Taylor's instant warm reaction to her plight, and what she felt was cold indifference from those who should have loved her.

'When I told Elizabeth, she had just cried and cried – and when she hugged me I could feel she was giving me something special.'

But there were no hugs for Aileen from the family, and she bitterly complained that 'No one in my family spared a tear for me.'

She was exaggerating, as she often did. Gail was desperately worried about her – as was her sister, Ariadne. But the fact was that, after so many recent tragedies, most of the family were finding it hard to face another – particularly one involving Aileen. They had heard too much about her troubles in the past. As Martine said, 'Aileen had a long history of drug abuse. So at first everybody thought she'd made it up – or just didn't want to believe it.'

Besides which, Aids was such a terrifying thing that, as Gail admits, she wanted to 'shy away' when Aileen first informed her that she was HIV positive. But the real problem was that at this stage almost everything to do with Aids was something of a mystery – particularly as it affected women, who still formed a small, virtually unresearched minority of its victims.

Trying to find out what was really wrong with Aileen, Gail asked her doctors; but none would say, on the grounds of her right to privacy, and they refused to discuss anything to do with Aids in even the most general terms.

'It can be a hideous thing trying to comfort somebody who thinks they're dying, when you can't even get the truth of what they're suffering from,' says Gail.

Elizabeth Taylor, on the other hand, as head of an Aids charity, and having recently seen her friend Rock Hudson die of it, knew exactly how to deal with the situation; also, as an actress, she was able to give Aileen the sort of emotional reaction she wanted. The Gettys couldn't.

Only when Gail found a sympathetic doctor who calmly and unemotionally explained the facts about her daughter's illness could she and other members of the family start to come to terms with what had happened.

The news was kept from Paul Junior for as long as possible, but finally he had to know. When he did, he became disconsolate, as those who knew him had predicted. All the old tragedies revived, together with the inevitable guilt and bitterness dating back to the divorce and even earlier. Would unhappiness never end?

Feeling he needed to talk things over with his oldest friend, but really needing consolation and reassurance, he asked Bill Newsom to fly over to discuss Aileen with him.

The worst thing was that there was little to be done – except to wait. In contrast with young Paul's situation, with Aileen the Getty money could make little difference. And once again there was the uneasy feeling that in some strange way the disaster was connected with a primal flaw within the family, and the chain of continuing unhappiness which seemed to follow them.

But one thing he could do was see Aileen again. He had to see her, and not long afterwards Bill brought her over. Thus illness and the threat of death had reunited yet another section of the family.

It was hard to see that Aileen had a great deal left to live for after Christopher Wilding divorced her and remarried in 1987, taking the children with him. Elizabeth Taylor, whom she called 'Mom' (Gail was 'Mummy'), continued to offer personal support, but wisely refused to be involved when Christopher gained custody of the children.

The loss of the children hit Aileen badly. She was desperate, and it was hard to tell which would get her first – Aids or her drug addiction. She was always in and out of clinics, trying to be cured but not succeeding. Then, at the end of 1988, she suddenly informed her family that she had met the man she wished to marry.

He was a good-looking young man whom she had met in her rehabilitation clinic. Gail advised caution. 'What's the hurry, and why marry straight away? Take your time.'

But Aileen, impetuous as ever, insisted she was free of drugs, and had set her heart on the marriage – which took place soon afterwards at the Monte Cedro Ranch near Gail's home in Santa Barbara. Gail, Ariadne and Martine attended, together with patients from the rehabilitation clinic. Afterwards Aileen and her husband left on a three-week honeymoon.

The day after they returned from their honeymoon, a friend of Aileen's called at their apartment and was alarmed to find her lying on the bed unconscious. She was rushed by ambulance to hospital, and the doctors had her stomach pumped out, suspecting a bad overdose of drugs.

Gail arrived as she was coming round, but the doctor said he was horrified by the sheer quantity of drugs that she had taken.

Soon afterwards Aileen's second marriage ended.

In contrast with Paul Junior's family, Gordon and Ann enjoyed reasonably untroubled relations with their children – for which they were profoundly grateful. Peter had just left college, where he had won a prize for a play he'd written. Having had it published, he was hoping to become a playwright. His brother Bill was enjoying a year at Florence University.

Gordon remained an easy-going father, and all his sons were very much California boys – relaxed, amusing, and not really wanting to live anywhere but San Francisco. This suited Gordon.

He always said how much he'd love the excitement of another major business deal, for in retrospect he felt he had enjoyed the drama of the sale of Getty Oil – even the broken nights, the law-suits, and the need to cope with all those possible disasters. It had been Gordon's time of living dangerously.

But when he did find himself involved in a deal, it rarely seemed to work, and it was clear that his coup with Getty Oil would never be repeated. On the other hand, his own creative work was flourishing. The series of songs on the theme of Falstaff which the Globe Theatre Trust had commissioned had grown into a full-scale opera, entitled *Plump Jack*, which received its first performance in 1989. Some critics liked it, others didn't, and, as with all his work, the reception was almost certainly affected by the fact that he was so extremely rich.

But Gordon's enthusiasm was unbounded, and at times he could hardly believe he'd done it. Hearing his own music professionally performed was more exciting than the sale of Getty Oil. One day perhaps the name Getty might really be remembered more for music than for money.

He was also excited by the economic theories he had been working on long before the sale of Getty Oil, and which, like Gordon himself, could be regarded as eccentric or highly original, depending on one's point of view. The first, on which he worked for several years, was a brave attempt to apply his interest in biology to economics. Starting from the proposition that the market operated upon economies much as natural selection did upon a species, he worked out a complex theory to account for the way this functioned.

The result, which he published in 1988 under the title *The Hunt for R* ('R' being the rate of return on an investment), is a highly esoteric exercise in economic theory calculated to scare off all but the most highly qualified of professional economists by the sheer complexity of its mathematics. This may account for its lack of impact so far in the rarefied world of higher economic theory.

But Gordon was also trying to devise an answer to a more pressing economic problem – inflation. Starting from the obvious fact that inflation tends to follow an increase in the supply of money, he began wondering if some other form of 'money' could be found which would not automatically fuel inflation in this way.

He reasoned that if only money could be made to have the same rate of return as that on other investments, an increase in its supply need not automatically raise inflation, for the simple reason that people would rather hold on to it than spend it. Even as he said this, Gordon realized that a sort of interest-bearing 'money' exists already – in the form of units in mutual funds; and his proposal, which he developed at length in the article 'Fertile Money', published in 1992, was that funds of this sort could easily become a form of currency, and that if only governments adopted his ideas, inflation could be cured.

In the real world, as opposed to the worlds of opera and of economic theory, the only apparent setback encountered by the thrice-blest Gordon Gettys at this time involved Ann's New York ventures following the sale of Getty Oil. It was becoming clear that they weren't working – and never would. The gossip had inevitably started, and back-biting and reproach, as Ann's publishing career was clearly not going anywhere.

She had originally thought that her son Peter might be interested, and one day even take over the enterprise. But although he, like his brothers, had literary ambitions, Peter wasn't driven.

It was bad that the Grove-Weidenfeld venture was showing signs of becoming a disaster. Disaster makes the rich nervous as they sense the fragile nature of their great possessions.

The situation of the publishing house inevitably meant the end of all the exciting ideas that Ann and Weidenfeld had so enjoyed discussing, but which would have to remain ideas – her precious Wheatland Foundation, the projected glossy magazine on the arts, the sponsored performances of great operas, and the conferences for writers and intellectuals – all might-have-beens,

as was the role she once envisaged for herself as a figure in the
world of art and literature.

For the sad truth was that for all the dinners she had hosted,
all the advances she had funded, for all the discussions, conferences, committee meetings she had once attended, the press had
not produced one genuine best seller.

Barney Rosset, working for years on the literary equivalent
of a shoestring, had published success after undeniable success.
But he was like a virtuoso gardener with publishing's equivalent
of the greenest of green fingers. Barney had had the knack. Ann
had only had the money.

Ann seemed to bear out the truth of Scott Fitzgerald's
famous dictum about the rich being different – but in a way
he'd not intended. The very rich like Ann are different because
money deprives them of a role – except the role of being very
rich, which stops them being taken seriously for anything else.
They can be flattered and indulged but things they undertake
have a way of ending badly.

Having lost an estimated $15 million on Grove-Weidenfeld,
the Gettys tried to sell it – but finding no adequate offers, left it
in a state of suspended animation. And the whole affair had left
behind a sour taste among many of the people Ann had wanted
to impress.

Harry Evans, former editor of the London *Sunday Times*,
had worked as an adviser to the company before becoming
President of Random House. He felt bitter at the way the whole
affair was handled.

'I didn't like the rich picking up a publishing house like a
plaything, and then dropping it when they got bored. It's part of
the vast carelessness of the rich. It's something maybe money
does to people. They just get a little casual.'

Casual or not, Ann returned gratefully to San Francisco, where
she licked her wounds, and started at the University of California

as an ordinary student majoring in chemistry. Weidenfeld once described her as 'a perpetual student' – as in his way was Gordon. (Out of interest he once spent a few weeks studying the university physics textbook by Halliday and Resnick, sat the first year undergraduate physics exam at Berkeley, and passed.)

But Ann was also fascinated by pre-history, ever since Gordon backed Richard Leakey's researches into the origins of man in Kenya. So as well as studying chemistry, she also soon became involved in field research in Ethiopia under the direction of the anthropological archaeologist, Professor Tim White. White was a colleague of Dr Donald Johanson, who in 1974 in a rocky site 100 miles north-east of Addis Ababa, found fame by discovering the fossilized remains of 'Lucy', a 3.2-million-year-old female hominid, which he claimed to be the oldest of man's non-ape ancestors ever discovered. Gordon had subsequently helped Johanson to create the prestigious Institute of Human Origins at Berkeley, with a $15 million grant. And Ann was currently hooked on Ethiopia, and the prospect of discovering even older fossilized remains.

Soon her life was becoming one of bizarre contrasts – between the great house on Pacific Heights and her personal Boeing which was being refitted at extraordinary cost – and the bleak valley in the Ethiopian hinterland, scratching through acres of rock and shale for fossilized hominid remains. Life in Ethiopia was tough, amenities non-existent, the climate dreadful, but Ann preferred it to New York.

Throughout this period, all three daughters of Gordon's brother George were sticking firmly by their original decision to avoid the limelight. Given who they were, and how rich they had become, this was a considerable achievement. They refused to be interviewed or photographed in public. They avoided gossip and avoided scandal. 'If you want a story, try my uncle Gordon. He enjoys publicity. We don't,' said the second daughter, Claire, to one of the few reporters to reach her on the telephone. Even when Claire unexpectedly gave birth to a son in 1979 – christened Beau Maurizio Getty-Mazzota – as the result of a love affair with an Italian she had met on a university course for foreigners at Perugia University, no further details reached the media.

The three girls also kept their distance from the other branches of the family. Indeed it was as if they could never quite forgive them for what they saw as the betrayal of their grandfather's achievement by agreeing to the sale of Getty Oil. They would keep in touch with members of their grandfather's entourage like Penelope Kitson or Barbara Wallace, but when George's daughters were invited to Mark and Domitilla's wedding the invitations went unanswered.

Ronald's life continued to be ruled by his exclusion from the ever-expanding Getty fortune, and it is only now that one can see the full extent of the damage this had caused him. By disinheriting him his father had made a sort of exile of him – from the family and from life itself – and he was spending an increasing amount of time with his wife Karin and his four children in their house in South Africa. Ronald and the family enjoyed Cape Town. He loved the climate, while the countryside around the Cape was beautiful and free from all associations with a past that haunted him. In South Africa Ronald wasn't constantly reminded of what he'd lost in California.

The children went to school there, but even with his children Ronald's exclusion from the fortune was having its effect. There was always a subtle difference between himself and them. All the children were destined to be included in the wider Getty family from which it seemed that he would for ever be excluded.

Despite his efforts to ignore this, he could already detect a different attitude developing among them – particularly with Christopher the eldest. He was a sturdy boy, shorter and less refining than his father, and already he had that touch of confidence the certainty of money brings. At the age of twenty-five Christopher would become a paid trustee for the money which would one day come to him and his sisters – and which, by rights, should have already come to Ronald on his father's death.

But Ronald hadn't given up, and had decided that if he couldn't inherit what he felt was morally his due, he would try to earn it. He was thinking big, just as his father always had, and as part of his plan to make that elusive fortune he invested in a company building a luxury hotel, the Raddison Manhatten Beach, close to Los Angeles Airport. The general partner managing the company was a friend and Ronald joined him as a non-executive partner.

It was a promising project, but by the early eighties there were problems. The Californian building boom had produced several other hotels in this once exclusive area, and when the recession followed, some went backrupt. To prevent his happening with the Manhatten Beach, Ronald joined his three other partners to guarantee the debts – but in spite of this the company finally collapsed as well.

Neither Ronald nor the other partners could meet their guarantees, but because his name was Getty, Ronald was the one creditors pursued for their money. When he discovered the astronomical sums for which he was liable, Ronald Getty's private nightmare started.

CHAPTER TWENTY-FOUR

SURVIVORS

I F THERE WAS a curse upon the Gettys, it seemed to be lifting with the new decade in 1990. At last the old man's influence, which had brought such trouble in the past, was
waning, and it was clear that Gordon – least practical but most
effective of his sons – had put an end for good to the conflict
and litigation in the family when he divided up the Sarah C.
Getty Trust. The sale of Getty Oil had more than doubled the
combined resources of the Gettys. And by putting aside his
money for the young trustees, Gordon had also ensured that
they too would have enough to keep them happy – and to
become involved themselves in the work of their respective
family trusts while they waited to inherit, probably fairly late in
middle age.

At the same time, the great fortune which Jean Paul Getty
spent his life creating showed no sign of disappearing like so
many famous fortunes in the past. On the contrary the way the
separate trusts were structured guaranteed that, with interest
steadily accruing, and barring unforeseen accidents and revolu-
tions, the capital would safely go on accumulating. As the
younger members of the family start producing children of their
own, the number of Getty heirs will also go on growing, but it
is hard to see a situation in which the family will ever cease to
be extremely wealthy.

Thus by 1990, financially at least, the future was already

looking rosy for the younger generation Gettys, but what of those still suffering from past disasters?

It was Aileen, possibly the most self-indulgent of the Getty casualties, who produced the bravest answer to her situation when it seemed most hopeless.

Early in 1990 came the first of the symptoms – in her case painful blisters in the mouth – signalling the onset of full-blown Aids, and the doctors gave their verdict. With luck she might have six months more to live.

From Aileen this produced a reaction few expected. She was still terrified of dying and knew that she could not evade her fate, but Aileen the rebel started objecting to the way that she was being treated. It was bad enough having people pitying her; what was worse was their refusal to address the subject of her illness, and she realized she was being treated as a source of shame.

This angered her, and out of her anger grew something that began to change her life. She says that Aids gave her something positive to live for.

For a period she was very ill; her nervous system was affected, making it difficult to walk. Physically and emotionally she had always tended to be fragile. She fell a lot, and hurt herself, so that for days on end she had to stay in bed.

But one thing Aileen didn't lack was courage, and she refused to hide behind some bland denial of her situation. 'What I wanted was to bring dignity to myself and to the disease.'

With this in mind, she openly admitted to the press that she was suffering from Aids. Her family supported her, and with the Getty name – and Elizabeth Taylor never far behind her – she gained maximum publicity for her fight 'to give a human face to the Aids plague for a world that didn't want to see it'.

What particularly incensed her was the plight of other women sufferers in the United States, where women and children had recently become the fastest-growing segment of the population testing HIV positive.

So she made no secret of the true cause of her own infection – not a blood transfusion as she originally stated, but through 'unprotected sex, out of fear of rejection' with someone she later discovered to have been HIV positive. The point Aileen was making was that however Aids was contracted was irrelevant, and that all its victims should be treated like sufferers from any other major illness – with care and dignity. Thanks largely to her name – and to her natural sense of drama – Aileen became a powerful voice speaking out for female Aids victims everywhere.

Soon she was on television pleading their cause. She worked with Aids sufferers in Los Angeles. She visited and campaigned for them, and planned a special hospice for afflicted women. With her name and looks she was becoming something she had never been before – a national celebrity.

This brought the challenge of putting her personal life in order. She did her best to come off drugs, and having re-established good relations with Christopher, who had now remarried and was living near her in Los Angeles, she was granted custody of her children four days a week.

Caleb was eight and Andrew seven, old enough to know what was happening, and she was open with them, answering their questions as truthfully as possible. She told them about her illness, and taught them how to cope with an emergency. Soon Caleb and Andrew were giving their mother the will to go on living – which by a miracle she has continued doing ever since.

Her life today is full – with her children and her work. Thanks to the Getty money she receives the best possible treatment – in her case so-called 'aggressive therapy', with the most powerful drugs available – the anti-Aids drug AZT and three separate anti-viral drugs taken simultaneously.

Along with this she has regained her self-respect through a cause she totally believes in. This, together with her will-power and determination, has clearly played its part in her survival.

She has periods of relapse, but on good days is unusually pretty and serene. She counsels other women sufferers, works for them, and does all she can to publicize their plight and help them. She says she now has little fear of dying, and that for the first time in years she's happy.

Aileen's situation provides her with an answer, however desperate, to what she had long seen as a problem associated with large amounts of money – its tendency to isolate the very rich from normal life and ordinary people. In her case, as an Aids victim, she had discovered a sense of genuine companionship with other sufferers.

In practical terms, her illness has had the effect of impoverishing her – by limiting her freedom and threatening to shorten her existence. But by concentrating all her interests and efforts in her struggle to survive, it has given her something in exchange – an overwhelming sense of purpose, and an urge to go on living.

Disaster has had a similar effect on another of the Getty casualties, Aileen's brother Paul, who after the kidnapping was practically destroyed by misery and drink. But now those closest to him think that the effects of the coma, however cruel, may well have saved his life. Until stricken, he had been locked in a never-ending cycle of disaster through drink and drugs – 'Hanging', as Gail puts it, 'above the abyss'.

Now, like Aileen, Paul insists that he is happy, and his friends confirm this. As with Aileen, the fight against his disabilities has given him a total sense of purpose. His days are underpinned with Getty money, but anything he wants requires extraordinary effort, forcing him to do something else the very rich are normally excused from doing – struggle hard for his existence.

Will-power drives him forward, and every day demands the constant slog of physiotherapy, along with exercises to improve his speech. The work is laborious and painful, but Paul has slowly grown stronger. Fourteen years after the coma, his speech is still improving. His stamina has increased and he has even taught himself to stand upright with his nurses to assist him.

But his real achievement is his resolution to live as if his handicaps did not exist. He regularly attends his favourite rock concerts; he loves restaurants; he keeps up to date with films and picture galleries; and by having many friends who read to him, he keeps abreast of contemporary fiction and the classics. With his team of nurses, he has devised routines for travelling. His cottage at Wormsley has become his base in England, and he stays there twice a year, including Christmas, which he usually spends with his father and the family. He is still planning to revisit Italy and Orgia, where Gail has been adapting the house to take him; but already he is telling her he'd rather stay in the centre of the village where, as he puts it, 'I can hang out with my old Italian friends.'

His marriage with Martine (or as she now calls herself, Gisela) ended in 1993, apparently amicably, and she returned to Germany, where she now runs a video company in Munich. They remain close friends, and speak regularly to each other on the telephone. He still falls in love as easily as ever, and has no lack of girlfriends, who adore him.

Paul has continued to enjoy a close relationship with his son Balthazar, who lives nearby in Los Angeles. Balthazar has inherited his father's old ambition to be an actor and finally a film director – and has had considerable success since appearing as a schoolboy actor in the film of William Golding's book *Lord of the Flies* with parts in films like *Young Guns II*, *The Pope Must Die* and *Red Hot*. His half-sister, Anna, is currently at the Sorbonne, but also plans to be an actress. Recently her stepfather Paul legally adopted her to make her one day eligible, like Balthazar, for her share of the Getty money.

But for all the courage and resolve of victims like Paul and Aileen, the fact remains that these are human tragedies – ruined lives, which all the money in the world can only cushion. The rest of the family will forget them at their peril.

★

Another of the family casualties – but of a very different kind – was their uncle Ronald, who by the early 1990s was facing total ruin as a result of the debts incurred building the hotel in Los Angeles. He had been naive and far too trusting; now he was suffering accordingly. The company's creditors were remorselessly pursuing him, but no one seemed capable of resolving anything – least of all the lawyers, who seemed to think that because his name was Getty he was made of money. In fact by now the unfortunate Ronald had lost his home in South Africa, and had few friends left and no resources.

One bright spot on a fairly bleak horizon was provided by his eldest daughter Stephanie, who would shortly marry Alexander Weibel, son of a prosperous Austrian textile manufacturer. Both Ronald and his wife would find some consolation for their troubles by staying with the hospitable Weibels in their house in Austria.

In 1993 their son Christopher would make an even more resounding marriage – to Pia Miller, one of the richest heiresses in America, whose father, Robert Miller, had made a fortune out of duty free franchises. Neither Ronald and his wife nor their daughter was at the wedding.

During this period, the family's star survivor continued to be its most unlikely candidate for redemption. Paul Junior, who had all but completed his transformation from the sick, reclusive victim of the counterculture into a respected, cricket-obsessed, oddly conventional pillar of the establishment.

What he had done was quite extraordinary. It's rare enough to inherit a fortune as immense as his in middle age. It's rarer still to do so when you're a drug-addicted bibliophile with a passion for the cinema and for high romantic nineteenth-century art and literature. Like a clever film director, Paul had created himself an intricate new role through his philanthropy, and had followed this by building wonderfully romantic scenery for himself, his family and friends at Wormsley.

When you can buy anything you end up buying dreams, and Paul's dreams seemed oddly reminiscent of a number of recurrent nineteenth-century romantic episodes in which rich unhappy men spent large amounts of money escaping from their sense of doom into magical worlds of private fantasy.

The most obvious parallels were with the rich reclusive writer William Beckford in the 1820s, fleeing from unhappiness and scandal by building his mock-medieval palace, Fonthill Abbey, not all that far from Wormsley, or with doomed King Ludwig of Bavaria, seeking salvation in the dreamlike castles which he built in the mountains outside Munich in the 1890s. A more interesting model may have been the hero of Jules Verne's novel, *20,000 Leagues under the Sea*, the mysterious, immensely rich Captain Nemo. Like Paul Junior, Nemo was a music-lover, a recluse and a would-be oceanographer, who used his fortune to construct an enormous submarine, the *Nautilus*, in which he sailed away from the world and its troubles, finding tranquillity by playing the organ to himself in the vast depths of the ocean.

From the beginning Wormsley had a touch of the same surrealist escapist fantasy, but thanks largely to his family and to friends as practical as Gibbs and as devoted as Victoria, the air of doom around Paul Junior was kept at bay, and the whole strange multi-million dollar enterprise was working. Paul Junior was beginning to enjoy his life at last.

He was no longer quite as rich as he had been when interest rates were going through the ceiling in the 1980s, and having given away something approaching £100 million, he was now needing all his income to sustain his building projects and his way of life.

This meant that his time of spectacular philanthropy was over, and most of his current giving was limited to income from the £20 million charitable trust set up in 1985. It was carefully disbursed and economically administered.

But Paul himself was increasingly enjoying life from his flat in London where he spent the week. Victoria would arrive there from her Chelsea home each morning, act as his devoted companion through the day, and stay as late as she was needed before returning to Chelsea and her children. She was an excellent hostess, and largely thanks to her, Paul's steadily increasing circle of friends included film stars like Michael Caine, writers like John Mortimer and the poet Christopher Logue, and a rich connoisseur collector like Lord Rothschild. Paul was even beginning to be seen at one of London's most exclusive dining clubs – Pratt's (proprietor the Duke of Devonshire), where he had recently become a member.

But it was at Wormsley that Paul relaxed and became positively benign. Here, the former recluse who once had rarely seen his own children had become an admirable father figure with Victoria's two sons, Tariq and Zain. He loved the countryside, was particularly proud of his herd of traditional English long-horned cattle and even remembered enough of his William Morrisite ideals to promise one day to establish a colony of happy book-binders on the estate. Often he would show friends something from his great collection of historic movies in his private cinema – or play them rare recordings (like Robert Browning reading his poetry or Oscar Wilde declaiming) from his equally great collection of historic records. At Wormsley it was hard to see how boredom could afflict him.

Yet in spite of all his current blessings, Paul Junior, like a true romantic hero, seemed fated never to discover lasting happiness. His private trip to hell was over, but the scorch marks seemed to set him noticeably apart from those around him – his middle years were wasted, lost in the *oubliette* of drugs for ever, two of his children had been practically destroyed by the same affliction, and he would always be a semi-invalid, condemned to live his life at one remove from everyday reality.

Nor did it seem that he could ever totally escape the death of Talitha, any more than devoted Victoria could take her place.

For Talitha's beauty was unchanging – as was the truth of whatever actually occurred on that July night in Rome in 1971. These were areas where his money could not enter, and it seemed that Talitha would always haunt him, unattainable and beautiful and young for ever.

Meanwhile from his Italianate mansion on Pacific Heights in San Francisco, Gordon was offering the family his personal example of how to stay sane and happy with a fortune of a billion dollars.

Unlike his brother, Paul, Gordon appeared curiously untouched by time or trouble. In his late fifties now, his looks had actually improved with age, but he was still essentially the same gangling would-be professor who forgot where he had parked his car, the same dedicated artist who would rather be remembered for an opera than a major fortune.

But although on the surface he appeared to treat his money as a slightly tedious irrelevance, this was really not the case at all. Gordon possessed a deep appreciation of the stuff, and in particular of the benefits that it bestowed.

Foremost among them was the privilege of being Gordon Getty. For one of the true advantages of very large amounts of money is the right to please oneself over almost everything – and Gordon did. He could travel as and when and where he wanted in the family Boeing 727. (When he purchased a new one, the man who did the interior decoration explained, 'it's the family station-wagon in terms of use'.)

He could also work at whatever he desired. As a workaholic, work was Gordon's greatest luxury and it was only large amounts of money which allowed him to indulge it as he did. Most days still saw him in his study, slaving at his music or his latest economic theory.

'As far as work's concerned, it's pretty much sunrise to sunset,' Gordon said.

But the most important aspect of Gordon's wealth was its

effect upon his personality. For it meant that absolutely nothing ever seemed to faze him. He had always been a man who pleased himself, and his fortune seemed to free him from the jealousies and insecurities which afflict so many people from a simple lack of money.

When a journalist was unmannerly enough to suggest that he was 'simply an artistic Walter Mitty', Gordon laughed and cheerfully agreed.

'Of course I am. I'm Don Quixote.'

And if other economists ignored his economic theories, he laughed again.

'They'll come round to accepting them in the end,' was all he said. 'They'll have to.'

As a businessman he had to rest content with his reputation as the man who had doubled the value of the Getty fortune, for few of his subsequent business ventures had succeeded. In March 1990 the Emhart industrial products corporation of Connecticut rejected the $2 billion takeover bid which Gordon tried to put together, and a month later Avon products were trying to sue him over another hostile takeover.

But business setbacks only made him more ambitious to succeed as a composer. Much of his time was spent 'polishing and perfecting' his opera, *Plump Jack*, for he found composing harder work than making money. As he put it, 'There is no such person as a lazy composer,' and writing his opera was virtually a full-time occupation.

By now Gordon was becoming a strangely amiable eccentric, and his real contribution to the Gettys was something they had always needed – concern and a touch of easy-going common sense from an older member of the family. Whenever he was in Los Angeles, Gordon would always make a point of visiting young Paul and Aileen, and Mark was always staying with his San Franciscan cousins when he visited California.

For families to function properly, their members need to like each other – and Uncle Gordon, with his extraordinary laugh, his latest pet enthusiasm, and his slightly rumpled sense of humour, was becoming an increasingly important source of family affection and belonging.

Hardly surprisingly, the place where this showed most clearly was with his own immediate family, and in their different ways all his sons had turned out somewhat like him. All were intelligent, original, rather private individuals. And whilst remaining very Californian and relaxed about life in general, all four of them had stayed immune to the Getty self-destructive streak which brought such havoc to other members of the family. So far they had been living undemanding lives as bright young men of independent means, able to please themselves about their future.

The eldest, Peter, was particularly like his father, to the point of even looking like him and trying to find farne as a composer – although it's hard to imagine Gordon composing music for the pop group which his son had founded and called 'Virgin-Whore Complex'.

Peter's brother, Andrew, was trying to write scripts for Hollywood; and Bill was on his way to becoming a Greek scholar who would opt for postgraduate research on Homer at the University of California at Berkeley. Only John, the noisy one of the family, would cause his parents serious worry when he left for San Diego, got himself tattooed, and joined a heavy metal group. But even he finally enrolled at the University of California at Berkeley, and ended up researching his father's heroine, Emily Dickinson.

As a rich boys' hobby all four brothers jointly financed an up-market wine merchant's shop in San Francisco – and as a measure of family solidarity they asked their father if they could name it after his opera.

'Well, I won't sue you if you do,' said Gordon.

So they called their shop Plump Jack – and under the management of Bill Newsom's son, Gavin, Plump Jack would start to build up one of the most interesting and reasonably priced wine-lists along the coast. It would also help to launch the previously abstemious Gordon on to a new enthusiasm – for vintage wine. Being scholarly and rich and surprisingly thirsty, Gordon soon became a most knowledgeable connoisseur.

But in the longer term, something more than an interest in wine and a wine shop will be needed to engage the full-time interests of the younger Gettys – which is why Paul Junior's son Mark seems destined for an important role within the family. Having personally witnessed so much past unhappiness, and with three young children of his own, he is quietly determined to do all he can to prevent the troubles of the past recurring.

Not that he talks about this much. Now in his mid-thirties, he has a certain wariness, and for all the quiet charm and easy-going diffidence, he is difficult to place. Studying philosophy at Oxford may have given him his air of rather cool detachment.

In fact the coolness is deceptive, for he is very serious about the family. It shows in his behaviour whenever his brother Paul arrives in London. Mark is always on hand to help him, look after him, and search out the sort of places and events he guesses will amuse him. Mark has also made himself the family's unofficial peacemaker and reuniter. He stays on warm terms with his father, and is devoted as ever to his Uncle Gordon, who refers to him as 'virtually another son'.

But if there is a key to Mark's character it probably lies in Italy rather than among the Gettys. People often forget that he was born in Rome, and marriage to Domitilla has strengthened his ties with Italy. For some years he has owned a house near Orgia and it is in Tuscany that he spends his holidays, keeps the horses which he races in Il Palio (the historic twice-yearly horse races around the city square of Siena), and he likes to hear his sons talking Italian and playing in the village where he used to play himself.

He still has many friends there. Remo's truck-driver son, Francesco, is godfather to his eldest boy, Alexander, and Mark admits the influence these country people have always had on him. Over the years they helped him reach certain conclusions which were not apparent to the Gettys.

The first was the importance which the villagers attached to skill and work well done. 'After all,' says Mark, 'whoever you are, your work is the most important thing you do. It helps define you and make you what you are.'

His second article of faith absorbed from the villagers concerned the prime importance of the family. At the time of the kidnap, when Mark's own family, for all its wealth, virtually fell apart, he could see examples of the way Italian families seemed to offer consolation and support to all their members. Later, in economic terms, he would also see how the Italian family still provides Italy with its basic and its most dynamic business structure. When he had married and become the first Getty of his generation to have to earn a living outside the family, what he had learned in Italy gave him food for thought.

By the time he was twenty-five, as a salaried trustee of his father's Cheyne Walk Trust, he was already involved in the investment policy for a fund currently standing at around $1.2 billion dollars; and by his early thirties his banking experience was giving him an increasingly important role within the family. Since then he has worked closely with his Uncle Gordon on family financial policy, and he currently runs Getty Investment Holdings. His cousin Christopher recently joined its board.

But Mark was still worried by the thought of the family declining, and concern for its future made him study how some of America's richest dynasties survived and prospered. What he learned confirmed much of what he'd learned already in his village in Italy.

The Rockefellers particularly impressed him with the way they managed to remain 'a flourishing, dynamic entity', in which different members of the family appeared to have a place. To discover the secret, he spent some time in the Rockefeller Center in New York, studying the organization which the Rockefellers created after the sale of Standard Oil to manage their investments and business interests, and to offer something of a niche for any member of the family who wanted it. The head of the family, David Rockefeller, told him from his own experience that any member of the family who was left out 'tended to become a problem'.

The way the Rockefellers had organized themselves helped convince Mark that there was no inevitable decline and fall facing his own family. On the contrary, it seemed as if the younger Gettys might well benefit from much the same advantages as the Rockefellers, provided that their elders were prepared to help them. He felt that what was needed was a sense of family identity and purpose, along with that magical activity which was as important to the rich as to the poor – the chance to work together.

In 1990, while still at Hambros he organized a Getty family investment in South Africa in an attempt to involve them together for the first time in a cooperative venture. He persuaded the three separate family trusts to make what by Getty standards was a fairly modest joint investment of $5 million in the South African based Conservation Corporation, which owns the famous Londolozi game reserve in Natal, and the Phinda reserve in Zululand. This was a glamorous project, started by the visionary conservationist, David Varty, who planned to turn Londolozi into the finest game reserve in Africa.

As there were few foreign investments in South Africa at the time, Mark made sure he had full approval of the African National Congress as well as of the South African government. With majority rule still some way off, the Getty investment was seen as a risky and idealistic gesture; and the corporation has since been cited by President Mandela himself as a model of how to integrate international tourism with the needs of animals and the local population. (Mandela has stayed at Londolozi on several occasions.)

But Mark denies that idealism played much part in his decision to invest in Africa, and says that his real objective was to help unite his family by using their talents and resources and arousing their enthusiasm.

When his uncle Gordon came to Londolozi together with Bill Newsom, his son Peter, and Ronald's son, Christopher, they were soon excited and particularly impressed by Varty and the Corporation's various locations. Later Mark's half-brother, Talitha's son Tara, was to work there. But for Mark himself involvement in a game reserve, however exciting, is not a big enough challenge to involve the energies and enthusiasm of the Gettys.

'Frankly,' he says, 'I don't see a future for us in the hotel and tourist business.'

He was seeking something altogether more demanding, and backed by his father and his uncle Gordon, he has been evolving what he calls 'a coherent strategy' between the majority of the trusts to spend £30–£40 million a time buying a number of related companies with long term prospects for growth. The first of these acquisitions has been a $30 million purchase of an 80 per cent holding in Tony Stone Images, a leading international non-news photo library, with thirty thousand colour images for use by magazines and advertising agencies for average fees of £400 per sale. Mark, with his partner, Johnathan Klein, is joint chairman of TSI. While he is confident that the company will continue to expand, he explains that the primary purpose of this strategy is to 'focus family interest and expertise in one area of investment, as happened when we still owned Getty Oil', and not necessarily to provide employment for future members of the family. However he is quick to add that he can think of 'few things more exciting than working in one's own family company', and he remains convinced that 'a family business is potentially the most dynamic organization in existence – provided the family has enthusiastic members who will work for it, a reliable source of family capital, and a common purpose and identity'.

By taking his long-term view, Mark is planning to harness the financial resources of the Getty trusts, and thus begin to build the sort of genuine Getty 'dynasty' which J. Paul Getty talked so much about but never understood.

As he puts it, 'Most of our troubles originated with my grandfather, who didn't understand families or what made them tick. Come to that, he never really understood people. It's time we did.'

1992 was an important year for the Gettys and for Paul Junior in particular. That September he would be sixty, and when the cricket season opened he resolved to celebrate the start of play on his new ground by staging something particularly close to his heart – the perfect game of cricket.

Country house cricket was making a comeback at the time, with Prince Philip fielding a team at Windsor, and the Duke of Norfolk doing likewise on his private ground at Arundel. But at the end of May, when Paul decided to follow suit at Wormsley, it is safe to say that not since Cecil Beaton staged the Ascot scene for *My Fair Lady* had a traditional English sport been staged with such precision and alarming dedication.

The setting was idyllic. The pitch had been nursed for months by Harry Brind, the chief groundsman from one of cricket's holy of holies, the Kennington Oval. The beechwoods were in leaf, and since W. G. Grace was captaining the great game in the sky, one of cricket's living legends, ninety-two-year-old 'Bob' Wyatt, England's oldest surviving Test captain, was there to ring the bell signalling the start of play.

Paul's team was captained by the most glamorous cricketer of the day, Imran Khan, captain of Pakistan; and the visitors had been organized by no less a body than the MCC itself.

Paul was enjoying one of the most enviable privileges of the very rich, of turning an elaborate dream into reality, and since a dream demands perfection, he had taken endless trouble, even asking continual advice from his friend, the *doyen* of cricket commentators, the late and much lamented Brian Johnston. Everything had to be totally authentic in a world that prides itself on authenticity – from the scorers and the sight screens by the pitch, to the neatly thatched pavilion, and the right sort of sugar buns for tea. It goes without saying that the lunch was faultless – cold salmon and new potatoes, followed by summer pudding, with Pimm's or cool draught beer or very good champagne. The outcome of the game was faultless too – the visitors winning with a boundary hit in the last over.

A perfect lunch, a perfect day – but the man of the match was not a cricketer, but Paul himself, who had survived the disasters that had seemed inseparable from the Getty inheritance and had put on this occasion as if to celebrate his own salvation.

He did it very stylishly, and without saying a word, as is his nature. As he sat there, wearing his MCC tie and blazer, watching the game from his seat in his own pavilion, he was flanked by his two guests of honour. On his left sat a self-confessed 'cricket fanatic' – the Prime Minister, John Major. And on his right and enjoying every minute of the game was Queen Elizabeth the Queen Mother.

For Paul it proved a splendid summer. The weather was indifferent, but cricket continued to the end of August. It was then that he told the cricket writer, E. W. Swanton, that 1992 had been 'my happiest summer since I was a boy'. And summer wasn't over.

When the season ended he gave orders for the marquee to be taken down, but nobody took any notice. Used to having his orders obeyed, he complained to Victoria, but still nothing happened, and when he arrived from London for his birthday on 7 September, he was annoyed to find the marquee still in place. It was bad enough becoming sixty, without having his orders deliberately flouted.

What Paul didn't realize was that for almost a year Mark had been organizing a party for his birthday, and that instead of the small family affair Paul was expecting, he had secretly brought down more than sixty guests by motorcoach from London.

Victoria, who was in on the secret, kept Paul in the house all

morning, and it was only when she took him for a stroll past the
marquee at lunchtime that he saw what was happening. Inside,
and waiting to wish him happy birthday, were many of his closest friends and relations, some of whom he hadn't seen for years.
They had come from all around the world. There were friends
from California and from Rome. There was a couple who had
once sailed up the Thames and moored their yacht opposite his
house on Cheyne Walk. There were some of his school-friends
from St Ignatius. And sitting on his right at lunch there was even
the woman who had once been closest to his father, the elegant
Penelope Kitson.

At the sight of so many long-lost friends Paul was moved to
tears. 'I never realized,' he said, 'that so many people cared.'

But there was more than this to the occasion. It was typical
of Mark, with his eagerness to bring the family together, to have
turned the party into an elaborate family reunion.

Apart from George's daughters, who were still keeping their
distance, almost all the family was there. Aileen was well enough
to have flown in from Los Angeles with Gail. Young Paul had
also made the journey with his nurses and his sister, Ariadne and
her actor husband, Justin Williams. Ann had felt unable to leave
her rocky valley in Ethiopia, where she was still searching for
the fossilized remains of her oldest ancestor, but Gordon had
flown over in the private Boeing, bringing their four boys, Peter,
Andrew, John and William.

The disinherited member of the family was not forgotten
either; for Mark had made a special point of inviting his uncle
Ronald and his family. By now Ronald was owing so much
money that he had frankly no idea of what was going to happen. But the party took his mind off his troubles and after so
many years of bitterness and rejection he was reunited with his
brothers. So it was an emotional moment for him as well as for
his brother Paul.

'It was,' he says, 'like entering the family at last.'

★

What does one give a billionaire with everything? In Siena Gail had found an antique silver and ivory paperknife with a handle in the shape of a tortoise which she thought appropriate. Bill Newsom had brought a yellow taxi-driver's hat from San Francisco. Penelope had found a Chelsea enamel box with a picture of a cricketer, and Christopher Gibbs a rare volume by the great Whig politician, Charles James Fox. It was entitled *On Wind*, and subtitled *A Treatise on Farting*.

But it was not until lunch was cleared and the birthday speeches were over, that Paul received his most important present of the day. It had been concealed behind a curtain at the end of the marquee, and when the curtain was pulled back he saw something he could not believe still existed – his red MG from Rome that he had sold years before to his half-sister, Donna. The children had traced it, and had had it carefully rebuilt and resprayed as a present to their father from the younger generation.

It was a present that meant more to Paul than any other, for it was also an omen for the future. There is a nostalgic feel to old motor-cars, and the MG seemed part of an existence that he had long considered lost for ever. It was associated with his youth, and with happier times in Rome before his troubles started. Now by returning it to him, it was as if the children were proving that even the past could be recovered and forgiven.

Against considerable odds, Paul's car had miraculously survived. Thanks to the care of those who loved him and the expenditure of a lot of money, the red MG had been wonderfully restored. And so had he.

CHAPTER TWENTY-FIVE

FULL CIRCLE

A NY TALK ABOUT the Gettys has a habit of finally returning to the true begetter of their story, the unpredictable
old man who simultaneously created most of the family's enormous fortune and most of their troubles – loner, financier of genius, and miser extraordinary, J. Paul Getty. The image
of him that persists is of a man of supernatural business skills,
immense financial power, and a personal life of utter
emptiness.

His was a genuinely strange existence in which money took
the place of almost everything. He was an alchemist of money.
For much of his life, working from some room in an hotel and
using nothing but a telephone, he had possessed the knack of
summoning up money which he magically converted into oilfields, refineries, and tanker fleets, usually in distant continents;
and such was his skill and such his cleverness that almost anything that he created seemed to summon up yet more money,
which in turn enhanced the Getty fortune and the tax-immune
income of the Sarah C. Getty Trust.

That was how it went, and the essential point about it all
was that for J. Paul Getty, most of what occurred in life – with
the possible exception of sex – took place in his truly extraordinary mind. He rarely saw the far-off marvels which he and his
money had created; he didn't care to. Nor did he ever spend the
money which he had piled away in such abundance in the Sarah
C. Getty Trust; he didn't dare to. It was entirely typical of him to

have built that strange museum out at Malibu which he would never see. And it was much the same with the scattered offspring he had casually produced but could not be bothered with for years on end.

So it was not surprising that there were problems when he decided that his adult sons were to join the family business, and start what he liked to call 'the Getty Dynasty'. To build a dynasty, one must first create a family, and J. Paul Getty, who had spent his adult life escaping from his wives and children, had really no idea of what a family entailed. Nor was it surprising that all his offspring in their different ways were scarred by contact with their father – that George should have destroyed himself, that Paul Junior almost did the same, that Ronald was tortured by his disinheritance, and that even Gordon had been forced to build himself his private intellectual world to take the place of what was missing in his childhood.

Mutual affection, understanding, generosity – the basics of any happy family – were not in J. Paul Getty's emotional vocabulary. Instead it was as if something of the old man's lack of feeling had been inserted in its place. This together with the vast amounts of money he was making, in theory to benefit his family, served to magnify the problem, helping to create jealousy, suspicion, and mistrust among the children, together with that fatal weakness which appears to have been somewhere at the root of the old man's curious psychology – fear.

With his fear for his possessions, fear for his person, and ultimately fear for his existence, Jean Paul Getty was that most unseemly spectacle, a fearful billionaire; and since fear is contagious, by the time of young Paul's kidnap he had turned the Gettys into a fearful family as well. Much of Paul Junior's reclusiveness had to do with fear, as had George's death and the family's behaviour during the kidnap and its aftermath. Gail was important to the family because she alone was not fearful.

But now that members of the family were emerging from the old man's shadow, fear was fading. Aileen had overcome it in her private Calvary, as had her brother Paul with his determination to go on living: so had her father when he came off drugs and faced the world again. Now with fear departing, the Gettys could start to pick up their existence as a relatively normal family.

Back in 1960 when the old man threw his monster party at Sutton Place for the daughter of a friend of a duke he barely knew, he felt no inclination to invite a single member of his family. But now, when Mark arranged the Wormsley party for his father, he had been anxious to invite all the Gettys he could muster. And the Gettys were increasingly behaving as a close and supportive family.

On 18 December 1992 the London *Times*, quoting an Associated Press report from San Juan, Puerto Rico, reported that a son of the late oil billionaire, J. Paul Getty, had filed for bankruptcy, claiming no assets and debts of $43.2 million. 'The claim by J. Ronald and Karin Getty was filed last month in San Juan.'

Although locally self-governed, the Caribbean island of Puerto Rico is in union with the United States and shares its legal system and its currency. Ronald and his wife had settled there after leaving South Africa, and on 18 December 1992, both appeared before the judge in the US Bankruptcy Court for the District of Puerto Rico to request an extension to file schedules and statements of their affairs. This was understandable, as Ronald owed money on behalf of his company to a formidable list of creditors. They included Merrill Lynch Private Capital Inc., Société Générale, First National Bank of Colorado Springs, Crédit Suisse, and the Security Pacific National Bank.

Ronald was personally liable for these debts, but ever since his company collapsed, he had been having nightmares with the principal creditors, some of whom had been prolonging the bankruptcy proceedings in an attempt to recover assets that he simply didn't have. He was sixty-two, a bad time of life to deal with this sort of crisis – and in the past he would have had to face the music on his own. But after his reunion with the family, things had changed. Gordon and Paul were on his side, and began to help in every way they could, advising him, paying for lawyers, and finally setting up a fund to pay a proportion of his debts and get a settlement. As a result, Ronald was able to discharge his bankruptcy.

By doing this, they helped their unhappy brother to recover peace of mind and a measure of self-respect, and since then they have arranged for him to have an income (of an undisclosed figure) as a paid consultant to his family trust. They are also helping him and Karin buy a house in Germany.

By doing so, the family has tacitly accepted that Ronald was unjustly treated all those years ago by his exclusion from the Sarah C. Getty Trust. They couldn't change that, any more than they could really make amends for Jean Paul Getty's behaviour. But they could at least ensure that after a lifetime ruined by trying to prove himself against his father, Ronald could end his days where he began and where he had always felt at home – among his mother's people in his native Germany.

In contrast with Ronald, Gordon remained the lucky member of the family, riding high on personal success, particularly with his music. Early in 1994, after attending concerts of his work at Newark, New Jersey and Austin, Texas, he had the unique triumph for a composer of flying in his own aircraft to Moscow to be present at a concert dedicated to his music, with the Russian National Orchestra performing *Plump Jack* and his 'Three Victorian Scenes', and 'Three Waltzes for Orchestra'.

It was the sort of accolade Gordon had dreamed of, and he seemed slightly overcome by the occasion. As he said, 'There's something very special about listening to a great orchestra like that playing your own music.'

In his role of latter-day Renaissance man he was also gaining public recognition for his economic theories from the Nobel economic laureate, Professor Franco Modigliani, who publicly praised the originality of the economic theories in his paper, 'Fertile Money'.

Simultaneously Gordon's wife Ann seemed to be sharing in the family success, as the money and the effort she had put into the search for man's earliest remains in Ethiopia finally paid off. That September it was confirmed that the team with which she worked had found what they were seeking. It had been established that the fossilized remains discovered some months earlier were 4.5 million years old and belonged to an ape-like hominid. Given the name *Australopithecus ramidus,* the creature was confidently claimed to be the long-sought 'missing link', joining the families of apes with humans.

The discovery was actually a triumph for the team's leader, Ann's tutor at the University of California, Professor Tim White. It was also a triumph in its way for Ann and Gordon, whose financial support had helped make Professor White's researches possible. But it also came in the middle of a bitter academic feud in which Ann and Gordon, in their role as financial benefactors, had inadvertently become involved.

Unlike his brother, Paul Junior, who has given to a wide variety of causes without strings attached, Gordon has always tended to become personally involved with the causes he donates to, treating them, as he puts it, 'just as responsibly as my business investments'. This was very much the case when he helped to found the Institute of Human Origins at Berkeley under the controversial Dr Johanson. Since then there had been a falling out between Johanson and his former colleague, Professor White, with Ann and Gordon increasingly supporting the Professor. White's success had given extra weight to his cause, and Gordon, true to his word, decided he would cease 'investing' in Dr Johanson's institute forthwith. Since this threatened the existence of the institute, Gordon inevitably incurred widespread criticism for his action. But he believes firmly that he was in the right. More to the point, he also has the money, which invariably

means that once Gordon has his mind made up, it takes something more than criticism to change it.

Ironically, just as his philanthropy was involving Gordon in con-
troversy, so a stroke of unexpected generosity was causing
embarrassment to his brother, Paul Junior, by publicly raising
the long-forgotten issue of relations with his father.

After a long and disappointing campaign to raise money to
buy Canova's neoclassical sculptural group, 'the Three Graces',
for a British gallery, it had looked as if the J. Paul Getty Museum
in Malibu was going to acquire the three life-sized marble
nymphs for the asking price of £7.4 million. They had been in
Britain since a Duke of Bedford purchased them from the Italian
sculptor back in 1820, and more than £1 million was still
required to keep them in the country. At the last minute Paul
Junior announced that he would personally donate £1 million
to the fund, provided the remaining money was contributed
from other sources.

Timothy Clifford, head of the National Galleries of Scotland, who directed the campaign, expressed his delight when
interviewed live on television – and when asked why Getty
should have backed a British gallery against his father's museum
in Malibu, he answered brightly: 'I believe that Mr Getty never
got on well with his father.'

Though broadly true, this was hardly tactful in the circumstances, and one can understand Paul Junior's annoyance when
he heard it. When you give away a million pounds you don't
expect to be reminded that you didn't like your father, particularly when this has little bearing on the reasons for your generosity. In fact the motive behind Paul Junior's gift lay, as usual, in
his genuine love of his adoptive country.

Uproar ensued when he expressed extreme displeasure and
added that he was thinking of withdrawing his offer. Faced with
full responsibility for the threatened loss to Britain of Canova's

'Three Graces', the unfortunate Mr Clifford did almost every-thing short of ritual disembowelment to express repentance.

He said he was profoundly sorry. He wrote to Paul saying he had made a terrible mistake. 'I know nothing,' he publicly lamented, 'about Mr Getty's relationship with his father.'

And that at last was that. Placated, Paul Junior confirmed his offer, and to the relief of Mr Clifford and the intense annoyance of John Walsh, director of the Malibu museum, Canova's three young ladies were permitted to remain in Britain.

The fuss about this relatively minor matter was a measure of the unaccustomed calm which otherwise had settled on the family, and one was left to wonder – could it last? Was the cycle of disaster truly over? Having endured almost every aspect of the curse of riches, could the Gettys possibly avoid it in the future?

In any family things always can and do go wrong for individuals, but what seems certain is that the epidemic of unhappiness that had scourged the family for nearly four decades was over, since so much of it depended on the interplay of Jean Paul Getty with his children, the circumstances in which his fortune was created, and the existence of the Sarah C. Getty Trust.

Also, families, like individuals, learn from their mistakes, and the Gettys have been forced to do a lot of learning. There was a sort of innocence in the way Paul Junior and Talitha first became involved with drugs in the 1960s – and also in the way Paul Junior's son, young Paul, made such tragic efforts to imitate his hippie father. But the younger Gettys are innocent no longer. By force of circumstance, they have become sophisticated and tough inheritors, schooled by the discipline of family disasters.

Young Paul's son, Balthazar, for instance, has always been adamant in his refusal to become involved with alcohol or drugs, and remains dedicated to his ambition to succeed as an actor and a film director.

Talitha's son, Tara, is similarly determined to enjoy life on his own extremely level-headed terms, steering very clear of drugs, preferring France to England, and remaining close to the person who largely brought him up, his step-grandmother, Poppet Pol. He is very good to her, has inherited his mother's charm, and gets on well with all the family.

Ronald's son, Christopher, is resolved to achieve the sort of business success his father didn't, and with his banking expertise, and connections with the family trusts, he shows every sign of doing so.

Paul Junior's youngest daughter, Ariadne, is similarly committed to her husband and her two young children. She misses Italy, but the experience of the kidnapping still makes her grateful for America and the privacy and safety of her own small family.

Ann and Gordon's children are all highly motivated, self-aware, essentially private people, who are very sure of what they're doing.

As for Mark, time alone will tell if his plans for a Getty business dynasty will work, but whatever happens he has his own life very much worked out, and seems certain to find riches as a merchant banker long before inheriting his full portion of the Getty money.

Remembering the Chinese curse 'May you live in interesting times', Mark says that he feels that the Gettys have been 'interesting' for long enough. 'I hope that from now on we can all become a little boring.'

But there is nothing boring in the situation of the younger Gettys. Thanks to Sarah Getty the money from her Trust looks like enriching the lives of her grandchildren and great-grandchildren as she originally intended. Their interests have been taken care of; the capital is safe within the separate trusts, and after the turmoil of the past, the younger members of the family are fortune's favourites. Having drawn their winning ticket in the lottery of life, they can look forward to the best of everything, and never feel the care and anguish that afflicts the vast majority of suffering mankind from lack of money.

But for them, unlike their elders, there can be no excuses if things do go wrong, and so they should not ignore the lessons offered by the sufferings and errors of their predecessors – or ever overlook their own immense good fortune.

POSTSCRIPT

WITH THE FATES apparently smiling on the Gettys, they had a final blessing to bestow upon the one who in his way had suffered most – Paul Junior.

Jon Bannenberg, the Australian naval architect who designed the *Queen Elizabeth II*, had been rebuilding his sixty-year-old yacht, the *Jezebel*, and early in 1994 the work was finished. The gleaming boat now rode at anchor on the River Dart, awaiting her new owner's pleasure.

With his yacht, as with his 'paradise' at Wormsley, Paul had been indulging his expensive passion for perfection. With a crew of nineteen looking after a maximum of twelve passengers in conditions of total luxury, the 90-metre yacht now ranked among the most glamorous vessels in her class – and was about to play a special role in the final stage of Paul's recovery.

Until now, Talitha's name had invariably been remembered with a touch of sorrow, but this changed mysteriously when Paul elected to rename his yacht *Talitha Getty*. Sailors are superstitious about changing names of vessels, but it was as if Talitha's spirit had been reborn in one of the loveliest ships afloat – and could offer Paul something he had not experienced for years – the freedom of the seas.

Born off the coast of Italy himself, he had always loved travelling by sea, but the damage caused to his feet and legs by acute phlebitis had made this impractical. With a spectacular ocean-going yacht at his command, and the chance to have his private doctor always in attendance, it was impractical no longer.

At the beginning of April he and Victoria flew Concorde to New York and on to the Caribbean where *Talitha Getty* was waiting to receive them both like minor royalty. For Paul, after twenty land-locked years this was the ultimate in freedom – and in Barbados he was even able to enjoy the amazing spectacle of Britain's Test cricketers beating a West Indian XI in Barbados for the first time for fifty-nine years.

Thanks to *Talitha Getty*, Paul was also able to revisit his beloved Mediterranean late that summer with Victoria and a few close friends for company. Then immediately after Christmas, which was spent with the family at Wormsley, the two of them flew once more to Barbados where the yacht was waiting. On 30 December, in Bridgetown harbour, on the deck of the *Talitha Getty*, Paul completed the love affair that had started so many troubled years before in Rome. Before a local minister, he married Victoria.

Before leaving for Barbados, they had told no one of their intentions, but there was a sort of rightness in the outcome of their journey. Her love for him had managed to survive rejection, drugs, ill-health and untold difficulties – and his for her had been dogged by troubles with his father, regret over Talitha, and a good proportion of the ills the flesh is heir to. But somehow, and in spite of all their problems, they had grown closer with the years. She was devoted to him and he depended on her utterly.

'Victoria is my inspiration,' he frequently remarked, which in its way was true, for she, more than anyone, had been constant through his troubles and had saved him from the depths of absolute disaster. When she was very young she had dreamed of marrying him. Now that she was young no longer, her dream had finally become reality.

Uncertainty was ended, the past was over if not entirely forgotten, and like the family itself, Paul and Victoria had earned their chance to enjoy their fortune and their days together.

Postscript to the 2017 Edition

'We look like you, but we're not like you,' John Paul Getty III, as played by Charlie Plummer, says in the trailer for *All the Money in the World*, the first glimpse moviegoers caught of Ridley Scott's film, screenplay written by David Scarpa, which was inspired by the kidnapping and ransom of Paul Getty as it appears in this book.

How true those words are. Peering into the world of the Gettys is like looking at an alien species through a looking glass. Perception is warped. Characters seem larger than life.

The vast money this dynasty attracted created opportunities like nothing else the world had seen. And yet in its wake the family fortune left a trail of devastation that fascinates us still.

In the years that followed the first publication of this book, it was hard to think what new revelations could ever emerge about J. Paul Getty and the dynasty he created. A memoir from his fifth and final wife Teddy in 2013, in which she disclosed his distaste at the amount of money she spent on sick Timmy's medical treatment, simply added to his miserly reputation, but the affection she clearly afforded him despite yet another failed marriage only added to the feeling that this was a family unfulfilled. J. Paul Getty once summed up his own regrets when he said, 'I would gladly give all of my millions for just one lasting marital success.' How many of his family would share his sentiments and trade their wealth for a second chance at happiness?

Marriage was not something at which the Gettys excelled. Even Gordon, someone who seemed to escape the worst tribulations of his relatives and whose stewardship of the family fortune brought some of its biggest returns, was found to have fathered a secret family. Although Ann was said to have known about the existence of her husband's three daughters with Cynthia Beck in Los Angeles for two years before their existence was made public in 1999, the revelations caused shockwaves for Gordon who had built quite the reputation as a composer and patron of the arts. When Gordon and Ann's son Andrew was found dead at his home, aged just forty-seven, naked from the waist down, having suffered what was described as some sort of 'blunt force trauma', it brought yet more unwelcome sentiment that this was a family cursed.

Money, the English philosopher Sir Francis Bacon wrote, is like muck – not good unless it can be spread.

So it has proved with the Gettys. Only when their vast riches have been shared or put to use other than to grow further fortunes have they come close to touching true happiness.

Arguably the greatest legacy of J. Paul Getty's riches has been the museum that bears his name – the one he hoped would be remembered as long as civilization lasted. 'The Getty', as the museum is known, has maintained its status as the world's richest, its activities having to be checked to prevent it gobbling up every priceless artefact on the planet. Following relocation to Brentwood, in Los Angeles, in 1997, the original Getty Villa was refurbished and opened in 2006. Today nearly two million people visit the two campuses every year, making the museum one of the most popular in the United States. Despite controversies surrounding some of its artworks, with several pieces returned to Italy and Greece after high-profile court cases, the museum boasts a world-renowned education programme and state-of-the-art exhibitions.

The benefits of philanthropy were also not lost on Paul Junior. Before his death in 2003 following a recurrent chest infection, Paul Junior had given away an estimated £120 million to the National Gallery, British Film Institute and other art institutions in his adopted homeland. For the last five years of his life he had been proudly able to use the title 'Sir', having received British citizenship in 1997. After being knighted by the Queen, he revealed she said to him: 'Now you can use your title. Isn't that nice?'

To Paul Junior, it was. 'It means a great deal to me,' he said. 'I am proud to be a subject of Her Majesty.'

Paul Junior's altruism continues today through his son Mark, who in 2015 also received an honorary knighthood for his contributions to the art world, in particular to the National Gallery. Like his more influential relatives before him, Mark has found the Getty name a magnet to money. Getty Images, a venture he started as a way to keep his own sons occupied, has grown into one of the biggest stock image suppliers on the planet.

Although Mark found a path away from the misery that blighted many of his namesakes, his brother, young Paul, was far less fortunate. Less than eight years after their father's death, young Paul died aged fifty-four. In many ways it was a blessing. Finally, he was free of pain.

One of young Paul's last public appearances was at the memorial mass for his father at Westminster Cathedral held five months after his death. Since Paul Junior had reverted to the Catholic faith of his childhood and given lavishly to the cathedral and church causes, he had earned an impressive service conducted by none other than the Primate of England, Cardinal Cormac Murphy-O'Connor.

So many of the characters from this book were there: Paul's widow Victoria, young Paul in the wheelchair, pushed by his brother Mark; Christopher Gibbs who had suggested the idea of Wormsley; and Mrs Thatcher, who gave him his knighthood. What made the service truly memorable was something utterly unexpected – the voice of God on the subject of wealth. Delivering the homily, the cardinal read the words of Jesus from the Gospel of Matthew: 'It is easier for a camel to go through the eye of a needle than for a rich person to enter the kingdom of God.'

'When one of his disciples asked Jesus, "Who then will be saved?", Christ replied, "With men this is impossible, but with God all things are possible"' – to which the Cardinal added, 'And I'm sure that God will remember our brother Paul and ensure his place in the kingdom of Heaven.'

Which must have meant that there was hope for at least a few members of that congregation.

Certainly, with the Gettys, anything is possible.

ILLUSTRATION CREDITS

At eighty-three, Getty had had three face-lifts, the last of which had failed, making him look inordinately old. (© Evening Standard/Getty Images)

Getty with his mistress, Mary Teissier. (© Evening Standard/Getty Images)

Paul II and his wife Talitha on the jungly patio of their house, Le Palais Da Zahir (the Pleasure Palace) in Marrakesh. (© Patrick Lichfield/Condé Nast via Getty Images)

On the hippie trail. Paul II at a peace demonstration in Rome in 1969. (© Keystone/Getty Images)

Paul III shortly after his kidnap in 1973. (© Bettmann/Getty Images)

John Paul Getty III with his wife Martine and children Balthazar and Anna in London, 1976. (© Hulton Archive/Getty Images)

J. Paul Getty in the dining room of Sutton Place, circa 1960. (© Archive Photos/Getty Images)

In the film, J. Paul Getty (Kevin Spacey) reconnects with his son John Paul Getty II (Andrew Buchan), his wife Gail Getty (Michelle Williams) and grandson John 'Paul' Getty III (Charlie Shotwell). (© Sony Pictures Entertainment)

Sixteen-year-old Paul Getty (Charlie Plummer) is kidnapped in Rome. (© Sony Pictures Entertainment)

The kidnappers call Gail and demand $17 million for Paul's return. (© Sony Pictures Entertainment)

Getty sends his advisor Fletcher Chace (Mark Wahlberg) to assess the situation. (© Sony Pictures Entertainment)

A desperate Gail pleads for the kidnappers to set her son free. (© Sony Pictures Entertainment)

The captors grow increasingly angry that the ransom has not been paid. (© Sony Pictures Entertainment)

Getty informs the press that he will not pay the ransom for his grandson. (© Sony Pictures Entertainment)

Fletcher Chace urges Getty to pay the ransom. (© Sony Pictures Entertainment)

INDEX

Other than in the entry under his name
J. Paul Getty (the elder) is referred
to as J.P.G.